BETWEEN
HITLER
AND
TITO
**Nazi Occupation and
Communist Oppression**

Also by Ljubo Sirc

Economic Devolution in Eastern Europe
Yugoslav Economy Under Self-Management
What Must Gorbachev Do?

BETWEEN HITLER AND TITO

Nazi Occupation and Communist Oppression

Ljubo Sirc

ANDRE DEUTSCH

First published in 1989 by
André Deutsch Limited
105 – 106 Great Russell Street
London WC1B 3LJ

Copyright © 1989 by Ljubo Sirc
All rights reserved

British Library Cataloguing in Publication Data

Sirc, Ljubo
    Between Hitler and Tito: Nazi occupation
    and communist oppression.
    1. Yugoslavia. Dissidents. Biographies
    I. Title
    364.1'31

ISBN 0 233 98405 4

Cartography by Sue Lawes
Typeset by Action Typesetting Limited, Gloucester
Printed in Great Britain by
St Edmundsbury Press, Bury St Edmunds, Suffolk

For Nadia — so that she would know
what her father was doing 'during the war'.

CONTENTS

Acknowledgements ix
Map x
1 Judgement on enemies of the people 1
2 Growing up in old Yugoslavia 4
3 Hitler's war and Tito's class war 12
4 Warnings go unheeded 37
5 Enslavement by the Liberation Army 56
6 Opposition legal but not tolerated 74
7 A trial on Stalin's orders 95
8 Wisdom from the solitary 121
9 Titoist re-education 137
10 Half-hearted rule of law 154
11 Postscript: Uphill struggle in freedom 175

Index 195

ACKNOWLEDGEMENTS

Getting this book into print was a major enterprise. At an early stage I was encouraged to persevere with the project by Charlie Allan, a university colleague, who asked his father, John Allan, the writer and broadcaster, to look at several chapters. Particular thanks are due to Lord Harris of High Cross, who offered invaluable advice and was instrumental in helping me to find a publisher. Nora Beloff gave incisive comments on reshaping the original typescript and an American friend, Richard A. Ware, offered his support and that of the Earhart Foundation, Ann Arbor, Michigan.

In the latter stages a fellow-Yugoslav educated in England helped by going through the final typescript with a toothcomb, and the altered script was patiently typed and retyped at the University of Glasgow by Miss A. F. Caldwell, Miss Linda Coates and Mrs Kate Livingstone.

Finally, I would like to thank Sue and Nadia, who have put up with my preoccupation with this book as they do with my other pursuits.

Ljubo Sirc

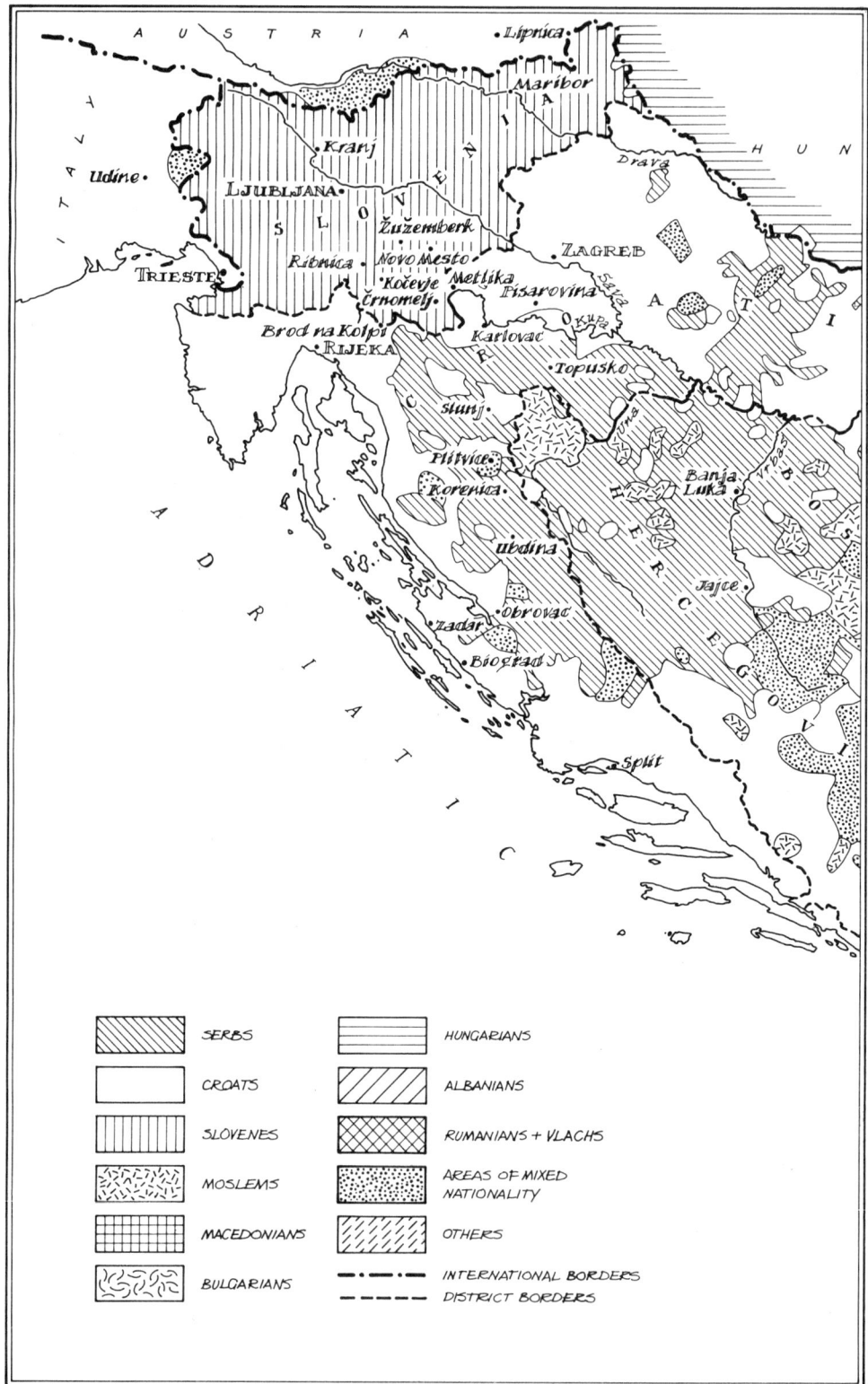

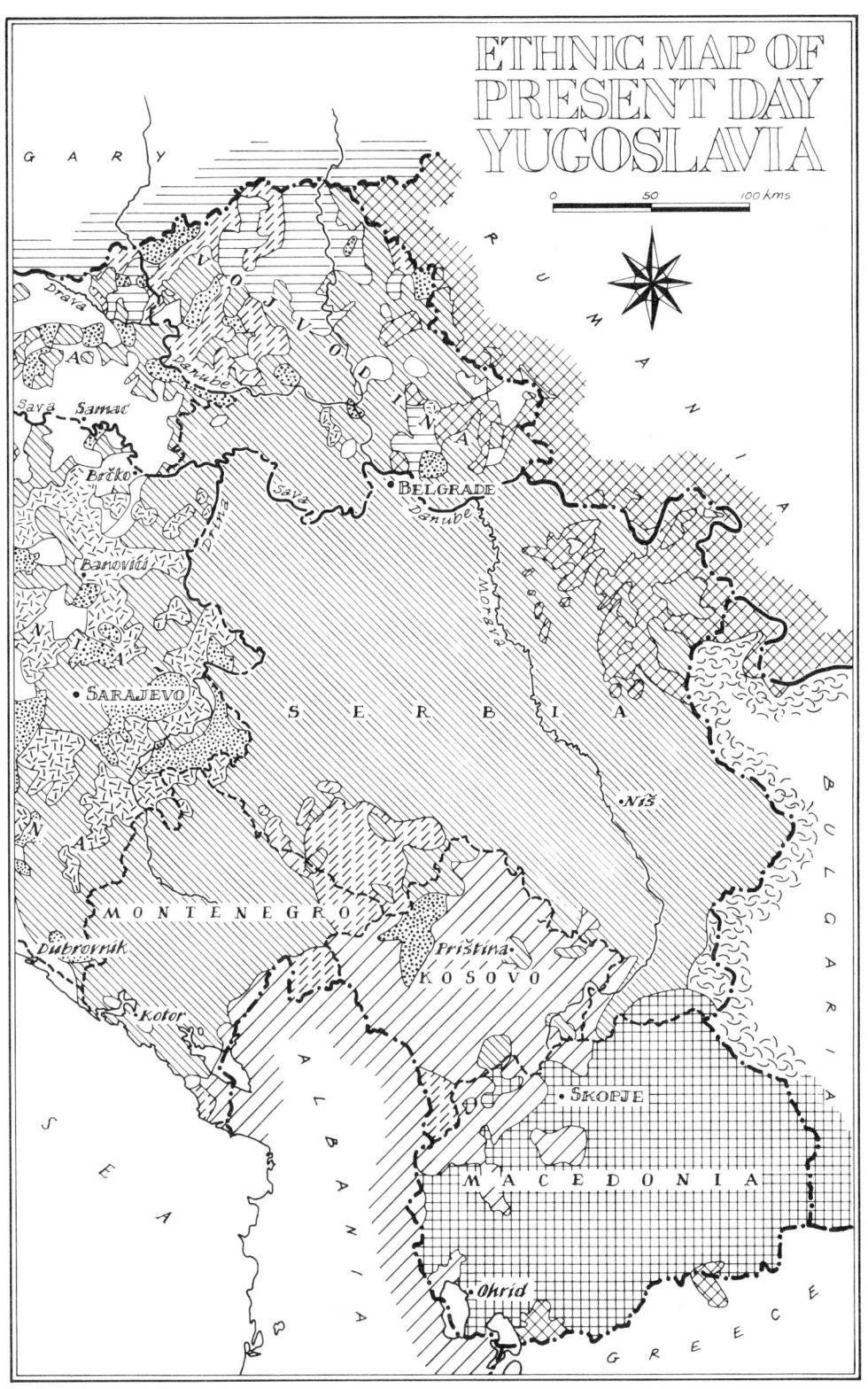

1

Judgement on enemies of the people

'Francis Sirc to ten years' imprisonment with forced labour'.

The Supreme Court of Slovenia, a constituent republic of Tito's Yugoslavia, had passed sentence on my father. I froze; suddenly I had no feeling left for anything. My own death sentence, pronounced only moments earlier, seemed a thing of the past, almost forgotten. Two more co-defendants had been sentenced to death by shooting, but by now I was so tired that all these words hardly meant anything. What could I do?

Yet dumbfounded as I was, the responsibility for my father cut across it all. I had been told earlier: 'The fate of your father depends on whether you behave.' It was not just that without me my father would never have been dragged through interrogations and court appearances. True, the Communists could not have liked him much, since he had formerly been a factory owner, but he had accepted their rule and worked industriously as a cog in their bureaucratic machine, much as he may have hated it. It was I who thought that I had to oppose the Communists, as I had once imagined I had to join the resistance against Hitler. This pride had brought disaster on my father.

By the time the Communists took over, he had had his fill of disappointment. After the defeat of Yugoslavia in 1941, our home town was occupied by the Nazis and everything my father had built up was confiscated because we were Slovenes, belonging to a small Yugoslav nation. We had to flee to Italian-occupied territory and my father fell ill. Now he was treated as a despicable criminal in a communist court.

Of course, the accusations against him were even more preposterous than the indictment against the rest. He had allegedly betrayed to me the secrets of the Slovene textile industry so that I could pass them on to the British Consul in Ljubljana. Apparently I knew from my father that Yugoslavia was short of knitting needles and that a UN Relief and Reconstruction Agency man called Liepschitz was looking for them in Belgium. This would have been top secret indeed.

But why not make a crime out of knitting needles if the prosecutor, and following him, the Court, classified as spying the fact that I had shown the British Consul a Reuters dispatch about a speech by Ernest Bevin, the British Foreign Secretary! It was claimed to be military espionage that I tried to find out what had happened to a wounded passenger in the American aircraft shot down by Tito's Air Force in 1946. The malice displayed in our trial was frightening.

The attitude of the Secret Police interrogators during the pre-trial investigation and that of the Public Prosecutors when they took over, was in itself part of the tremendous pressure on all of us. Everything one said was immediately turned into the confession of a terrible crime. Step by step, any prisoner exposed to this treatment must lose all sense of reality, in particular if he is not allowed to sleep for weeks on end.

All this did not exculpate me, I thought, when we were led away from the courtroom, an armed soldier in between every two of us. I should have known what was going to happen if I became enmeshed in anything displeasing to the communist leaders. 'You could not have known how evil they are,' an extraneous voice seemed to say to me. No matter, I should have desisted for my father's sake.

I saw my father's back in front of me in the line of prisoners, as he disappeared behind a door. His grey head was hanging as he dragged his feet with difficulty. He did not try to turn round to see me. Between Professor Furlan and me, both sentenced to death, there stood only Professor Leo Kavečnik. Furlan looked thoughtful but hardly dejected. From the post of Dean of the Faculty of Law, he had been demoted to our co-defendant. He was accused of being a British and American spy and, just like the rest of us, of conspiring against the State because we had attempted to organise an opposition to Tito's government – though Tito himself had consented to this in his agreement with the Yugoslav government in exile in London*. Professor Furlan was no stranger to political persecution either; between the wars, he had had to leave his native Trieste to escape arrest by Italian Fascists for being one of the leading Slovenes in the city. During the war he was sentenced to death by a fascist court *in absentia,* but by that time he had arrived safely in the United States to support the Yugoslav war effort. He became very enthusiastic about Tito's partisans and returned home for this reason. Reality was very different to what it had seemed from London and New York, and Professor Furlan was particularly worried by the arrogance of Tito's people towards the Western Allies.

Although sentenced to death, he was not shot, but kept in solitary confinement for four years, after which he was released as an invalid and died a few years later. Similarly, for unknown reasons, I was not shot either, but Dr Nagode was. In court, he headed the list of defendants – I sat next to him – and he whispered to me as if in apology for the fact that we had all ended up in

---

*Resistance to the advancing German armies had broken down within a fortnight of the invasion. Just before that, the Yugoslav government escaped by aeroplane to the Middle East and then moved to London, where it acted in exile as did governments of so many Allied countries overrun by Hitler.

front of communist judges: 'They told me that only I would be shot.' Why they picked on him is difficult to know. He had never been a Communist, but at some stage he was what is usually described as a fellow-traveller – in fact, before the war he was secretary of the Yugoslav-Soviet Friendship Society in Slovenia. His main mistake was that he was far too decent to approve of communist tactics as devised by Lenin. It was also alleged that Kidrič, Tito's economic dictator, disapproved of him; apparently he considered him a rival, but why is entirely obscure.

After Dr Nagode had been shot, his mother somehow found out where his grave was, lay down on it and took poison.

In this way, the opposition in Slovenia was successfully eradicated. It would seem that the instructions to eliminate it root and branch had come from Stalin. There is no reason otherwise why there should have been similar trials of democratic politicians at almost the same time in Zagreb and Belgrade, and also in Bulgaria and Rumania. The non-communist Hungarian Premier, Ferenc Nagy, withdrew to Switzerland and the Polish peasant leader Mikolayczyk escaped by plane. The culmination of this East-European purge was the Prague *coup* in February 1948.

In the wake of our trial, the British and French Consulates in Ljubljana closed.

2

Growing up in old Yugoslavia

The traditions, values and discipline in which I was reared ruled out the possibility that I could – as alleged – have collaborated with the Nazis and Fascists who occupied my country in 1941. No doubt it was also this background that prevented me from compromising with – or serving – their Stalinist successors who, during the period of my trial, and in the very same interrogation prison and courtroom that the Nazis had used, showed themselves to be equally totalitarian. On both sides, my family could trace back several generations of artisans, small shopkeepers and professionals: their standards of self-reliance, rational thought and respect for human dignity were attributes I grew up taking for granted.

Slovenia, where I was born in 1920, was a backward region in an even more backward, newly created State of Yugoslavia. Kranj was a dreamy, formerly Austrian, provincial market-town of about 4000 people. Some centuries earlier, its position on a promontory overlooking two rivers and guarding their bridges would have qualified it as a valuable fortress. Its decaying walls and its churches, two Gothic and one Baroque, were symbols of a great past, but after the First World War it did not seem to have much future. All this changed when tariff barriers were erected around Yugoslavia, cutting Slovenia off from the industrially better developed parts of the former Austro-Hungarian Empire and opening up new markets in less well-developed Yugoslavia.

During the long decades of mismanagement by the Communists, many Slovenes have come to blame their low living standard, relative at least to neighbouring Austria and Italy, on having joined the State of Yugoslavia. But our town of Kranj proved that Yugoslavia had opened up opportunities for all those eager to seize them. In the 1920s, my grandfather Pirc became mayor of Kranj and my father set out to attract investment to our town.

My father was very proud of this accomplishment, so much so that he told me at one of our very last meetings to remember that it was he who had made Kranj into an industrial centre; he was very ill then, about to leave prison to die. Indeed the 1970 Kranj *Almanac,* produced under communist auspices, recognised that my father was involved in the establishment of almost all the textile factories in our town.

He had always been bursting with energy, looking rather like an Italian tenor about to sing an aria. His looks were hardly surprising, since his maternal grandfather had been an immigrant stonemason from Vicenza. But otherwise the Italian forefathers had left little trace, for my grandmother, the stonemason's daughter, did not know one word of Italian. My father's other grandfather was either a small peasant or an agricultural labourer, like the majority of Slovenes. Very few Slovenes were town-dwellers; in the larger towns even shopkeepers and artisans were often German-speaking.

Father must have inherited most of his energy from his mother, a formidable woman who buried two husbands and, ruling with a rod of iron, managed both a grocery store and an inn which stood on opposite sides of the Sava bridge. Rather than graduating from the local high-school, my father chose to go to the Commercial College in Prague. In those days, studying in Czech was a protest against the imposition of the German language in non-German parts of the Austrian Empire. He did well at commerce and finished his studies, but he turned his back on his mother's petty ventures and found work at a Czech bank in Trieste.

His work was interrupted by the First World War. As a lieutenant in the Austrian Army reserve, he spent most of the war, after a short spell on the Russian front, in the Tyrolean Alps, doing his best – as a good Slovene in sympathy with the Serbs and their allies – to dodge his military duties. He used to tell me how his divisional commander joked: 'We all know, Sirc, that you are a traitor to Austria.' Apparently the *camaraderie,* or the high incidence of 'traitors' in the Imperial service, prevented sanctions against the disaffected. My father's younger and only brother, Vinko, ventured further: he let himself be captured by the Russians and in captivity he joined the Yugoslav volunteers to fight with the Serbian Army against the Central Powers on the Salonika front.

Before the end of the war my father married Zdenka, the first of the five children of a Kranj local dignitary and the first Slovene girl ever to study pharmaceutical chemistry. Their family names were not very common and coincidentally rhymed, his being Sirc (pronounced Sierts) and hers Pirc (Pierts). When she married, she abandoned her professional ambitions and devoted most of her time and attention to my father's business where she acted as his secretary. After my father's death she dedicated herself with the same zeal to helping me with my work and indeed typed the first draft of this manuscript.

My mother's father, of a far less practical turn of mind than my father, would have preferred his daughter to marry a professional rather than a businessman. My father respected his integrity but laughed at his small-town habits and views and his Utopianism about the outside world.

Grandfather Pirc was a big presence in my life. Since our houses were only a few hundred metres apart, I spent much time in the home of my maternal grandparents, called 'Little Laurence's House' after an ancestor who moved there in 1680. At the back there were workshops full of all sorts of strange equipment — the family had been substantial master-dyers. In some places, the walls of the house were several feet thick and I would roam around for days on end in an enormous attic full of niches. Some of the beams were covered with inches of dust.

By my grandfather's time, however, the new generation was no longer satisfied with being master-craftsmen and aspired to the professions. My grandfather's brothers became high-school teachers and agronomists and he himself studied law in Vienna before returning home to take over the family business, or what remained of it, when his elder brother died.

The dyer's trade was eventually abandoned, partly though neglect, and partly because markets dried up: local peasants no longer wove their own cloth but bought machine-made and cheaper dyed textiles. Newer medicaments also replaced 'Laurence's salve', a side-product of Pirc's, although not before I had it applied to a thumb I had hit with a hammer. All that remained in the family was a retail textile shop run by my aunt. My grandfather could then concentrate on his true interests — town administration and politics.

The Pirc family took part in the 'national reawakening' in the second part of the 19th century. All the energies of the Slovene people, then numbering around a million, were concentrated against absorption by the Germans and in cultivating their language, which is similar to, but distinct from, Serbo-Croat. My grandfather Pirc's contemporaries attended all-German schools and reacted by zealously trying to preserve their mother-tongue. All notables, including politicians, had to become poets or writers or artists of some kind to keep the national flame alive. I often used to laugh happily at the stories about the couplets in Slovene composed by grandfather, who sang them on New Year's Eve and other festive occasions before enraptured small-town audiences in the local Slovene reading club.

Grandfather Pirc was a rather short man and, perhaps for that reason, very belligerent. At his wedding in 1890, he created an uproar by insisting on saying *da* (Slovene for 'yes') when asked if he would take the 'here present maiden Mimi Sajovic' as his wife. The priest's will finally prevailed and he had to say *ja*, the German word used in the Carniolian dialect, but grandfather claimed that was only to protect 'maiden Mimi'. I was rather proud at school to find this earth-shattering event described in a history book.

My patriotic Slovene grandfather Pirc married, appropriately, a great-niece of Janez Bleiweiss, a veterinary surgeon and conservative politician who, in the mid-19th century, became so influential that he was known as 'the father of the Slovene nation'. The Austrian government hardly favoured his cause but his standing was so high that the Emperor felt obliged to knight him. By my time, Bleiweiss with his 19th-century reputation was dismissed as a reactionary and reproached for making life difficult for the Slovene national poet France Prešeren, a free-thinker. I cautiously kept quiet about my noble relation. In the immediate post-war period, the Communists even went so far as to change the names of various 'Bleiweiss Streets'. Now new generations are digging up old traditions and his reputation is reviving.

Unlike Bleiweiss, grandfather Pirc was a free-thinker, a persuasion presumably acquired during his time at Vienna University. He was politically active and sat at one time in the Carniolian Land Diet. Of this period he loved to recall how he blew a hunting horn when he and his fellow-deputies were 'obstructing' the proceedings; the Chamber was dominated by German gentry and their Slovene collaborators, elected with preferential votes.

In spite of his interest in politics, my grandfather always identified with his small town and angrily rejected the suggestion that he should become a senator in the Yugoslav National Assembly, spending his time in Belgrade instead of in his beloved Kranj. His furthest travels were to Vienna, and to Venice for his honeymoon. Sometimes he had to go to nearby Ljubljana but even these short journeys caused such a domestic upheaval that I still dread to think what would have happened if he had been required to do any serious travelling. If his train was due to leave at ten, everybody in the house would have to be up at six o'clock in the morning and then remained in a state of high animation until the moment of departure.

He was invariably immaculately dressed and was a stickler for punctuality. He checked the accuracy of his gold watch twice a day by Radio Vienna. From 10 till 11.30 he attended to business at the municipal chambers, then proceeded to the café 'At little Peter's'. There he sat in winter under a mirror in the main lounge and in summer at a table surrounded by chestnut trees on the veranda. At one o'clock he would play cards before attending another session at the chambers and then take a walk before returning home. Lunch was always served at twelve noon precisely, dinner at seven o'clock during the week and at seven-thirty on Sundays.

As a boy I was usually at my maternal grandparents' house when grandfather came home. I would draw up a low stool and insisted that he tell me how we would 'go a-hunting' bears, wolves and lynxes in the supposedly inaccessible forests of Southern Slovenia. He never tired of inventing increasingly dramatic stories to delight me. I also enjoyed walking with him and his dog in the fields and hilly woods around the town.

In my adolescence, of course, I became highly critical of grandfather Pirc. I was furious when, at the centenary celebration of the Kranj high school, he finished his speech with the Latin words *Vivat, crescat, floreat*. Could he not speak Slovene? Like my friends, I thought that the political division into Clerical and National-Liberal parties in Slovenia at that time was absurd. Our democracy appeared silly and inefficient. For a brief spell we thought that a national-socialist dictatorship must be better: at least it got things done. But, when Czechoslovakia was invaded, our qualified admiration for Hitler vanished. A threat to the Czechs was a threat to ourselves. We shifted our quest for efficiency from Germany to the Soviet Union.

Communism infuriated my grandfather Pirc. Although he was certainly not a wealthy man, he scorned 'social sentimentality' or, in his German phrase, *soziale Gefühlsduselei*. My father, 'the capitalist', would tease him about his anti-socialism and claimed that he himself was a Socialist.

But on one point grandfather Pirc and I were in full agreement: unquestioning enthusiasm for Yugoslavia. During the pre-1914 opposition to the ruling Austrian Germans, many Slovenes had pinned their hopes on the Kingdom of Serbia, which under King Peter I — the King who translated Milton's *Paradise Lost* — presented the appearance of a democratic and efficient State. The Serbian victories in the Balkan wars against Turkey in 1912–13 had aroused unconcealed expectations that this small kingdom would ultimately defy the Austro-Hungarian Empire. Grandfather Pirc's belief in Serbia was so great that, after the First World War when the Kranj municipal council was asked to suggest a name for the new State of Serbs, Croats and Slovenes, he proposed that it should be named the Kingdom of Greater Serbia.

Today this may sound absurd but at that time neither my grandfather nor many others, including myself, appreciated that a similar language is an insufficient base for a unitary State. For centuries the Turks had ruled Serbia and Bosnia and they remained in control of Macedonia until 1912. The Croats lived as a self-governing part of the Habsburg Empire in an uneasy arrangement with Hungary. The Slovenes on their part were administratively divided amongst four crown-lands and, together with Dalmatia, belonged to Austria.

The Serbs, the Croats, the Bosnian Moslems and the Montenegrins, who consider themselves Serbs anyway, speak the same language, especially where they live in mixed communities; they are intermingled over large areas due to migrations during the century-long struggle against the Ottoman Empire. Of the Yugoslav population 73% speak Serbo-Croat. As explained, the Slovenes speak a related language and so do the Macedonians, adding another 14% to the Slavonic-speaking majority of the population. In the 19th century, a strong movement for cultural and political unity of Yugoslavs developed, originating in Croatia. It was intended to protect the Yugoslavs against the inroads of Austrian Germans, Hungarians and Italians. The establishment in 1918 of the Kingdom of Serbs, Croats and Slovenes was the crowning success of this Yugoslav movement (also called Illyrian after the Roman province of Illyria on present Yugoslav territory). But the prevailing enthusiasm made those in power forget that the Yugoslav territories straddled the divide between the old Byzantine East and the Roman West, a factor which created considerable differences between various regions despite linguistic similarities. Against the opposition of the majority of Croats and Slovenes, and even against the advice of some wiser Serb politicians, a simple majority of the constitutent assembly adopted a centralist constitution.

Commotion followed, but finally wiser counsels prevailed and the Croat Peasant Party under Stjepan Radić joined the government led by Serbian radicals. It all ended in catastrophe – a Montenegrin deputy took offence at some remarks and shot at the Croat deputies, killing two (in full Parliament) while Radić died later.

King Alexander first made the Slovene Catholic leader Korošec Prime Minister, and it looked as if he was veering towards decentralisation and autonomy for the various regions. But then he changed his mind, and proclaimed his personal dictatorship in 1929 with a general as head of government. The name of the State was changed to Yugoslavia and the differences between Yugoslav nations proclaimed non-existent in favour of unity. Although considering himself a liberal, my grandfather supported this political course; after all, did not the arch-liberal Voltaire think that enlightened despotism was required in some instances? It all came to an end when Croat Ustashi and Macedonian revolutionaries killed King Alexander on a visit to France in Marseilles in 1934.

Prince Paul and two other Regents took over. Paul understood that he had to change direction and dismissed the Alexander man who had become Prime Minister after victory in a suspect election. Now the Slovene Catholic People's Party joined the government, and one consequence was that my grandfather was removed from his mayorship and even charged with a fabricated offence, later dropped. 'This could not have happened under Austria,' he complained. With regard to the 'rule of law', Yugoslavia still had a lesson or two to learn from the Habsburgs.

Despite political turbulence and the world depression, Slovene business flourished. After a few false starts in banking and printing, my father found his true vocation when, in 1928, he was able to raise enough money to set up his own small textile factory. The enterprise thrived and he spent much time travelling around Yugoslavia, visiting his main customers.

My father became virtually one-track-minded: he talked and dreamt cotton. He encouraged me to study languages, but with a fixed purpose. At the family table, for example, we were once discussing whether I should study Spanish. 'Oh,' exclaimed my grandfather, 'you will be able to read *Don Quixote* in the original.' 'So what!' was my father's rejoinder, 'he will need Spanish to buy cotton in South America.' He also wished me to switch from the high school to a textile college. But this would have meant no university and I almost fell ill with disappointment. He finally relented, but on condition that I should regularly attend the factory during the long vacation and learn how to work a loom.

My father was a jovial man – in a café or a restaurant he would know everybody and pass from one table to another talking and laughing. It was all the more surprising that we could not talk to each other. An express train left at

7.05 in the evening for Belgrade and this he usually took on his frequent journeys. I would carry his suitcase on the five-minute walk to the station and I was always planning what I was going to say to him as we marched side by side over the bridge. But when I saw him deep in his own thoughts, my heart would sink and in the end I would not say anything.

In October 1934, when I travelled to Belgrade with my father and grandfather to attend King Alexander's funeral, I did not feel well. Upon returning home, I had several bouts of influenza one after another and the specialist said that my lungs were showing signs of tuberculosis. It appeared that I had contracted it from my youngest uncle, my ski-ing teacher, who had died a few years earlier. After a year in bed in an Austrian sanatorium, where I was sent so as not to waste time but learn German, I came home and lived more or less normally for a year and a half. In the early summer of 1937, I was irresistibly drawn to visit Bulgaria, which in my view should have been part of Yugoslavia, the Bulgarians also being Southern Slavs. It was easy for me to learn enough Bulgarian for conversation and correspondence. A fortnight later, on my return home, the specialist ordered absolute rest, saying that he could detect two tubercular cavities in my lungs.

My father took me away again, this time to Leysin in Switzerland where I was to polish up my French. But when we arrived, we were told that I might have the fatal galloping form of the disease. When my father heard this he sat down on my bed and began to weep, and only then did I realise how much emotion there was hidden behind the face which had always seemed so stern to me. But I recovered after two more years on my back, returned home, and passed my final examinations at the high school at a time when dark clouds were gathering over Europe.

My great worry was that I would not be accepted for military service, so I engineered a deferment rather than risk immediate invalidity. In reality I still had a so-called 'bilateral pneumothorax' which persisted until 1942 − air was pumped fortnightly between my lungs and the pleura on both sides so as to compress the cavities and give them a chance to heal. There was no chemotherapy as yet.

No physical exertion was allowed, but otherwise I was in circulation, studying and debating with my colleagues. In such discussions I was often worried by my father's fortune, although he was rich only by our Slovene standards. True, my father and my mother worked very hard; my father thought nothing of working all night, filling the office with smoke, when it was necessary or he was in the right mood. But talk about Socialism was rife in the 1930s and I had a guilty conscience about being a capitalist's son. I found it embarrassing when my father's wealth was mentioned. I remember such an occasion later on at the University. University education in pre-war Yugoslavia was free except for those whose parents could afford it, and they paid fees in relation to their income. I blushed furiously when the cashier grabbed my tax certificate, almost shouting: 'This one pays the maximum,' and the whole queue turned towards me. I could not believe that my school-fellows, among them some children of my father's employees, liked me, even when they elected me chairman of a school pupils' association.

At the end of the summer of 1939, I was registered to study law at the University of Ljubljana.

3

Hitler's war and Tito's class war

On 3 September 1939, Hitler invaded Poland early in the morning. The news was being broadcast when I was on my way to enrol at the University of Ljubljana.

A sombre mood prevailed in the student body, divided as it was into Catholic populists, liberal nationalists and left-wingers, mostly Communists. I cannot remember anybody having any sympathy with Nazism, let alone with the invasion of Poland by the Nazis, even among the right-wingers whose main feature was that they were strongly in support of a unitary Yugoslavia.

Unitary Yugoslavia, however, was in the process of being taken apart. At least, since the assassination of King Alexander I, attempts had been made, first by the Serbian opposition parties and then by the government, to work out an agreement between the Serbs and the Croats. But negotiations had not come to a head until August 1939, a few days before the start of the Second World War. The Croats, represented by the Croat Peasant Party, had been given an autonomous territory and their leader, Maček, had been appointed deputy-Prime Minister in the Cvetković government. The final move had been inspired by Prince Paul, so that the agreement was virtually between him and Dr Maček, something the Serbian opposition parties resented bitterly. To everybody's amazement, the Slovene Catholic leader Korošec did not press for autonomy to be granted to Slovenia as well. He died in the autumn of 1940, causing a great loss in dangerous times. His successor was the Rev. Kulovec, padre in the same Austrian division as my own father in the First World War.

I cannot remember much debate among students about the solution of the Croat question. We were far more preoccupied with our communist colleagues, who had been taxing our patience for some time. We had had running battles with them because they were always denigrating the Army, protesting against the partial mobilisation of the reserve and resisting measures everybody knew were needed to withstand the mounting German pressure on Yugoslavia. They claimed they wanted peace and were opposed to all imperialisms. At the beginning of 1941, the underground Communist Party of Yugoslavia had issued a resolution attacking the English and French imperialists who 'had helped to kindle the new war conflagration, not in order to defend freedom, democracy and independence of small peoples, but in order to defend their colonial empires and hegemony'. In the very same resolution, the Soviet invasion of Poland and the Baltic States in alliance with Hitler's Germany had been hailed as the 'liberation of 23 million working people from the national and capitalist yoke'. Some of us remembered the statement made by Molotov in 1939, after the non-aggression pact between Hitler and Stalin, that it was criminal to wage an ideological war for the destruction of Hitlerism disguised as a fight for democracy.

The Communists became even more exasperating when the Soviet Union attacked Finland. They tried to ridicule anyone sympathising with the Finns, while many, especially my grandfather, rejoiced over every Finnish success.

My thirst for information about Communism and the Soviet Union was, curiously enough, eventually partly satisfied by my own industrialist father. By then he had acquired a reputation as a leading expert on cotton textiles. Raw materials were scarce because many normal trade routes were cut by the war in Europe, and the Association of Yugoslav Cotton Spinners elected him member of a commission of three entrusted with the task of searching for raw cotton and cotton yarn. They travelled to Italy. They also travelled to Turkey, and, in the summer of 1940, we had two Turkish politicians selling cotton as guests in our house. Finally, the Commission went to Moscow, early in 1941.

I was looking forward to learning from my father what the much-praised Soviet Union was really like. He reported shortages of some commodities and wages no higher than in our country, where they were low enough; but he praised the discipline in a textile mill he visited. He admired the Soviet theatres and reported that there was plenty of good food in the hotels for foreigners, but that people avoided talking to foreign visitors if they possibly could. Nevertheless, in my father's view, the Russians liked us other Slavs and would, no doubt, come to our aid if we were attacked by Hitler. According to him, the communist system in Russia was certainly a great step forward. He sounded exactly like so many other 'capitalist' visitors to communist countries later on. What was surprising, however, was that as soon as the new Yugoslav Embassy opened in Moscow just before the war, a few Yugoslav workers who had gone to the Soviet Union because they were of communist persuasion came to the Embassy and asked to be repatriated from the workers' homeland. To make sure they would not be forgotten, they simply settled in the cellar of the Embassy. What was one to make of this? From Moscow my father also brought an enormous can of caviar and several volumes of Marxist-Leninist works which I lent to my eager communist colleagues before I had even looked at them properly.

Our student life still consisted of argument and examinations. However, we sensed that pressure by the Nazis was constantly growing and wondered what we could do about it. Somebody who claimed to have a link with the military suggested that we should compile a list of potential German spies. I went to see a schoolmaster in Kranj who allegedly already had a register of the local

Germans who had come to our town with the new industries. He gave me short shrift: 'First go and ask your father about the Germans in his factory.' My father was livid − his technical director was a Jewish textile specialist who had had to leave Vienna when the Nazis arrived in 1938.

On 25 March 1941, we heard that the Yugoslav government had joined the Tripartite Pact between Hitler's Germany, Mussolini's Italy and Japan. And the next day students began converging on Ljubljana in order to stage a protest march against this pact and against the possibility of German munition trains being allowed through Yugoslavia to the Greek front, where Mussolini's soldiers had got bogged down. And protest we did, but with the police, on horse and on foot, at our heels.

Fellow-students in one hall of residence had the greatest fun: they were throwing empty cans at the passing police and yelling 'Long live our Japanese brothers!' The police found the carrying-on less amusing, so they invaded the hall, arresting everybody in sight except those in their pyjamas sitting behind the chimneys on the roof.

On the morning of 27 March, I was on my way to the University when a communist friend flung himself at me, shouting that the government had been overthrown by the military and that General Simović had taken over. Another communist student joined us, raising his fist in the communist salute as if to say: 'This is our victory!' We all ran to the editorial offices of the liberal daily nearby and found a scrap of paper on the door announcing that the military were backed by the young King Peter. Although just under 18, he had been declared of age by General Simović, thus removing Prince Regent Paul.

Suddenly wild shouting was heard from the direction of the Opera House. It was the procession of students who had been arrested the night before when demonstrating for the Japanese, and who had been promptly released by the police. They were carrying a large Yugoslav flag and giving vent to their approval of the overnight change in the political situation. People from every direction joined in, and soon the whole of Ljubljana, just like Belgrade, rapidly turned into one great demonstration in support of the new government. Complete strangers embraced each other, people wept and sang, and on every corner there was a gathering with people making patriotic speeches. I too climbed up on a monument and made my début as a public speaker. Who my audience were and what I said, I no longer recollect.

Then word reached me that I should go immediately to a meeting of student representatives. The delegates of all hues assembled and I was included, as chairman of the students' club of my home town. In great excitement, we appointed a commission of three to draft a manifesto, but they soon ran into an impasse because the communist member refused to accept any sympathetic reference to what he insisted on calling 'imperialist Britain'.

The demonstrating in the city continued into the night. By then the Communists had completely withdrawn, but members of the Slovene People's Party (in present terminology Christian Democrats) which had been represented in the overthrown government, and even right-wingers, came joyfully into the streets. But as I marched with a column of students past a big café, I noticed my father standing at the window, and he beckoned me in. 'Don't be too enthusiastic,' he told me, 'you don't know what will happen next.'

Clearly the military authorities were also worried and advised us to disperse lest 'our Northern neighbours', the Germans, should misunderstand the situation. The foreign consulates had been asked to take down flags they had hoisted in honour of King Peter's accession; all the same, huge crowds gathered under the windows of the British Consulate and burst into cheers when the consul showed the Union Jack.

Then came a sobering period, even for us students. We learned that the demonstrations against the Tripartite Pact in Slovenia and Serbia had not been taken up in Croatia, and that Maček, the old Croat leader, was in no hurry to go to Belgrade. He had been invited by General Simović, who wanted all political parties to participate in his government. Certainly, nobody could accuse Maček, or even Prince Paul, of having sympathies with Hitler or Nazism. Nor could one level that charge at other members of the overthrown government – they were cautious, conservative men trying to procrastinate, while the hot-headed military and the more adventurous politicians plotted against them and their delaying tactics. It also seems that some Croats saw the *coup* as directed against their newly won autonomy rather than against the placating of Hitler. Finally Maček did decide to go to Belgrade.

On 6 April 1941, I stumbled to my feet from the couch in my student's digs to the wailing of sirens. So, this was it: the war which everybody had been expecting, yet which everybody had been hoping against hope would not come. My alarm clock showed half-past-seven and, true to form, the Germans had chosen a Sunday. All railway traffic had already been put on a war-time schedule, but I managed to catch a train to take me home to Kranj, twenty miles up the Sava valley in the Carniolian Alps. From that evening, the bright lights around the many factories of Kranj no longer came on; there was a complete blackout.

Three days after Hitler had invaded Yugoslavia, an appeal was broadcast to all students to report immediately to a special unit called the Academic Legion. I rushed to the town square where my fellow-students were assembling at the Headquarters of the Frontier Guards. We were seizing and putting on any available items of uniform when a senior student reminded me that I was ill and that the doctor had told me to keep out of trouble. As they all marched off to the station accompanied by half the town, I was left alone, saddened that I was unfit to go with my contemporaries. Instead of going to the war, I was sent to the nearby sanatorium, so as not to be at home when the Germans arrived. Nor did the Academic Legion cover itself with glory. First they were divebombed, then they met German tanks and dispersed, many to be picked up by local Fascists or by the Germans themselves and taken into captivity, while others trickled surreptitiously back home.

It was on Easter Saturday 1941, which happened to be my twenty-first birthday, that the Yugoslav High Command capitulated. The end of Yugoslavia was even more inglorious than it need have been. Some Slovenes took a devil-may-care attitude: 'Well, at least under the Germans we shall have order.' But what kind of order?

A few days later, I was called back to Kranj; I hardly recognised it decorated with swastikas. An industrialist of German extraction had warned my father that unless I left without delay, I would be arrested because I was chairman of the students' club. Ljubljana was the only possible refuge as it was not under German but under Italian occupation.

Soon after, my parents and other relatives and friends followed me to Ljubljana. My father had learnt of the German intention gradually to deport all Slovenes to the Eastern parts of Yugoslavia so as to ensure free access to the Mediterranean for their Reich. The first to be deported would be those who could be expected to give the people a lead: priests, teachers, industrialists and leaders of peasants and workers. For a week or so nothing happened and many began to wonder whether my father had not been misled. Then the occupation authorities, mostly manned by Austrian Germans, began to arrest people from a list and assemble them in a Catholic high school.

Those of us who had avoided being herded into this transit camp by slipping over the German-Italian demarcation line into Ljubljana, awaited anxiously what was to happen to our less fortunate friends and neighbours. At the beginning of June 1941, it was rumoured that the trains deporting them were going to pass through Ljubljana, since this was the only possible route. Of course, we all wanted to get at the trains, but the Italian occupation authorities had the main station blocked. So we ran to a suburban station, crawled in through the windows and managed to reach the first train – to the obvious discomfiture of the German guards. I immediately came across my former maths master, a school-fellow, and a carpenter, our neighbours, and began grasping them by the hand. When the schoolmaster realised how upset I was, he said soothingly: 'Courage, Ljubo, courage!' But they did not even know where they were being taken. They were lucky: in fact, that train went to Serbia where the deportees were released to the welcome of the Serbian population and authorities.

Among them was also the Jewish manager of my father's factory. My father had tried to persuade him to come to Ljubljana with us, but he kept repeating that his documents were in order. In a way he was lucky to be taken to Serbia rather than to a camp. He was settled in a remote village and died after being bitten by a rabid dog.

The second train we did not even see. The stations were sealed off by Italian troops, but we could hear the deportees singing and joined in with them. Soon the dense crowd in front of the station was shaking with emotion. The Italians ordered us to disperse and pointed their rifles at the singing multitude. To my intense shame, I was seized by panic and ran into the darkness, almost knocking down a child. In the end, the unrest in Ljubljana was such that the Italian command prevailed upon the Germans to stop the deportations for fear of an open revolt.

The deportees' property was confiscated by the occupiers, as was that of people who had escaped to Ljubljana. And in July 1941, the German administration of Kranj put up a notice to the effect that the property of my father, my mother and myself 'was inimical to the German State and people (*Volks- und Staatsfeindlich*) and had therefore been seized for the benefit of the Reich Commissioner for the strengthening of Germanism'. German officials came to the factory and one of them made a speech telling the assembled employees that they should thank Hitler for having brought them justice and liberated them from the 'bloodsucker Sirc'. Another one said that a Slovene was not worthy of possessing a factory.

The Reich Commissioner soon sold the factory to a Berlin company, which turned it into a plant for the manufacture of aircraft parts. All the textile machines and all the stocks of raw materials and finished goods were sold and the proceeds transferred to the Reich Commissioner's account. My father thought he was completely ruined, particularly as the Germans refused to pay his debts to the banks in Ljubljana. But, worst of all, my father's activity was abruptly stopped and this plunged him into a kind of torpor from which he never entirely recovered.

The Nazis not only took our factory, they seized our home as well. Together with our furniture, it was sold to a German. Only my paternal grandmother, who had been living with us, was allowed to remain with her belongings in one solitary room, where she was cared for by one of our former employees until she died in 1942. In the hiatus between the formal confiscation of our property and the arrival of the new German owner, my aunt, our cook, and our nearest neighbour smuggled out everything they could carry – even a fairly large Persian carpet which my aunt tied firmly around her waist and concealed with a cloak before she waddled up the hill to my grandparents' house. Most of these meagre belongings were later spirited over the demarcation line which divided Ljubljana from Upper Carniola and even cut off Ljubljana from some of its suburbs. But about 1000 of my Slovene books, which we had hidden in a village, were found, taken to the paper-mill and pulped – the German occupiers intended to wipe out any trace of the Slovene language. Grandfather Pirc died in Ljubljana soon after his arrival there in May 1941, disappointed and broken-hearted.

In Ljubljana, Sunday morning after Sunday morning, Verdi's cheerful arias would echo from the corner of Bleiweiss and King Alexander streets. An Italian military band, placed at this vantage point, thus tried to sweeten the bitter pill of occupation for the citizens who liked to take a preprandial walk in Mediterranean fashion. In May 1941 the weather was glorious and the trees in full bloom. Through the branches, the walkers in the Tivoli could see the grey castle rising from the old part of the town behind church steeples.

To begin with, the occupation changed little outwardly. Many Italians, taken in by fascist propaganda, believed that they were not invaders but that they had liberated the Catholic Slovenes from the yoke of the Orthodox Serbs. The next logical step was the formal annexation of the *Provincia di Lubiana,* a violation of international law. The impression that the Slovenes desired this was strengthened by the invitation sent to Mussolini by some frightened Slovene politicians at the start of hostilities asking him to take Slovenia under his protection. The invitation was later withdrawn, but the mistake could not be corrected. Humiliating as it was, Italian occupation turned out to be far better than the Nazi variety.

The annexed Slovene territory was administered by a civilian High Commissioner, an official, a Fascist, nominally assisted by a Consultative Council of Slovenes. Some leading politicians initially made the grave mistake of accepting council membership, although they soon resigned. Had they refused to become members, the stigma of collaboration would not have been imprinted on the clerical and liberal parties from the very beginning.

Before long the Fascists showed their hand in matters which may seem of minor importance. They began by renaming several streets: King Alexander Street became Via 3 Maggio in honour of the day Ljubljana was annexed, Gaj Street was rebaptised Via Verdi. All inscriptions had to be bilingual, the Italian rendering coming first. Then the Fascists had the statues of the Yugoslav kings Peter I and Alexander I demolished: the first one, made of stone, was hammered to pieces, the other of bronze tied to a military truck and pulled from its pedestal. Demolition workers had to be brought from Italy to do this job. Many a passer-by wept.

The Italian Army distributed thousands of Italian flags and ordered house-owners to fly them for fascist festivities. Each evening, the flag at the Army headquarters was ceremonially lowered and people in the square had their ears boxed if they did not stop and raise their arms in the fascist salute. One could feel how the backs of the population, bowed by defeat, now straightened and the town seemed to whisper a stubborn 'No!' Sunshine and operatic tunes were all around, but innocent-looking people out for their daily constitutional began conspiring. In twos and threes they walked up and down the Tivoli, whispering and planning how to make life unbearable for the occupying Italians.

I joined forces with two fellow-students. We fancied ourselves as the first resistance cell and decided that we would contact other small groups to throw a net of conspiracy over the town and then extend it to the countryside. My first two fellow-conspirators were arrested by the Italians because they had been involved in the anti-fascist activity of the Slovene minority in Trieste. Then others got in touch with me and together we searched further. I came across Miloš Lokar who had assembled some thirty students and young Army and Navy officers, while another colleague found a group of professional people named *Pravda* (Justice). Merging with these two organisations seemed the obvious thing to do. At the beginning of August 1941, I was taken to see Dr Nagode, *Pravda's* leader. We walked to a residential area of Ljubljana and climbed to the first floor of a corner villa. The door was opened by an old lady, dressed in what I thought were 19th-century clothes, clearly Dr Nagode's mother. The small hall was adorned with dark oil paintings and wooden Baroque angels and smelled strongly of fish. The smell was not surprising since under the occupation Ljubljana had been inundated with Italian wine, rice and stock-fish.

Dr Nagode, a big man of about 40, received us in his modestly furnished study which contained only bookshelves, a simple desk, a sofa and a few chairs. He sat there in an open-necked shirt and worn trousers and began telling us about the programme of his group. *Pravda* was firmly in favour of the Yugoslav State, but of having very close ties with the Soviet Union. The Yugoslav economy should be planned on the basis of an inventory of the natural resources of the country. This last statement betrayed his profession: he was a doctor of geology, graduate of the Sorbonne, specialising in transport problems.

The great thing was the Soviet Union. Dr Nagode had been secretary of the regional Society of Friends of the Soviet Union which had brought him an invitation to dinner at the Soviet Embassy in Belgrade. He did not like the Slovene Communists very much, but held the view that the Soviet Communists were certainly different. At any rate, Yugoslav foreign policy after the war should be attuned to the policy of the Soviet government and the governments of other Slav countries. Internally, Yugoslavia should find ways of exploiting her own economic resources. Foreigners would no longer be allowed to profit from our country. Nor would any man be allowed to work for another: people would be self-employed or work for the State. Commerce was useless as it produced nothing and only raised prices. 'Our first demand', said Dr Nagode, 'is honesty. Nobody whose national and social attitudes are not "pure" can become a member of *Pravda*.'

The group consisted mainly of intellectuals – engineers, professors and journalists, old friends of Dr Nagode's. They were organised in sections according to the tasks they thought would have to be performed, among which the preparation of plans for post-war reconstruction figured prominently. As my colleagues and I were students of law and social sciences, we were considered not really much good. So we were allotted to the propaganda section which would print an underground paper and leaflets to keep the population informed about war developments and explain *Pravda's* programme on how to organise a better Yugoslavia when the war was over.

I was instructed to go and see the chief of the propaganda section, a schoolmaster from my home town who had taught me at high school. To my amazement, he denied any knowledge of the organisation and sent me away. When I next spoke to Dr Nagode, he told me that I would not work in propaganda but would assist him personally in the preparation of economic plans. A few days later, two student friends met me in the street and dragged me into a corner. 'Everybody hates you and your family,' they told me in great excitement. 'The best you can do is pack your bags and take refuge somewhere outside Yugoslavia.' 'Oh, don't be so silly,' I retorted, wondering what it was all about. 'No, no,' they insisted, 'you and your family must go away.'

Finally, Dr Nagode explained what had happened. My former schoolmaster had refused to have me under his command because I was the son of a capitalist and thus socially 'impure'. He had demanded that I be expelled from the group. Dr Nagode agreed to remove me from the propaganda section but not to turn me out of the group, and so the schoolmaster had left instead. In spite of his leftist views, Dr Nagode, whose father was a justice of the Supreme Court, thought that entrepreneurs were hard-working people and that their drive and initiative must somehow rub off onto their children. Even 'under the new social order', such people would be needed to give a lead in the life of the country. So despite my 'impure capitalist origin', he invited me to attend the regular weekly meetings of the executive committee of *Pravda*.

By then it had become known that the Communists, Christian Socialists and the left wing of *Sokol,* the nationalist gymnastic organisation, had joined forces and organised an association. Initially it was called 'The Anti-Imperialist Front' but was changed into the Liberation Front when Hitler invaded the Soviet Union on 21 June 1941. Until this date, the Communists had equivocated and so had the Soviet government. After the occupation of Yugoslavia by the Nazis, Stalin broke off diplomatic relations with the Yugoslav government in exile.

Relations between the two countries were resumed only when Hitler invaded the Soviet Union. The main issue at the first meeting of *Pravda* I attended was whether we should join the Liberation Front. Contact with the Front had been established some time previously, but it had not been possible as yet to iron out the differences in our programmes. The statute of the Liberation Front did not mention Yugoslavia at all and omitted any reference to the social and economic system that was to be adopted after the war. The explanation offered regarding Yugoslavia was that a decision would have to be taken by 'the people' as to whether Slovenia would be part of it or not. Meanwhile, the Liberation Front had to insist on the right of the Slovene people to self-determination and secession.

The communist-orchestrated propaganda of the Liberation Front blared full blast against Yugoslavia all the time, always referring to it as 'former Yugoslavia', just like the occupiers. The communist underground paper *Delo* declared itself against a return to 'Versailles Yugoslavia or any other imperialist State system fettering the Slovene people'. The Yugoslav government in exile was persistently inveighed against and ridiculed for having gone to London. While they were in this way offending all the people who were firmly for the continuation of Yugoslavia, the Communists claimed they could not include any programme for social or economic reforms in the Statute of the Liberation Front, because this would cause disunity.

Despite such equivocations, and the apprehension they provoked, *Pravda* eventually joined the Liberation Front on 16 August 1941. The young communist leader Boris Kidrič and Dr Nagode signed a document according to which *Pravda* accepted the statute of the Liberation Front, while the latter took note of *Pravda's* programme.

We were invited to send our representatives to the local committees of the Liberation Front spread all over Ljubljana. However, when we asked whom our people should contact, we were told that this could not be disclosed because it was too dangerous. No solution could be found, in particular as the Executive Council of the Liberation Front suddenly decided that groups would no longer be allowed to recruit members for themselves but only for the Liberation Front. Almost simultaneously, in another rule, the Council decreed that groups which did not have substantial membership could not remain in the Liberation Front.

This manoeuvring was bad enough, but we were soon also involved in controversies about economic plans and Yugoslav territorial claims. *Pravda's* position was that work on economic plans for the post-war period should start immediately and that we should also work out what kind of social and economic system there was to be. As a first step, *Pravda* prepared an organisation scheme. Since no one among us knew very much about economics, the scheme concentrated on the question of ownership. It was generally agreed that the introduction of public ownership would alter everything by facilitating planning and opening up unexpected possibilities.

Having just passed an examination in economics at the University, I had some doubts — although not very strong ones — about whether a change in ownership would bring about miraculous economic progress. Even if my doubts had been stronger, I would not have dared to mention them, because I was afraid that my friends would take this as a defence of my selfish capitalist interests. My slight knowledge of economics was by no means considered an advantage; I was told that I should study natural sciences if I really wanted to understand economic problems. I was nevertheless given the task of working out a plan for the reform of ownership under Dr Nagode's supervision. Everything was to be nationalised, with the exception of the retail trade, artisan workshops and peasant smallholdings. Retail profit margins would be strictly limited. A land reform would give a maximum of five hectares to each peasant. This kind of economy would be administered by a huge bureaucratic apparatus of government offices and co-operatives, not unlike the system our Communists actually introduced when the war was over.

The organisation plan was published in one of our underground papers and we expected to earn high praise from the Liberation Front, or at least from the Communists. We were in for a great disappointment. The Liberation Front propaganda machine opened a heavy barrage of invective and insult against *Pravda* as 'plan-mongers'. Dr Nagode tried hard to clarify the position and finally succeeded in contacting Boris Kidrič, who promised to come to his villa for a discussion. We all knew that Kidrič was high in the communist hierarchy, but who would have expected that this slender man with a Stalin moustache and knickerbockers would eventually become the economic dictator of Yugoslavia? When we met he was about 28, a failed student of chemistry turned professional revolutionary. His father was Professor of Slovene Literature at the University of Ljubljana and his mother was Viennese.

Later on, during the war, Kidrič became political Commissar at the partisan headquarters in Slovenia, and after the war the first Premier of the Slovene government. He went on a short planning course in Moscow, then took over the Yugoslav Ministry of Industry and inspired the initial Five-Year Plan and the first socialisation of enterprises in 1946.

'No,' Kidrič said vehemently at the meeting with *Pravda*, 'we do not want any plans for the future. Everything has to be concentrated on the resistance effort. Plans only hinder our present activities. No, we must be patriots and fight, regardless of our social and political views.' 'Surely,' Dr Nagode was saying soothingly, 'you realise that the immediate post-war period is going to be the best period for social reforms, since everything will have to be started from scratch.' 'No, no, no,' Kidrič repeated, 'the Liberation Front is not interested in social change. All we want is a united fight for freedom.'

The meeting with Kidrič warned us that the Communists labelled any attempt at planning for post-war social and economic changes a diversion from the liberation war. But there was another surprise in store for us. When the borders of Yugoslavia had been drawn after the First World War, about half a million Slovenes, one-third of their total number, had been left outside the new State in Italy and to a lesser extent in Austria. Our group requested the Liberation Front to organise a commission to discuss the question of Yugoslav territorial claims. The commission, of which Dr Nagode was a member, eventually met, only to be told by the Communists that the borders would no longer matter because they would be 'porous'. They said the Party was no longer free to discuss any territorial changes because they were bound by an agreement concluded between the Communist Parties of Yugoslavia, Austria and Italy. The spectre of the Communists trying to take us out of Yugoslavia and drag us into some kind of union with Germany and Italy began to haunt us more than ever.

Pravda's frustrating discussions with the Communists about the Liberation Front were followed by savage attacks on its individual members. Rumours were spread that Dr Nagode had connections with unspecified capitalists and he was questioned about these nebulous contacts by Dr Rus, an important member of the Liberation Front and then still an active judge. I myself was told by a communist student that he no longer wanted to see me because I was the son of a capitalist and organiser of the 'White Guard', a group of anti-communist military units. The funny thing was that he seemed to believe this, although no White Guard existed at that time, and anyway he knew my father was hardly capable of organising any kind of military unit after his nervous breakdown.

Circulating rumours about events and persons was one of the most successful propaganda weapons used by the Communists. Such rumours were readily transmitted by a network of committees organised by the Liberation Front throughout the country. These committees 'whispered', as we used to say. Most of their members were not Communists and would have probably sworn initially that the Liberation Front had little to do with Communism. The whispering was supported by slogans written on walls and in underground newspapers. Very often the 'activists' doing this sort of job were caught and sent to prison, but nobody seemed to care. They were soon replaced by others equally willing to sacrifice themselves, whilst the leadership seemed to welcome a few arrests here and there to cement the solidarity of the population and strengthen their resistance. The accepted slogan was: 'There must be victims!' (in Slovene: '*Žrtve morajo biti*').

The Communists never advised caution, but kept asking for more action and sacrifices. They kept the population going by promising, in 1942, that the war would be over in two months. If anybody expressed doubts, he risked being branded a traitor. Once my father was giving vent to his fears that the war might continue for another three or four years, when the communist actress who lived in the same house as ourselves menacingly exclaimed: 'No, the war is going to be over in two months, but the butchering of the people's enemies will have to continue for at least another six months.'

The nationalist-liberal students' club, which turned itself into a resistance group, started so-called 'abstention evenings' on the birthday of the exiled King Peter in September 1941. People were asked in leaflets not to go into the streets between certain hours. The Communists immediately took over and the Italians were more and more incensed by the picture of the completely deserted town.

At the end of October 1941, *Pravda* was finally given Liberation Front contacts at the University and was asked to send its representatives to various students' committees. I myself went to the first meeting of the committee at the Faculty of Law. The four students present, a Communist, a Christian Socialist, a nationalist from the former students' club called 'Yugoslavia' and myself, began our meeting with a discussion of the abstention evening planned for 1 December, the day of the foundation of the Yugoslav State in 1918. The Communist said they would not celebrate the day of 'former' Yugoslavia and we parted. In the end the Liberation Front gave in, though, and co-operated in the organisation of abstention, obviously fearful of a public opinion which did not as yet distinguish between the former Yugoslavia and the Yugoslavia to come.

The abstention evening was a great success and the Italians became nervous and angry. From then on they tried to counter any attempt at 'abstention', which was always timed by the organisers to begin one hour before *copri-fuoco* and go on until curfew. The Italians countered by moving the curfew forward an hour; this went on until curfew had been brought forward to three o'clock in the afternoon. Tension was then almost at breaking point, so that further demonstrations of that kind had to be abandoned.

During this upheaval I narrowly missed arrest. When my parents fled to Ljubljana, I moved in with them. The Italian police were now looking for me at my student's digs so I went into hiding. I learnt from there that it all had something to do with my fellow-student Hubert, a Communist.

His parents, being Slovenes from Trieste, had left Ljubljana before the Italians arrived so that he was on his own in a largish villa. My aunt and her husband rented the first floor when they too had to escape from our home town. On Hubert's ground floor there was always a surprising number of people making merry, until one night in the autumn of 1941 Italian troops surrounded the house, searched it without finding anything important and arrested Hubert. Before the Italians got in, Hubert had managed to conceal a few bundles in the upstairs bathroom and these turned out to be the Liberation Front radio transmitter. The bundles were soon collected by Aleš Bebler, a prominent Communist. Despite being the son of an industrialist he had fought in Spain, and after the war became, *inter alia,* Tito's UN Ambassador.

Hubert's statement to the Italian police, found in 1945, showed that he had given his interrogators quite a few names of fellow-students who had nothing to do with him politically. This was in line with Communist Party instructions that arrested Communists who could not refrain from talking should name non-Communists, since Party members were too precious. A trial took place in which Hubert and his two co-defendants were sentenced to several years' imprisonment to be served in Italy. Unfortunately Miloš Lokar, a member of *Pravda,* who hardly knew Hubert, was involved and died in the Modena prison.

Towards the end of August 1941, Radio London announced that Colonel Mihailović was leading guerrillas in Yugoslavia and that the Yugoslav government in exile had appointed him Supreme Commander of the Yugoslav Army at home. Before his arrest, Hubert had told me that the Communists would never accept this appointment because, according to them, Mihailović was just one of the guerrilla commanders on the Serbian-Bosnian border.

One day in November 1941, I was received with more hush-hush than usual when I came to see Nagode. I learnt that he had just talked to a certain Colonel Avšič of the regular Army, introduced to him by some other officers. He told Nagode that Mihailović had appointed him commander for Slovenia, with a Major Novak, another regular officer, as his Chief of Staff. Nagode was to help Avšič contact the Liberation Front. According to Avšič, in Serbia, too, Mihailović detachments were fighting alongside communist Partisans, despite difficulties. The argument was about whether to start large-scale operations, or to wait cautiously for better opportunities. Mihailović was for caution, while the communist commanders pressed for risky actions despite danger of reprisals against civilians.

Early in December, a Liberation Front underground paper published a savage attack on Mihailović, claiming that he did not want to fight the Germans and that his troops were fighting Partisans. *Pravda's* underground paper riposted by printing the story as told by Colonel Avšič. Further exchanges followed. For example, it was said that Mihailović had links with officers serving in the Army of the Serbian quisling Nedić, but reports from Serbia explained this in that the aim was to transform Nedić's units into a reserve force of resistance guerrillas. Furthermore, Mihailović wanted to avoid clashes between Serbs, as the Serbian population all over Yugoslavia had suffered more than enough.

After its defeat in April 1941, Yugoslavia was broken up into pieces. North-Western Yugoslavia, Slovenia, was occupied in part by the Germans, in part by the Italians, and the Hungarians had been given a small chunk too. Northern Croatia was occupied by Hungary, Dalmatia taken by Italy and the rest of Croatia, with Bosnia, turned into an Independent State of Croatia, which – the joke had it – was 'neither independent, nor Croat, nor a State'; it was handed over to the Ustashi, the Croat Fascists, who arrived from abroad in the Italian and German wake. The southern part of 'independent Croatia' was occupied by Italians, and Montenegro was placed under Italian supremacy. Serbia proper was administered by General Nedić, a former Yugoslav Minister of Defence, under German supervision; the Yugoslav North-East or Vojvodina was divided between the Hungarians and the Germans and the South-East or Macedonia was occupied by the Bulgarians. A considerable part of Yugoslavia was allotted to Albania, itself under Italian rule. There were blocks and borders everywhere.

When the first signs of resistance became noticeable, the German occupation authorities in Serbia relentlessly killed large numbers of hostages. In the autumn of 1941, thousands of Serbs, including high-school pupils and their masters at Kraljevo and Kragujevac, were shot. Entire Serbian villages and their inhabitants were exterminated after an uprising organised by communist Partisans. For their part, the Ustashi decided to do away with most of the Serbs in their 'independent State'. Approximately 300,000 perished, while those who could escape into the woods and mountains became the hard core of the resistance, Partisans or Chetniks, according to circumstances.

It was hardly surprising that nationalist guerrillas, mostly Serbs, were opposed to the precipitous actions clamoured for by the Communist Party. In this they were supported by BBC broadcasts insisting that lives in occupied territories should not be risked without urgent need. The Communists riposted that this advice was prompted by British fear of the people liberating themselves and deciding their own future without waiting for the Western Allies.

In Slovenia as well, the Liberation Front (influenced by communist recklessness) called for action at any cost and for people to join the Partisans, regardless of whether they had arms and were able-bodied. Anybody who advised taking only calculated risks was branded a traitor. Warfare for the Communists was an extension of political propaganda and they wanted victims so as to gain support from the dead men's relatives.

Late in the autumn of 1941, at Dr Nagode's, I met a group of men from my home town who had come to ask him to intercede with the Liberation Front for Jože Pesjak, a doctor of law slightly older than I was. Pesjak had abandoned a promising post with the Central Workers' Insurance in Zagreb, and the Communists' military headquarters in Slovenia had appointed him commander of the Kranj battalion. The unit consisted of only 40 men instead of the planned several hundred. They were ordered to 'liberate' our town but Pesjak refused, fearing he could only hold it for a few hours and that reprisals would follow. Instead, his men had fought Germans in the mountains of Upper Carniola until the late autumn when they asked permission to withdraw to the Italian-occupied territory and rest. Having received no reply, Pesjak came to Ljubljana on his own to make contact. He was eventually met in a secret place by two youngsters on behalf of the military command and ordered to go back. He asked them to accompany him and persuade the remaining men to carry on slogging it out. While they were walking through a forest, one of the lads hit Pesjak over the head with a hatchet concealed under his coat. He fell, but being a very strong man recovered and went for the youngsters, who fled. *Pravda* did intervene, only to be told that Pesjak was a deserter. So he went back to Upper Carniola and soon after that was killed by the Germans.

'Liquidations', that is the murder of people whom the Communist Party disliked (hardly ever the invaders), had become common practice at the end of 1941. One day in December, a girl friend told me in tears that she had just seen Fanouš Emmer, a metallurgical engineer from Kranj, lying dead with bullets in his chest in front of a small suburban church. He was alleged to be both a collaborator and a common thief. Fanouš was a cousin of Jože Vilfan, a prominent Communist, who, after the war, became 'secretary general' to Tito and a Yugoslav Ambassador. Emmer's real offence was that he had contacted the nationalist guerrillas and then gone to negotiate with the Communists, who shot him. A socialist trade-union leader was killed soon afterwards.

As members of the Liberation Front we felt in part responsible for these atrocities. What could we do? For some months we tried to persuade non-communist resisters to join the Front, hoping to moderate its excesses. The Communists, however, refused to share control over it with anybody and insisted on vilifying the State of Yugoslavia. The 'New Yugoslavia' severed all contacts with the Front when it started attacking the Mihailović guerrillas in Serbia.

Worse things were to happen. The Front leadership sent us two points to add to its programme: the Front was to be the repository of the sovereignty of the Slovene people and nobody would be allowed to fight the enemy outside the Front. If anybody did, he would be considered a traitor and liquidated. The communist underground paper called on all Front members to 'nip in the bud any attempt to organise, on Slovene territory, any armed forces outside the Slovene National-Liberation Partisan Units and People's Militia'. Unambiguously, the Communists meant units fighting the enemy without accepting communist leadership.

Initially, the Front had had an Executive Committee of Communists and fellow-travellers and a Plenary Council including other groups. The meetings of the Council were discontinued at the end of 1941. When *Pravda* objected to the extension of the programme the Executive Committee announced that the additional provisions had been unanimously adopted.

Nagode wrote a letter on behalf of *Pravda,* to ask what all this was supposed to mean. The crucial question was where the Central Committee stood regarding the State of Yugoslavia and the London government recognised by all the Allies including the Soviet Union.

A *Pravda* representative, himself a judge, handed two copies of the letter to the Executive Committee member Judge Rus, who was later to become a member of the Yugoslav State Praesidium. Within two days, Rus returned one copy saying that he could not accept it on behalf of the Executive Committee, for procedural reasons.

As a consequence, we were expelled from the Liberation Front, in February 1942. Total submission to the Communists was evidently a precondition for remaining in the Front. The Communists' underground paper underlined its stand: 'Whoever, at the present time, in any way attacks the Communist Party, acts against the people and sides with German and Italian Fascists.' Simultaneously it stated that anybody claiming that the Front was left-wing was wrong. The aspirations of the Slovene Communists to political supremacy were pretentious. The party was weak numerically, and for that it was criticised at the Vth Conference of the Yugoslav Communist Party. In Slovenia, in the Trbovlje collieries, there were only 100 party members out of 15,000 miners and in Jesenice steelworks 12 out of 4000. The communist underground paper claimed that the communist cause (presumably the abolition of private ownership and of the market) was so sacred that no method used for its promotion could be deemed immoral.

Boris Kidrič denounced *Pravda* as of a clearly Fascist-Trotskyite character and as hiding behind 'radical' and 'sovietophile' phrases, but he invited individual members to remain in the Front. Our group now split – some became individual members of the Front and served the Communists. Others claimed that the Slovene Communists were Trotskyite on the grounds that they were internationalists. Even after our expulsion we could not bring ourselves to attack the Front as it seemed to us to represent the Slovene struggle against the Fascists. Our restraint was not reciprocated – among other things, the Communists spread rumours that Nagode was 'a Churchill hireling'.

Before taking any further action, we wanted to consult Colonel Avšič, Mihailović's representative for Slovenia. We had last heard from him when, at the end of 1941, he had sent another officer to ask that *Pravda* should intercede with the Front for Colonel Vauhnik, the last Yugoslav military attaché in Berlin, known for his intelligence skill. Vauhnik was afraid the Front might have him killed after he had noticed cyclists suspiciously circling around him. The Front 'liquidators' often arrived by bicycle, gunned down their victim and cycled away. The occupying authorities were by then confused, could not understand who was killing whom and eventually forbade the use of bicycles since no authority could allow people to be simply gunned down in the street whatever their politics.

I was sent to find Avšič but was told by the contact-man that he was hiding. I was assured that he still supported Mihailović but thought that co-operation with the Partisans was imperative. Perhaps a week later, we learnt that Avšič had changed sides and joined the Partisans who soon made him a General. Many years later, in 1982, when Avšič died, his communist obituaries claimed that he had been in cahoots with the Slovene Communists well before going to see Mihailović. Why did he then praise Mihailović when he visited Nagode?

The burning question in 1942 was: Who was Mihailović's representative for Slovenia now? To our great relief, an investigator, a judge by profession, arrived from Mihailović's headquarters and called upon Nagode, at whose house I also met him.

He promised to let us know his findings. We discussed the need for a political programme for Mihailović and the possibility of establishing a radio link, since a radio engineer had built a transmitter for *Pravda*. A few days later I met the investigator in the street, and gave him *Pravda's* political suggestions, while he handed me an envelope containing technical instructions for a wireless contact. There was no indication as to who should be considered Mihailović's commander for Slovenia nor a code-book for the radio link.

We got the code-book from Major Novak, which seemed to confirm that he was the new commander. He came to see Nagode, and asked him to organise a meeting with moderate political leaders. But it all came to nothing – the moderate leaders did not want to meet at *Pravda's* invitation, and the radio contact did not work. In the end, the Italians even found the transmitter but, fortunately, never discovered to whom it belonged. The judge from Mihailović's headquarters had also invited *Pravda* to send a representative there. But for my tuberculosis I would have been chosen and gone. As it turned out, nobody went, for the situation was becoming ever more confused.

The Communists carried on as before. They attacked, *inter alia*, the clandestine printing office of the *New Yugoslavia* underground paper and destroyed its machinery, while Kidrič encouraged his followers in the underground newspaper *Delo* 'to destroy the filthy literature of other groups'. Such attitudes certainly did nothing to enhance solidarity in the fight against foreign occupiers.

These clashes between Slovenes bemused the Italians and made them ever more restless because they did not understand what was happening. They reacted by pressing Slovenes into fascist organisations, which all of us abominated. The Communists talked about everybody simply joining the Partisans, yet when this turned out to be impractical, they did not object to workers joining the Italian *Sindicati* (trade unions). But children in schools would not become members of *Gioventù Italiana* and students refused to be browbeaten into what was called the University Organisation. I myself received an invitation to become the Organisation's representative in the Law Faculty. The letter was sent back unopened by my mother and I went into hiding.

A barbed-wire fence was erected all around the town of Ljubljana and permits were required to enter or leave. Parts of the town were cordoned off in turn and searched for 'rebels' without much success, though a large part of the male population was sent to camps in Italy.

The Italians had been magnanimous to Yugoslav regular officer natives of the territory occupied by them. They were considered prisoners of war in provisional freedom and were paid adequate salaries. But in March 1942 the Italian Army arrested all officers thinking that they were the main movers behind the unrest in the 'Province of Ljubljana'. My second maternal uncle, Boris Pirc, was arrested in our house and deported with his brother-officers to camps in Italy. If Mihailović's movement ever had a chance in Slovenia, the Italians had now destroyed it, for these officers would have become the movement's backbone.

It did not help much that the non-communist groups did finally get together and organise a political body called the All-Slovene Union to support Mihailović in Slovenia. The organisation was complex – a niche was reserved for the Communists, although there was hardly any hope that they would join. *Pravda* was invited and did join, but not for long. Our contact-men soon reported that there were too many 'old politicians' among them. Moreover, the communist 'liquidators' killed a theologian, Professor Ehrlich, the spiritual leader of right-wing Catholics, and later with two students who had thought it expedient to join the Executive of the Italian University Organisation. *Pravda's* underground paper condemned the murders but also objected to participation in Italian organisations in any shape or form, which made us very unpopular with at least some member groups of the All-Slovene Union.

I was told to contact Major Novak, since Nagode had not seen him for a while and wondered what Novak's views were. After a long search, I met him in an architect's studio, and he started by reproaching me for *Pravda's* criticism of membership of the University Organisation. He approved of people joining Italian organisations because, according to him, this was the only way to persuade them to give arms to Slovenes. I never saw him again.

Novak was obviously primarily concerned with fighting the Partisans. As we did not believe these were instructions from Mihailović, we thought that the Major was acting on his own or, at best, with some of the old politicians. Mihailović had to be warned – somebody would have to escape via Italy to Switzerland and communicate with London and the exiled Yugoslav government there. I volunteered my services.

It was not difficult to obtain an Italian permit to travel to Italy for the purpose of studying Italian at the *Università per Stranieri* (University for Foreigners) in Perugia. Moreover, an Italian Carabiniere officer, who had rented rooms in Boris Pirc's flat since his arrest, urged repeatedly (this was the beginning of June 1942) that I should leave either for Italy or Croatia without specifying why. Then the Italian Command in Ljubljana announced that 10 to 25 hostages would be shot for every murder in the street. When I next went to the cemetery, to visit my grandfather's grave, I saw 20 wooden boxes awaiting burial. The next day, I left for Italy intending to escape promptly to Switzerland.

Once in Italy, I started contacting friends who might know how to get across the border and almost got myself arrested because my travel permit was originally limited to Perugia while I had to go North. In Milan I learnt from a friend who had just arrived from home about negotiations between the Italian occupation authorities and certain Slovenes for arms to fight the Communists. Apparently no agreement had yet been reached because of the Italians' mistrust. Before leaving Ljubljana, I had been told by one of Major Novak's aides about the continuous requests they were receiving for arms so that peasants could defend themselves against the Liberation Front and the Communists' attempts to murder leading villagers.

Though the Communists had been talking about the armed White Guard in Slovenia since the beginning of the war and had killed many a public figure as White Guard leaders, their underground paper *Delo* admitted in November 1942 that the so-called White Guard had obtained arms from the Italians only at the end of the previous summer.

The report was followed by an appeal to 'fight against the civil war', a war the Communists had quite clearly started themselves. In his novel *Ukane* (Tricks) which appeared in Ljubljana in 1971, a former partisan officer, Tone Svetina, wrote:

> the population, although religious, had been in its heart for the insurrection, but then political and military mistakes were made. Many people were murdered quite needlessly and others were mysteriously disappearing... Not only the priests, but the Partisans themselves helped to create the White Guard, because they were incapable of treating people as human beings.

He then described how the Partisans shot an entire family. 'Before judging the collaborators there are many things one must know ...' Many people, especially the Ustashi, collaborated with the enemy from the beginning, but many others were pushed into the enemy's hands by communist terror. It is now known that in the year between June 1941 and June 1942, the Communists killed some 1000 men and women, mainly people connected with the Catholic People's Party. This was in the so-called Province of Ljubljana alone, i.e. Italian-occupied Slovenia, with a population of barely 300,000. The Communists murdered them because they considered them opposed to the aims of the Communist Party.

In the lulls between my trips to North Italy, I attended lectures on Italian culture in Perugia. The University for Foreigners was overrun by German girls being trained as interpreters. But to my amazement, I met a young German in the corridor with whom I had spent several months in the Austrian sanatorium in 1935. We had been great friends then – his father was Czech, his mother German and they had lived in the disputed town of Tesin, which was occupied by Poland in 1938 when Hitler took over Czechoslovakia. My friend went to Germany and joined the German Army. He told me so himself, when I glanced in surprise at the stick he was using to walk with and at his stiff leg; he explained that he had shot himself in the leg when cleaning his gun. I never understood whether he did it by accident or on purpose, but he did tell me that he thought Germany had lost the war, which could almost qualify as perceptive thinking in 1942. I thought nothing of going for walks with him or of having our photograph taken by a street photographer, so far as I remember. It never occurred to me that this photograph could be submitted to a court as evidence that I had consorted with SS men.

In August 1942 my father came to Perugia to give me the Swiss banknotes he had bought with the proceeds of a load of cotton. The load had, by coincidence, ended up on a truck at a siding in Ljubljana station, although it was addressed to his factory in Kranj. We said goodbye, since the Swiss francs were meant to pay for my stay in Switzerland, but a few days later a telegram summoned me to meet my father in Rome. This time he told me about a new Italian decree in Ljubljana threatening relatives of 'rebels', persons who disappeared from home without trace, with sanctions including imprisonment and confiscation of property. My father asked me not to escape to Switzerland and promised to try to obtain an Italian pass for me under the excuse that I needed further treatment for my lung condition. Now I was stuck and uneasy, so that I felt glad to learn (at the end of 1942) that my mother and my aunt were in Italy trying to visit Captain Pirc in his camp and were expecting me to join them and go back to Ljubljana. Before leaving, I wanted to travel to Rome and see whether there was any news about my pass for Switzerland.

A few weeks earlier, a young Croat had been sent to Perugia by the Italian authorities and interned there. He was the son of a Croat politician, member of the Yugoslav government in exile in London, Juraj Šutej. His mother had been arrested by the Croat Fascists and imprisoned in the Jasenovac concentration camp, while young Šutej succeeded in escaping to the Italian-held territory. He stayed in Italy till the end of the war and then emigrated to South Africa where he eventually became a judge at the South African Supreme Court. In 1942 he wanted to communicate with his father, so he asked me to take his letters to the Yugoslav Legation in the Vatican, which of course was still operating.

Šutej alerted me to the possibility of sending a report to London myself without waiting to get to Switzerland. In Rome, my first step was to take a letter to Father Mandić, a high-ranking Croat Dominican friar, who was welcoming and friendly. He was keen to tell me that Serbian Chetniks were indiscriminately killing Croats in Bosnia. I was not prepared to believe that, but unfortunately it was true. After Ustashi had been murdering the population of entire Serb villages, including women and children, the Serb men who escaped organised themselves and began revenge massacres. It was horrible; of course, they would have been fully justified in searching out the villains and executing them, but there could be no excuse for killing innocents, even under serious provocation. The terrible blood feud that ensued diverted attention from the original criminals, the Ustashi whom the Nazis and Fascists had brought with them. They finally turned out so bloodthirsty that even the occupation military commanders criticised them for their behaviour and the chaos it was causing.

When I told Father Mandić I wanted to go to the Yugoslav Legation at the

Vatican he gave me his visiting card, as he thought it would help me to get in. So I went there, taking Šutej's letter and my own report. I had written it in a note-book the evening before, stressing that in Slovenia, after the initial shock of defeat, people wanted to resist; that the resistance, however, had become monopolised by the Liberation Front which threatened to do away with anybody fighting outside its ranks. The old politicians had prevaricated, enabling the Communists to accuse them of collaboration and push them into the hands of the occupiers by killing off their followers. I said that, because of communist tricks, our group *Pravda* welcomed Mihailović's presence in Slovenia, but that we had become apprehensive when it turned out that Mihailović's representative was Major Novak, and that he was interested in fighting the Communists rather than the enemy. I emphasised that, in our view, the way to restrain the Communists was to fight the Nazis and the Fascists. Nagode, to whom I later showed a copy, thought it was very good. We hoped that the report would be sent to London and reach Mihailović by this roundabout way and make him admonish or remove Novak.

I doubt that this report ever got anywhere. The attitude of the Chargé d'Affaires, Monsignor Moscatello, a Croat priest, and of the Legation Secretary, a Serb diplomat, was disconcerting. The Monsignor looked at Šutej's letter superficially and began impressing on me that the war was almost over, that Šutej should keep quiet and should certainly not try to slip out of Italy. I was so put off that I handed my report to the Secretary only after the priest had left.

The Secretary promised to re-type it and send it on, but then launched into a diatribe against the Croats, wondering how I could still be in favour of Yugoslavia after what had happened between the Serbs and Croats in Bosnia. I left downcast. The Nazis and the Fascists were devastating Yugoslavia, yet here in the Yugoslav Legation there was no will to fight. Surely, conflict between the Serbs and the Croats was precisely what the Nazis wanted and the best response would be to unite against them.

Such unity, alas, was not to be. Not only was there a blood feud between the Serbs and Croats, but the Slovenes too were fighting each other, as I discovered when I reached Ljubljana just before Christmas 1942. On the way there I was told that in Ljubljana mass arrests were being carried out by Slovenes under Italian protection. My aunt, Captain Boris Pirc's wife, had just been to her home region of Dalmatia where she too saw armed people with Yugoslav flags in the streets shouting 'Long live King Peter' under the eyes of Italian soldiers. They were apparently Serb refugees from the Ustashi State who had been given arms by the Italians.

On the way home from the station, I could see for myself armed people mostly wearing blue berets as their only piece of uniform — these were the so-called White Guards. Apparently a fortnight earlier, some 20 officers had been released from Italian concentration camps and were now directing the White Guard actions. A friend of mine was among them, and from him I understood that upon their return they were ordered by Major Novak, expressly referring to Mihailović, to organise arrests of left-wingers. By way of explanation, I was told that even in concentration camps the Communists would not leave others alone. Anybody who would not toe the Communists' propaganda line was threatened with shooting once back in Slovenia. The Slovene Communists were greatly helped by the Communists among the Italian soldiers.

I was so angry about this new turn of events, not understanding how anybody could venture to collaborate with the Italians, that I spoke out furiously against it when some of us met again at Dr Nagode's. To my amazement this earned me a sharp rebuke from Judge Benedik, a sober and calm man, who accused me of meddling in matters I did not fully understand. He had become a member of Novak's staff and claimed that it was impossible to fight the occupying forces while under constant danger of being stabbed in the back by the Communists. What was more, amongst the officers on Novak's staff there were some whom I would never have dared accuse of cowardice or immorality. For a moment I thought, and so did Dr Nagode, that everybody was playing a clever game together so as to deceive the Italians, and that one aim was to get the officers out of the camps.

We all believed the Allies would eventually land in the Balkans, in which event it could be of great importance to have well-organised troops in Slovenia able to turn against the Axis. But very soon we had to dismiss as wishful thinking our hopes of well-thought-out deception plans with Mihailović and the Partisans working jointly. The bitter truth was that there was an all-out civil war.

The situation was even worse in reality than we thought. Unknown to us (or at least to me), in the spring of 1943 the Communists had terrorised their main allies, the Christian Socialists, into giving up their separate identity and merging into a conglomerate, still called the Liberation Front, while the Communists preserved their separate organisation and 'forced themselves upon the other as real leaders'. This was claimed much later by the Christian Socialist leader, Edvard Kocbek, who had himself failed to support *Pravda* when it tried to prevent the Communists from imposing the Liberation Front (meaning their own) monopoly in fighting the enemy.

Against this background, the way F.W.D. Deakin, a leading British liaison officer, describes his meeting in the autumn of 1943 with Kardelj, whom he considered to be the head of the Slovene Liberation Movement, seems somewhat ill informed. About six months after Kardelj's Communists had used 'silent terror', as Kocbek put it, to persuade their allies in Slovenia 'to acknowledge their Party's actual and formal primacy', Deakin still thought that Kardelj was not simply what he looked, 'a bookish Marxist intellectual', and praised him as the creator 'of the only genuine regional all-party United Front'. He fell victim to communist tactics, as so many others did, partly out of naïvety and partly because they wanted to believe them, being left-wingers themselves. At that time communist deception was working full blast. Thus, in February 1943, Tito's headquarters guaranteed the 'inviolability of private property and full opportunity for private initiative' in post-war Yugoslavia.

All these 'all-party fronts' and 'guarantees of private property' were fraudulent, simply attempts at deceiving, aimed at foreign observers in particular. Djilas clearly describes in his *Memoir of a Revolutionary* (New York 1973, p. 388) how, as early as the spring of 1941, Tito had formulated a communist takeover to be implemented after the defeat of Germany. The Communists wanted to organise themselves militarily to attack their enemies at the time of the German defeat, and be poised to seize power themselves. They decided to denounce groups of officers preparing in the mountains to fight the Germans, and to begin an armed struggle against them, as well as against the Ustashi fighting on the side of the Germans. Everybody who could obstruct a communist seizure of absolute power was to be done away with in one way or another. Whether the opponents of Communism fought the enemy or collaborated did not matter.

In the spring of 1943, the Central Committee of the CP of Yugoslavia also stated that 'the aim of our national-liberation struggle is to realise the age-old dreams of the best generations of Yugoslavs: the Union of all Southern Slavs from the Black Sea to Trieste.' No question any more of self-determination or secession for the Slovenes. Now the slogan of 'Brotherhood and Unity' of all Yugoslavs came to the fore.

While the Communists were thus cleverly adjusting both their hidden and their open stances to the requirements of the moment, Major Novak also finally seemed to move. After most professional officers had returned from prisoners' camps in Italy, quite a few of the younger ones were ordered, in April 1943, to leave Ljubljana and form fighting units. We all hoped that operations against the Italians would begin, but some of the officers soon came back disgruntled and complaining that the assembled units had been ordered not to attack the Italian troops. It even transpired that the Italians knew where they were hiding. Moreover the Italian Commander in Ljubljana, General Gambara, revealed to a group of officers who returned from prison camps in May 1943, that he knew some of their colleagues were in the woods, and said he did not object to their actions because he had heard they were fighting the Communists.

Dr Nagode and I were again appalled, blaming Novak for this imbroglio, and we would have started having serious doubts about Mihailović himself, had Nagode not been visited a month or so earlier by another emissary from Mihailović's headquarters. This man was a journalist, a former correspondent of the Belgrade newspaper *Politika* in Slovenia. He was known as left-wing so that his adherence to Mihailović was the more impressive. He explained to Nagode that the Serbs firmly supported Mihailović, while the Croats were all for the Partisans. Should the Slovenes fail to join Mihailović's movement, Yugoslavia would be in great danger. Further Nagode was told that Mihailović was acting in agreement with the Allies and his tactics were to mobilise his full strength only after the Allies had launched a large-scale attack in South-East Europe. He also asked for information about German military plants in Slovenia for the use of the Royal Air Force. In his turn, Nagode suggested to the go-between that Mihailović's tactics should be explained to the Slovene population in leaflets dropped from planes, but no leaflets ever came.

We were far from happy, and Novak irked us even more. Some people outside *Pravda* were not enthusiastic about him either, but did not necessarily resent the contact with the Italians. A nationalist leader, a respected university professor, told me in June 1943 that it could hardly be wrong to collaborate with the Italians at a time when they could be considered potential allies. My opinion was that the Italians should change sides first. Until they did, our own people, who were keen to fight the enemy, would not understand our dealing with them. The professor laughed and said that Slovenia would no doubt be occupied by the Western Allies and they would most certainly not support the Communist Liberation Front.

I did not like what the professor was saying, did not believe his conclusions and had a sinking feeling. The BBC had caused a good deal of confusion, first praising Mihailović as a hero and then switching its support to the Partisans. The right-wingers disregarded this change and claimed to have had word from London that many people in Britain did not support the communist Partisans and were sympathetic to anti-communist feeling in Yugoslavia. I did not think that these reports were a good enough reason to discontinue the resistance.

On the other hand, it was true that the Communists had no liking for the Western Allies, so that the assertions that they were preparing to oppose any Allied landing in Yugoslavia did not sound too far-fetched, and, in fact, they were not — as we were to discover.

In the spring of 1943, the Communists were not letting on about their ill-feeling towards the Allies. On the contrary, they used to great advantage the arrival in Slovenia of Major Jones, the British liaison officer. After he had spoken at a meeting of Partisans, his photographs were circulated and pieces of parachute were passed from hand to hand to prove Allied deliveries had come. The name 'Tito' also appeared on walls. Nobody knew as yet who he was, but the Communists were obviously out to popularise him.

While all this was going on, I was told that my Italian travel permit to go to Switzerland had been refused. I reverted to my original plan to escape over the border.

4

Warnings go unheeded

The early summer of 1943 found the Communists in the Slovene Liberation Front as dominant and intransigent as ever, and the rest of the membership as hapless in trying to oppose them as they had been from the beginning. In Slovenia in general, most of the adversaries of Communism felt no affinity with Hitler, but a considerable number allowed themselves to be pushed into co-operation with the Italians. This spelled disaster, not just for the people concerned but for democracy in Slovenia, for it was precisely the leading democratic party, the Catholic Slovene People's Party, that was manoeuvred into a false position by the communist leaders.

A year earlier my associates in *Pravda* had asked me to escape to Switzerland through Italy, following the previous escape of a Slovene Catholic politician, Koce. Their purpose was two-fold: to protest and warn against any kind of collaboration with the enemy and to describe the way the Liberation Front and the Communists operated. The developments in 1942–3 seemed to make this task more urgent than ever. The warnings and recommendations would be directed at the Yugoslav government in exile in London, some of whose members were acquaintances of Dr Nagode and other *Pravda* members. They had supplied me with proof that I was sent by them, for instance, part of a letter to Nagode from the Serbian scholar turned politician, Professor Slobodan Jovanović. We had little idea of the inefficiency of the government in exile or of its internal quarrels. When I was about to leave, these squabbles had just come to a head and a government 'of civil servants' had been constituted, including Naval Captain Ivan Kern, whom I knew well because we were related by marriage. I thought this would give me an even better contact.

Politics were my greatest concern but by no means an exclusive one. I still felt that it was any young man's duty to take an active part in the war, and I thought that this ambition would be easier to fulfil abroad. If I stayed at home, joining an armed force would mean participating in the civil war, which I would not dream of doing. Yet I felt in better physical shape than ever – the treatment for tuberculosis had been successfully completed almost a year earlier, in 1942.

Seen from Slovenia, the war did not seem to be approaching a quick end. It was true that the Allies had landed in Sicily in July, but the Germans still appeared determined to defend 'Fortress Europe'. Towards the end of August, somewhat shabby German troops, perhaps a full division, passed through the streets of Ljubljana, maybe to frighten the population. The Italian authorities had forbidden civilians to leave the town until the German movements were completed. The Italians were still in command, although Marshal Badoglio had replaced Mussolini as Prime Minister, and the former dictator had been confined in a hotel on the mountain of Gran Sasso d'Italia. I had climbed there in 1942, trying to get fit for my escape to Switzerland.

Since the summer of 1942 I had been in league with two fellow-students trying to find a way over the border. As I travelled through Venice and Verona to the South Tyrol, trains carrying German troops, tanks and guns were rolling south from the Alps in quick succession. In Meran, my fellow-students had found an Austrian journalist, very anti-Nazi, who gave us a contact with South Tyrolean smugglers willing to take us into Switzerland for 18,000 Italian lire (probably worth about £2000 in today's purchasing power). The next evening we were on our way, climbing a steep slope south-west of Glurens (Glorenza). To my dismay, I developed a bad headache and finally began vomiting violently. We three escapees had to hide during the day while the smugglers went back to the valley and returned in the evening. We set off again and were making good progress, when we suddenly panicked because we thought we had been spotted by Italian border guards. As luck would have it I fell down a slope and broke my right leg. We wondered what to do next. Eventually, my two companions left for the nearest Swiss village with one smuggler whilst the remaining three smugglers helped me towards the border, still some distance away. The path was too narrow for two men to carry me between them, on the other hand only one of the three was strong enough to carry me on his back.

After five hours, we at last crossed the frontier – they bedded me down under a pine-tree and made a fire. The man who had accompanied my two companions returned and told us they were both down at an inn. They had promised that I would give him another 100 francs for his efforts (they themselves had no money left), but the smugglers' leader would accept no more. They all wished me luck and disappeared. It was 2 a.m., 1 a.m. Swiss time, when my fire went out. It was dark and, to add to my troubles, pouring with rain. As I lay there I wondered how long it would take for my leg to get better.

Slowly, the shapes of trees re-emerged. I began shouting to attract anybody looking for me, and at about seven o'clock there was an answer from below. To my great relief I soon saw a group of soldiers climbing the slope. The medical NCO rebandaged my leg and I was put on a stretcher. A cup of coffee and a piece of cheese soon raised my spirits; everybody was very kind. On the way down, they told me that the Allies had landed at Anzio the day before, which made me curse my bad luck. Why had I not gone south? When we met the local frontier guard commander and police officer who were waiting for us, they told me that my two companions were in jail at St Maria.

At the local hospital, the doctor examined my leg while a police officer searched my luggage. When I showed him my money, he took it away, together with my documents, saying that I was not allowed to contact anybody. Later that afternoon I was given an injection and fell asleep, to wake up at noon the next day, a Sunday, and find my leg in a cast. The nurses gave me newspapers so that, in spite of all that had gone wrong, I spent an enjoyable afternoon reading: it was wonderful to have access to a free press again, after the force-feeding of propaganda.

On Monday a Swiss policeman brought my two fellow-students to say good-bye. We were told that they would have to go back to Italy as the Swiss frontiers were closed to all refugees, and that I would have to follow them as soon as I could walk. Our repeated pleas against being sent back to greater danger achieved nothing.

My dejection lifted when visitors appeared: first a Protestant pastor, then a Catholic priest. A Catholic theology student from the nearby village brought me books. Even a military patrol dropped in to see me. Finally, one of the nurses gave me a pen and paper, so that I could write to the Yugoslav Legation in Berne, home to Ljubljana and to a Swiss family with whom I had spent several weeks in 1936, and to whose address I had arranged my parents should write. I told the Legation that I had a report for them and needed assistance. A few days later, I wrote again and the nurses posted my letters in contravention of official orders, but they did not seem to be much worried about that.

On 8 September 1943, news of the Italian capitulation came through. Although happy about the success of the Allied armies, I was naturally unhappy about my own setback, thinking that the war would soon be over and my sole contribution would have been to break my leg. But on the following Sunday, a young Yugoslav appeared in my room, introduced himself as Serge and said he had come on behalf of the Yugoslav Legation. He was not in fact a diplomat but the Secretary to Mihailović's representative in Switzerland. The Yugoslav Envoy had received my letter, but he would only have thrown it into a waste-paper basket, had Serge's boss not happened to call.

When we discussed the situation in Slovenia, I emphasised the need to remove Major Novak because his policy was harmful. However, Serge had more recent news than mine: after the German take-over in the Province of Ljubljana, the first thing the Partisans had thought of was to attack the Chetniks' camp at Grčarice and massacre the whole detachment. He also disclosed that his boss was sending Yugoslav government money to Major Novak through Northern Italy. Eventually we agreed that Minister Kern (my relative) would be notified of my arrival in Switzerland and that I would write a detailed report on conditions in Slovenia.

To my enormous relief and puzzlement, a few days later I received a letter from my two companions. It was posted in Berne where they had arrived safely and hoped I would soon follow. The policeman escorting them to the frontier had explained in detail how they could return to Switzerland without detection. Had we all crossed the Italian-Swiss border just two days later, nobody would have bothered with us anyway, for after the Italian capitulation the Swiss frontiers were thrown wide open and at least 30,000 Italian troops had flooded in.

I got down to work on a report for Captain Kern which followed the lines of all my communications — that the resistance forces must unite; and that the anti-Communists must not fall into the trap of collaborating with the enemy; if they did, they would be swept away and the Communists would take over. I admitted that it was not easy to stay calm while the Communists indulged in Goebbels-like propaganda, trying to blacken everybody else. They were exploiting to the full the newly established link with the British.

It now seemed absolutely clear that the Communists were out to capture power, and that they were a force to be reckoned with. Even more importantly, a very large number of their followers sincerely believed they were fighting for a better Yugoslavia and were entirely unaware of the secret plans of their leaders. My estimate was that there were about 2000 Partisans in the Italian Province of Ljubljana after the capitulation of the Italians and before the arrival of the Germans. The toughness inculcated by the Communists in their followers was remarkable — in spite of repeated terrible setbacks, they invariably rallied.

The so-called White Guard, fighting the Communists on the side of the Italians and sometimes under their command, was far more numerous. I wondered what these 8000 men would do now. I predicted that some would take to the mountains and others be disarmed, but I did not venture to forecast that any would be blind enough to join the Germans.

My suggestion was that, since there could hardly be any hope of finding a solution within the country, an energetic officer should be sent from outside to organise all those who refused to work with the Communists on an entirely military basis. For this, strong support from the BBC would be needed. Unfortunately, the BBC broadcasts were not very informative and my associates in Slovenia had impressed on me that I must request the BBC to widen the scope of its talks. While everybody knew, or at least surmised, what the Communists wanted, the democratic powers were not making it clear enough what their aims were. All my acquaintances were hoping for a lead from the new government.

I read and re-read this rather lengthy report for Captain Kern, hoping that Serge would come in person to collect it. However, he failed to appear and, after a fortnight, I mailed the paper to him. He confirmed that he had received it, condensed it and sent it to London. But it never reached Captain Kern.

While waiting for Serge and for my broken leg to heal I was busily reading Swiss newspapers and trying to figure out what had happened in Yugoslavia after the Italian capitulation. It appeared that the Italians had decided, or were forced, to hand over their arms, mostly to the Partisans. Consequently, the Mihailović-controlled area had shrunk, according to the Swiss *Weltwoche,* to about one-tenth of Yugoslav territory. Moreover something seemed to have gone wrong with the Yugoslav government of 'civil servants' in London, which had apparently shifted to Cairo though Captain Kern had resigned before its departure.

From time to time, I was glad to read something different so I jumped at the German translation of *Mission to Moscow* by the former US Ambassador Joe Davies. The impression I obtained from this book was that the Soviet Communists were greatly superior to our Yugoslav variety. I was particularly interested in Davies' description of how Trotskyites and Bukharinites confessed and repented of their crimes, and I had no foreboding that in a few years' time I myself would experience how such confessions were extracted.

At last the big day arrived when the cast was to be taken off my leg. When the hospital doctor who had only just returned from a short spell in the Swiss Army cut the plaster, it was obvious even to me that the broken bone had not knitted. The doctor suggested I should go to Berne for an operation and I eagerly accepted.

I rang Serge, and he soon called back saying that his boss, the Mihailović representative in Switzerland, would arrange everything provided I tell the Swiss that I had been linked with Mihailović headquarters in Slovenia, so as to pass for a military person. Since the Swiss had no objections, I armed myself with a pair of crutches and boarded a bus with my rucksack. In Berne, I was taken straight to the Lindenhofspital and operated on. Again, my days were spent in bed, but here intriguing visitors began arriving. Serge came first, bringing very bad news. After the bulk of Major Novak's followers had been massacred by the Partisans at Grčarice, the remainder had gathered in Ljubljana and agreed to serve under the Germans.

I thought this development terrible, but my next visitor did not agree. He was a Slovene from Geneva, an elderly gentleman and a former official at the League of Nations. I could hardly believe it when he told me that the situation in Slovenia was good, that the Germans had forced General Rupnik to assume power over the former Italian-occupied Province of Ljubljana, that he was organising some kind of police, most probably with the intention of attacking the German occupiers at a suitable moment. This man appeared to be an intermediary between some Slovene politicians in London and others in Ljubljana. At least he said that the expert studies by Dr Nagode had passed through his hands on the way to London. During the First World War, this same man had escaped from Austria to Russia and become a Yugoslav volunteer in the Serbian Army. His wife was of Russian origin, but he hated Communists. When Serge came to see me again, he warned me that I should not be too trusting when talking to this man. When he had shown him his own condensed version of my report to Captain Kern, the Geneva man had apparently accused Serge of being a Communist.

Eventually Serge's employer, Dr Anić, came to see me himself in the company of a professional colonel who had commanded Chetniks near the port of Rijeka. The colonel had been arrested, like all career officers, in the spring of 1942 and had escaped to Switzerland at the Italian capitulation. Dr Anić himself, whose real name was Dr Felix Engel, was a Jewish lawyer from the Croat capital of Zagreb. He had become involved with Mihailović after the Ustashi, under the influence of the Nazis, had killed his father, and had been obliged to escape to the Italian-occupied zone of Croatia. In his view nobody in Slovenia had ever considered Novak a particularly clever man, but then the idea of collaborating with the Italians was not Novak's. The order had come from his superiors because Serbs in Croatia and Bosnia had to fight both the Ustashi and the Partisans and so were driven to accept Italian protection. Some Serbs also came to regard the Ustashi and the Partisans equally as an embodiment of Croat hatred for the Serbs, although there were undoubtedly many more Serbs than Croats in the partisan detachments.

In my opinion the Mihailović movement was in grave danger of complete defeat. When I voiced these misgivings, I was told that the Yugoslav government in Cairo was recognised by all the Allies, and therefore everything was all right. Many people did not want to face the facts. Dr Anić asked me to write an article about Slovenia. My description was realistic, but when the article appeared in some Swiss paper it was amended to absurdity. While I truthfully said there were hardly any Chetniks in Slovenia, the article read that they were well hidden and would come out into the open at the right moment.

My misgivings were not reduced by information obtained by Dr Anić from a Spanish diplomat on his way home from Budapest. Contrary to the British assessment that the partisan army was about 200,000 strong, according to the Hungarians their number was probably no more than 50,000. The discrepancy was a result of misleading partisan terminology whereby some 250 men were called a brigade while normally a brigade numbers several thousand men.

Whatever their numerical strength, the partisan leadership organised a National Committee, in reality a rival government, at a meeting in Jajce; this was reported by the Swiss press on 5 December 1943. The Yugoslav government in Cairo reacted violently, accusing the Partisans of terrorism, claiming that they were helping the enemy by causing dissension, and blaming the Allies for not allowing it to explain the real situation to the population in Yugoslavia.

By Christmas 1943 I could move around again although I was limping badly, and I spent the festive season with a Swiss family not far from Berne. After Christmas, the Swiss authorities allowed me to stay in a boarding house instead of going into a camp because I needed further physiotherapy. On 31 December 1943, I unexpectedly received a postcard from my uncle, Naval Captain Boris Pirc, telling me that on Christmas Eve a group of Yugoslav officers from Ljubljana had crossed the Italian-Swiss border safely and explaining that they had escaped because they did not want to be press-ganged into the collaborating military formation of *Domobranci* (Home Guards). When these fugitives came to Berne some months later, they found it hard to express their horror that so many of their brother officers in Ljubljana were agreeing to serve in a formation under German sponsorship. They drew up a list of such men and asked Dr Anić to send it on to London, but this had no effect.

The situation was devilishly difficult. A young professional officer, a friend of mine, tried to escape to Switzerland, but was stopped by his contact in Trieste and sent back to Ljubljana to serve with the *Domobranci*. Another former fellow-pupil of the Kranj high school, Naval Lieutenant Marko Česenj, felt it his duty to join the Partisans, although his family was strictly Catholic; but the Communists murdered him the first night as they suspected him of being a nationalist. He was by no means the only one treated this way.

I felt it imperative to communicate to my associates in Ljubljana what political reality in the outside world was like, and I was glad when Dr Anić offered to send a letter to Dr Nagode via Trieste. First of all, I explained that after Eden's visit to Moscow in November 1943 the Allied commander in the Near East had issued a warning, saying that whoever fought on the German side against the Partisans should realise that the Allies disapproved most strongly.

Further, I stressed the prevailing leftist mood in the West, including a general demand for planning, and advised that *Pravda* should not lose its contacts with the left wing in Slovenia. I regretted that relations between Yugoslavs abroad were no better than at home, especially among the politicians in London. The only hope was an agreement between Partisans and Chetniks, at least until free elections could be held, which a new committee in London, consisting of three leading intellectual figures, including a Slovene, my university teacher Boris Furlan, could help bring about, although the committee was supporting the Partisans.

Another letter went by open mail straight to Ljubljana and surprisingly arrived at its destination. It was addressed, as arranged, to an old lady, written in French and in veiled terms, referring for instance to Mihailović as *Monsieur Michel*.

A later second letter to Dr Nagode reported the strictures against General Mihailović, for the benefit of my associates in Ljubljana. He was being criticised for his alleged acceptance of arms from the Italians – to restrain the Germans – and for his alleged backsliding into a narrow-minded Serb nationalism. A British Minister told Parliament that the British government supported the Partisans more than Mihailović because they were more active, but that it was not yet time to accept the National Committee proclaimed in Jajce as the freely elected government of Yugoslavia. Most curiously, the British papers, as reported in the Swiss press, claimed that a delegation of Partisans had visited the Yugoslav King and asked him to become their leader.

Since the Swiss authorities allowed me to live in Berne, I applied to work for a doctorate in economics in Fribourg until my leg was in walking order again. Fribourg is 20 minutes by train from Berne and I chose it rather than the University of Berne because I wished to study in French. Fribourg was full of Polish officers interned in Switzerland – two Polish divisions had entered the country in 1940 when France fell – and there were also a few Yugoslavs, among them the Croat Monsignor Juretić whom I met from time to time. He seemed to have come to Switzerland as a spokesman for Archbishop Stepinac, but he was also a political follower of the Croat leader Maček. I learnt from Juretić that Mihailović had been trying to establish contacts with Maček, the Croat leader who remained in Croatia and was kept under surveillance. This information did not bear out the allegations of narrow Serb nationalism. On the other hand, of course, it was also silly to pretend, as some inveterate Serb nationalists did, that the Partisans were an entirely Croat movement.

Towards the end of March 1944, an answer in code from Dr Nagode arrived by ordinary mail. In his view the worst forebodings we had when collaboration with the Italians began had come true. He was desperately looking for a way out. He considered that an agreement might be reached with the Partisans, but that the Province of Ljubljana would be the most difficult area to work in, as it was the centre of conflict between the Communists and the Catholic Party. He thought negotiating could be tried in other parts of Slovenia. Yet he admitted that the partisan communist leaders had not changed.

Dr Anić again forwarded a letter from me to Dr Nagode written on 3 June 1944. By then Churchill had repeatedly expressed his sympathy with Tito, but hoped that the King would succeed in bringing the sides together. Churchill's attitude made it clear that Mihailović's passivity and local collaboration with the occupiers had cost him the Allies' support and induced his failure in Croatia and Slovenia. However, a Spanish diplomat passing through Switzerland claimed that Serbia proper was still solidly behind him.

On behalf of Dr Anić, I asked Nagode whether there was any chance of groups getting into Slovenia from abroad and whether they could hope to reach an agreement with the Partisans if they introduced themselves as Yugoslav nationalists.

On 3 June, Dr Nagode was also writing to me, angrily describing the confusion in Slovenia and blaming it on both Communists and anti-Communists. The way he was writing then about willingness to support Serbian policy showed that he and other people in Ljubljana still had not grasped that the government in London and Mihailović had completely failed. I can no longer find a copy of this letter amongst the papers I left with my friends in Switzerland. Presumably I carried it on me and it was impounded in Ljubljana when the Secret Police searched our flat in 1947. Dr Nagode's copy must have disappeared in a similar way, so both copies may have ended up in the files of the Court that tried us.

I still possess a letter though from Naval Captain Vlado Naglič who had escaped from Slovenia to Southern Switzerland at about the same time, and who wrote to me in the same vein as Dr Nagode. When Italy capitulated, he joined the Partisans, but broke his leg and came back to Ljubljana pretending that it was an accident. His fracture saved him from arrest by the Germans when they rounded up all professional officers who would not join the *Domobranci*; he then made his way to Switzerland.

Captain Naglič reported that he had asked officers joining the Home Guard whether they were not worried that the Germans might send them to fight the British or the Americans or the Russians. They all thought they would be able to escape if it came to this, but they may have been underrating the Germans. In fact much later, at Christmas 1944, the Germans did arrest a group of officers who were organising themselves for an emergency. In April 1944, the German occupation authorities coerced the *Domobranci* into swearing an oath, the nature of which was not quite clear, although the local SS Commander claimed they had promised to fight side by side with his troops. Some leaders of the *Domobranci* hoped that there would be a separate peace between the Western Allies and Germany and that they would all turn against the Soviets. Naglič wrote that my father agreed with him in thinking that such expectations were nonsense. Slovenia was divided: the so-called Province of Ljubljana was for the *Domobranci* General, Rupnik, the rest for Tito.

Still under the influence of this letter, I ran into the Swiss Colonel Wattenwyll at my Swiss friends' house. On hearing that I was from Yugoslavia, he told me that the last pre-war Yugoslav military attaché in Berlin, Colonel Vauhnik, had just come to Switzerland from Italy and was passing most interesting information and views to the Swiss military. Vauhnik is mentioned earlier in this book. Everybody praised him, but I could never quite figure out what he was doing. In the spring of 1943 in Ljubljana, he rather childishly told my uncle Metod Pirc, in my hearing, that he was working for British Intelligence. Yet Walter Schellenberg, head of German intelligence after the execution of Canaris, considered Vauhnik important enough to mention him in his *The Schellenberg Memoirs* (André Deutsch 1956). It appears that in June 1944, Colonel Vauhnik had come to Switzerland to offer the services of the Slovene *Domobranci,* of some Croat soldiers and some Chetniks to the British. And it also appears that he was unceremoniously turned down.

By then I was anxious to leave. I could now walk normally and limped only when very tired. For a while I considered going back to Slovenia. But, as the news of internal clashes worsened, I tried to find a way into, and possibly through, France. My contacts in the French resistance in Geneva suggested that there were too many people in the *maquis* as it was. After the Allied landing in Normandy, I redoubled my efforts to leave Switzerland and do something useful in the war.

On 25 June 1944, my last letter was despatched to Dr Nagode complaining that it was more and more difficult to communicate in any direction. It reported that it was hard to understand the real relations between Americans, British and the Soviets, but that a separate peace between the West and Hitler was not on the cards. Even if the British leaders wanted to conclude such a peace (which they did not), public opinion would prevent them.

The only viable policy seemed to be co-operation with the Šubašić government, now installed in Britain after the dismissal of Purić in Cairo, with the purpose of reaching an agreement with Tito. I wrote that it was, of course, silly to say that Tito had 300,000 soldiers, but he did have Churchill's support and an incredibly efficient propaganda machine. Mihailović could reckon on only possible help from American right-wingers and Serb hatred of Croats. I was sorry he had allowed himself to be manoeuvred into this corner, because I did not doubt his patriotism.

In suggesting support for Šubašić in my letter, I actually assumed he was acting in full agreement with the Western Allies, especially Churchill. I regarded this as a guarantee that Britain and the United States would prevent Tito's introducing a communist dictatorship. It would help matters I thought, if there was a non-communist organisation fighting the Axis, or at least a large number of non-Communists amongst the Partisans.

Personally, I intended to press on with my plan to join the Yugoslav armed forces. In Geneva there were other young Slovenes wanting to do the same, among them Dr Milok, a former carpenter from near Trieste, who had been sentenced to 30 years' imprisonment by the Fascists as a Slovene nationalist. My French contacts dissuaded us from leaving immediately, and then the Allies landed in Southern France.

It looked as though there could be no more obstacles in our way and so I left Berne for Geneva with a Swiss travel permit. There I was told that the French border was sealed and nobody was allowed to enter. After long negotiations, my French contacts obtained a visa for me but none for Milok.

In spite of a regular visa, I was told to cross the border at a particular post and meet a French Red Cross man in Annemasse. My astonishment was great when the Partisans at the border, looking morose, were far from welcoming though they let me pass. It turned out that in the French department of the Haute Savoie, the Communist Party and its armed guerrillas were in full control.

In Annemasse the Red Cross man took me to the local Liberation Committee Chairman, a physician and son of the French communist leader Dr Cachin. He looked quite civilised, but then a less pleasant character turned up and started questioning me, primarily about whether I had been under the command of Tito or of Mihailović. When I said neither and pointed out that there was now an agreement of co-operation between all Yugoslavs, the interrogator took this amiss and I was told to wait.

In my frustration, I got entangled with the *Milice Patriotique* because I had heard that they were issuing travel permits. I soon learnt that this communist partisan police treated people without protection as criminals; they were not even allowing Frenchmen to enter, their pretext being that such Frenchmen had not come when there was any fighting to be done. When I told them my whole story and said I wanted to join the Yugoslav or any other Allied Army, I was escorted to the Swiss visa office to be sent back, but the Swiss said I had signed a commitment not to return, which was true.

At long last, it became clear that a Yugoslav partisan officer had arranged that no Yugoslavs would be allowed through without his permission. The *Milice Patriotique* wanted to arrest me, yet let me go to a hotel when I protested, keeping my documents but leaving my other belongings untouched.

To me these obstacles seemed preposterous — I was firmly convinced that the Tito-Šubašić agreement was internationally recognised and I could not quite see why any 'Yugoslav officer' should be interested in keeping me at Annemasse. Day after day, I went to ask whether the *Milice Patriotique* had established contact with the mysterious Yugoslav and then watched the bus leave for Annecy. In the end an Englishman who said that he was the Allied liaison officer in Annemasse, although he was in civilian clothes, advised me to get out of Annemasse without further discussions because the place was 'like a brothel'.

So I took a bus to Annecy and started looking for an office where I could get a travel permit. All offices were duplicated, one for *Francs-Tireurs et Partisans Français* — communist Partisans — and one for the *Armée Secrète* — Nationalist guerrillas. Eventually I discovered an AS office issuing permits and I would have got one, had it not transpired that I was a Yugoslav. The man then produced some kind of instruction, signed by the Gaullist commander of Haute Savoie, Colonel Nizier. It stated that an officer from the Yugoslav National Liberation Committee in Switzerland had arranged that Yugoslavs crossing without the Committee's travel permit should be returned to Switzerland, and those with a permit sent to *camps de triage* — selection camps. By now it had dawned on me that the Yugoslav Communists did not want people from abroad to come back to Yugoslavia, because they did not want anybody to dilute their movement and endanger their control. But why should Gaullists help them?

Wandering around Annecy, I came upon the Partisan to whom the Red Cross man had introduced me in Annemasse. He offered to give me a travel permit already filled in with a French name. So on I went by train to Chambéry but in

Aix-les-Bains, I was stopped by a partisan officer. First I lied to hide that I was a Yugoslav and almost finished up in a police prison, an unpleasant prospect which prompted me to tell the truth. I was taken to the *Casino des Bains* where German collaborators were imprisoned but kept apart from them. A man from French Intelligence, certainly no Communist, came to interrogate me and seemed to believe my story, but said he had to send me back to collect my documents.

On about 10 September 1944, I travelled back to Annecy accompanied by two communist youths who did not quite know what to make of me. Nor did they know where to take me, so that it was only after a long search that we went to D'Essaix barracks. Upon my insistence that all I needed was to have my documents returned, we were told to come again in the afternoon. When the two had had lunch on me and left, I went back to D'Essaix barracks, to be triumphantly told by a malevolent Communist in charge that they knew now that I had left Annemasse without a permit, and that I would have to wait. Before I grasped what was happening, I was searched and taken to a former riding school, turned by Germans into a garage and now used as a prison. There were about a hundred prisoners of all sorts there, predominantly alleged collaborators.

Nobody paid much attention to me when I lay down on some straw. A few days later, however, several people were moved and I was told to occupy the lower part of a two-tier bunk by a group consisting of a lawyer, a hotel manager and a common thief. When they heard that I had left Switzerland to join the Army, they fell about laughing. But they shared their private food with me, which was important since the prison food was insufficient.

I was interrogated by a polite and sensible man who seemed to regret my luck but could do nothing about it. My letters to various friends and authorities requested intercession, but only a few seem to have got through. One day we were all lined up for an inspection by Colonel Nizier, and I could hardly believe my ears when the bad-tempered Communist accompanying him pointed to me, saying: *'Et cela c'est un Yugoslave qui faisait de l'espionage pour les Allemands.'* Highly alarmed, I tried to speak to Nizier, a young man of my own age, but he only said: *'Oui, oui, plus tard!'*

After a fortnight, I was taken to the office, given back my documents and told I was free. A postcard from Dr Milok was amongst my papers, from which I gathered that he had crossed the border by stealth and looked for me at the D'Essaix barracks. They would not allow him to see me and behaved so threateningly that he preferred to make off. It would seem that I was released at the very moment when De Gaulle had disarmed the French Communists and stripped them of the power they had arrogated to themselves in parts of France. Maybe I was luckier than I realised because, during their short reign, the French Communists are reported to have killed tens of thousands of people under the pretext that they had collaborated with the Nazis.

I left for Grenoble and Lyons in search of Dr Milok, or any sensible Yugoslav representative or Allied body prepared to help me. After much toing and froing, a former Yugoslav Consul in Lyons gave me some kind of *ordre de mission* for Paris with which I boarded a train bound thither. It appeared useless to try to go to Marseilles because the connections south were still cut and there was no way of knowing whether one could get from Marseilles to Italy and on to Yugoslavia.

Communications in France were chaotic. My first train went as far as Paray-le-Monial, where we walked for a while because a bridge was down and then boarded a train to Moulins. There the same operation was repeated so as to travel to Nevers. We took three days to reach Paris, the train finding its way through pulled-up tracks. It was evening; I had a frugal meal and spent the first night in a small hotel near the Gare de Lyon.

Although there was no electricity, Paris was the old city of light: liberated, it could breathe freely again and it was visibly pulsating with life. The Métro did not work as yet, but I was happy to walk for miles to see a theatre performance or go to a meeting where the present and the future of France were discussed. French dailies such as *Le Figaro, L'Aube* and *L'Humanité* were getting to grips with French problems — not so different from Yugoslav ones. I was enthusiastic about the sensible articles by François Mauriac in *Le Figaro*. But the French Communist Party seemed the most active. Its slogans were everywhere, including the one demanding that the communist leader, Thorez, should be allowed to return, *Thorez à Paris!* He had been sentenced in his absence for deserting the Army during the validity of the Hitler-Stalin friendship pact. While I was in Paris, people as famous as Joliot-Curie and Pablo Picasso joined the Party.

After a few days entirely on my own, staying at the hotel where I had stayed with my father in 1936, I noticed in the newspapers an invitation to a meeting issued by the Yugoslav Liberation Committee, based at the Yugoslav Legation, and addressed to all Yugoslavs in Paris. In spite of misgivings, I went there and almost fell over Dr Zalokar, a friend from Geneva. He too, with another Slovene from Geneva, had crossed the Swiss border into France about a month after me, and they were duly stopped by the communist journalist Partonić in Lyons. This man, later to be Tito's Ambassador to Tokyo, was obviously the same so-called liaison officer who had made life in France so difficult for me. Dr Zalokar and his companion had been told by Partonić that they must go back to Switzerland, as they lacked a travel permit from a Liberation Committee: and yet the slogan 'All Yugoslavs home — our country needs us!' was being repeated *ad nauseam*. Dr Zalokar had refused to go back, but his companion had complied, as he was an officer in the Army reserve and considered himself subject to Army discipline. The result was that it took him more than a year to get to Yugoslavia.

At the meeting, we were supposed to elect a Yugoslav Liberation Committee for Paris. Some people were clearly better organised than others, so that only one list was put forward. General Ilić, a Spanish civil war veteran, became president, a student became secretary, and the most vociferous member was our old acquaintance, Partonić. It soon transpired that they were all Communists.

The Committee organised endless demonstrations in league with the French Communists, allegedly to popularise Yugoslavia in Paris, but propaganda for Yugoslavia soon turned out to be propaganda for Communism, using Yugoslavs. Among ourselves we were mostly harangued about the rottenness of the pre-war Yugoslav régimes. The rather elegant building of the Yugoslav Legation in Paris was time and time again described as the house that the last Yugoslav Envoy before the war had built for himself with money squeezed out of the Yugoslav workers.

In the kitchen of the Yugoslav Legation, the welfare section of the Liberation Committee established a mess for Yugoslavs without permanent Paris residence, dispensing food provided by the French authorities. Dr Zalokar and I ate there with all sorts of other people until somebody shouted: 'Eating at a red table is not allowed to just anyone.' Although the secretary rebuked the man, saying that we could not start distinguishing between red and green and other tables, Zalokar and I were told to stop coming to the Legation for meals and go to the barracks, where a group of Yugoslav ex-prisoners and ex-workers were incessantly treated to communist propaganda.

The dominance and manoeuvring of the Communists did not augur well for the fulfilment of the Tito-Šubašić agreement, but all I could do was to write again to London and then pack my rucksack and find my way back to Yugoslavia. The question remained how to travel – the Liberation Committee in Paris was eager to keep everything under its control, it urged everybody to assemble under its auspices for the return. At the same time, it stated openly that it did not want to rely on the Western Allies, but would ask the Soviet Embassy for help. This was preposterous.

At the French Foreign Ministry a sympathetic diplomat accepted my letters for London, in which I wrote that I would like to report on the situation in Slovenia and then join a fighting unit. He said he regretted that the Yugoslav Embassy was in the hands of Communists, but a regular mission should soon arrive. My visit to the newly opened British Consulate was a let-down, since the Consul said that even with a visa, I could travel to Britain only via Spain, and the Spaniards would not give me a transit visa before I had a British one. He was not in the least interested in what I wished to tell Yugoslavs in London.

At the end of October a Yugoslav military mission, consisting of an Air Force lieutenant-colonel wearing the old Yugoslav uniform and two communist red-star captains, finally arrived from London. The colonel had a message for me from Captain Kern saying he had left for the Mediterranean to become

Commander of the Yugoslav Navy under the Tito-Šubašić agreement. The message for me personally was that the only recognised armed force I could join was the National Liberation Army, and that for this I would have to go to Italy. Alternatively I was offered a post in the Yugoslav diplomatic service, but at this stage I had no wish to finish up in an office.

The military mission from London exhorted us all to go home as soon as possible to fight with the Liberation Army. The Air Force colonel, who had been in Belgrade with Šubašić, explained that all differences had been unravelled and that there was now full understanding between Tito's National Committee and Šubašić's government. He himself had witnessed the enormous effort which had been made to win the war but my own past experience left me sceptical. In a private conversation, the colonel confirmed that Tito's Committee had taken over the whole military organisation, and that the Liberation Army was indeed the sole force. But when his red-star colleagues came into the room he looked strangely anxious and fell silent, something I did not like at all. In the colonel's opinion it would take time to organise repatriation transport for Yugoslavs and so he advised me to try on my own.

Before leaving, I wanted to have another go at writing to London. This time I wrote directly to Šubašić himself, because I knew he was a friend of the Croat branch of our family. Explaining the vexed situation in Slovenia all over again, I offered to return there and bring the different parties together; such an attempt would, of course, require support both from the London government and from Tito. At that time, I still surmised that Tito might be less sectarian than the Slovene Communists.

The Yugoslav colonel told me that he could not forward the letters, so I went back to the Quai d'Orsay and pressed them onto a very reluctant French official. The letters never arrived – not that that had any immediate consequences. Almost a year later, though, a friend was told at Tito's Foreign Ministry in Belgrade that they were in possession of a very 'nasty' letter I had written to London from Paris. What could have been 'nastier' than to try and mediate between the Communists and their adversaries on Slovenia?

By the beginning of October trains were running again from Paris to Lyons and on to Marseilles. What was troublesome was to obtain ticket and seat reservations, because enormous crowds were besieging ticket offices at the Gare de Lyon. Once I had managed to get onto the train, it took only ten hours to reach Marseilles. Poles were coming there in droves in an attempt to get to Italy and join the Anders Polish Army; with help from them and the French military, I found a Yugoslav liaison officer who was a committed Chetnik but willing to help any Yugoslav coming through. Although I told him that I was in favour of the agreement between Tito and Šubašić, he promised to take me to the Allied repatriation camp at Madrague, not far from Marseilles. First, however, we went to the building of the former Yugoslav Consulate-General, where a

Liberation Committee had installed itself. In the general confusion, the only information to be extracted there was that the British and the Americans were not to be trusted. They would allegedly take Yugoslavs to Africa and recruit them for the Royal Guard.

So all one could do was to go to the Allied ex-POW repatriation camp at Madrague. The British officer in command, Captain Eagon, made it clear that they could transport any Yugoslav to Italy only if he was prepared to volunteer for Tito's Army, which of course I accepted.

While I was settling down in one of the tents, a group of Russians arrived and started making themselves comfortable. They all seemed rather intelligent workers and laughed uproariously when I wondered what they were doing in a British camp, since our Liberation Committees insisted that Soviet ships would soon come to take the Russians and the Yugoslavs home. 'Anybody waiting to go by Soviet boat will have to wait for a long time,' they exclaimed, clapping me on the shoulder.

The Liberation Committee in Marseilles must have come to a similar conclusion, since the next day its leaders brought 52 Yugoslavs to be repatriated from Madrague. They wanted Captain Eagon to sign a formal undertaking that these men would be sent to Italy to serve exclusively in the Yugoslav National Liberation Army. He shrugged his shoulders, sighed and signed.

We all stayed at the Madrague camp for a fortnight with permission to come and go as we wished. The Liberation Committee people wanted to impose a pair of Communists on us as leaders, but the Yugoslav group almost unanimously refused to accept them and said that I had served them well as liaison so far and I should continue to act as liaison with the camp authorities. I felt flattered but kept in the background. All I did was to try to keep our men quiet and to prevent them from quarrelling with the Polish inmates. The Liberation Committee people had somehow convinced them that all Poles were Fascists, to which the Poles did not take at all kindly, understandably enough. Another bee in my compatriots' bonnet was a perennial hankering after collectives. Any odd group had to form a 'collective', which meant that everybody had to pay in all his money and was given an equal share in the yield. Our Russian comrade thought this habit excessively funny, which dampened the zeal for instant Communism amongst the Yugoslavs.

All along I hoped that the group of Yugoslav officers assembled in Switzerland would come to the repatriation camp too, but they never showed up. I was told in Paris that they were coming and Captain Eagon had confirmed that he was expecting them. Presumably the Communists did not want them to return too early; as it was, they only got home after the war.

Eventually, in mid-November, the day arrived when we were to leave for Italy. The camp officer escorted us Yugoslavs and the 10 Russians accompanying us, to the port of Marseilles where we embarked on an American troop transporter. In addition, there were a large number of Poles and, according to our own estimates, about 1000 Soviet soldiers and about 400 German prisoners. We Yugoslavs had a good look at everybody, since the Americans detailed us to organise the traffic from dormitories to the boat's dining compartment. It was standing room only, around some 15 tables for 10 persons each.

The Soviet troops astounded us by their primitive behaviour. They were quite prepared to go down on their knees if they thought this could earn them one more sausage or cup of coffee. The contrast with the 10 Russians who were with us was striking, but when we asked them the reason for this difference, they just shrugged their shoulders. My Yugoslav compatriots who had been exposed, as I had, to propaganda on the great dignity of Soviet soldiers were at a complete loss to understand what kind of human cattle these people were. Our first encounter with Soviet men was puzzling, to say the least.

The Americans manning the ship were harsh. I was treated as an equal by the officers, and a lieutenant even ironed my trousers before I disembarked; but the sailors behaved towards the other Yugoslavs with condescension. That did not prevent them from coming to our dormitory to sell us chocolate and clothing for any kind of money that was going.

When our boat arrived in Naples, the Poles departed for General Anders' Army, the Soviet ex-prisoners disappeared, and we Yugoslavs with the Russians accompanying us were taken to a repatriation camp called Ricino next to the excavated ruins of the old Roman city of Herculaneum. The camp was in the grounds of a magnificent villa and was under British control.

It soon turned out that the British here were far less enthusiastic about the Yugoslav Partisans than their counterparts in France. There was still a full-time Yugoslav liaison officer with royal insignia attached to the camp who obviously enjoyed their sympathies. He worked closely with Lieutenant Moore who, after my companions had insisted they were leftists, lined us up and found out which of us were former German and Italian soldiers and should, he said, go to prisoners' camps. As if to underline his hostility, he pointedly warned that we should have no illusions about Trieste − it had never been and never would be Yugoslav. Nonetheless, the 20 or so of us Yugoslavs who remained were issued with full equipment, apart from weapons.

After settling in, I had a long discussion with the Chetnik officer, who turned out to be a friend of my father's friends in Belgrade, a lawyer by profession, who had spent the war as a prisoner in a camp in Italy. Although I explained to him that the agreement between Tito and Šubašić was finalised and that, as a result, a mixed partisan-royalist mission had arrived in Paris from London, he tried to talk me out of going back to Yugoslavia. Indeed, he suggested I should go to Rome and see the Slovene politician Krek, who was still the Yugoslav representative on the Allied Control Commission for Italy, with a view to enrolling at the University of Rome. 'I have no intention of studying while the war is on,' was my reply. Then the officer wanted to send me to a royalist camp — where again there would be nothing to do. In the end he loyally gave me the address of the Titoist repatriation office in Naples.

When I got there, I found everybody who had been turned out of the British-controlled camp. Most had discovered a Committee of the Italian Communist Party and been directed by them to the headquarters of the Partisans. This consisted of two private apartments in adjacent buildings, too small for the multitude of Yugoslavs who had come to report, so that the candidates for repatriation slept all the way down the staircase in one building. I was received with much rejoicing by those who knew me and informed that the partisan liaison officer would be back soon — he had gone to collect the remaining Yugoslavs from the camp where I had been.

In fact, they all arrived shortly on a truck and the liaison officer whose name or rank I never learnt instructed me to go with him immediately to the British repatriation headquarters to interpret his complaints about the way he was being treated. And off we went. The partisan liaison officer would not wait for me to tell the lieutenant on duty in English what it was all about, but launched into loud complaints about Lieutenant Moore, all in bad Italian. It appeared that the Partisans considered Italian the diplomatic language in which to deal with the British, while the British refused to accept this arrangement and demanded English interpreters.

When I explained that I was one, the liaison officer and I were ushered into the office of a grey-haired major, the commander of Allied repatriation camps. The Partisan immediately began spouting another deluge of complaints, this time in Serbo-Croat, gesticulating wildly, while I translated, trying to keep up with him. 'You must translate everything word by word,' he admonished me every time he thought that I was speaking calmly. The gist was that the British, especially Lieutenant Moore, were treating the Yugoslav Partisans, the speaker in particular, badly, and staging a propaganda war against the National Liberation Army although the Partisans had saved so many British pilots.

The major offered us cigarettes and then commented, more in sorrow than in anger, that it would hardly be surprising if the partisan liaison officer met with unpleasantness, because he was so rude himself. Turning to me, he asked to be sent a liaison officer whose name and rank he would know (the Communists gloried in never wearing rank insignia) and who would have a proper letter of introduction from his headquarters. On the way back to the partisan offices, we stopped at a military hospital to visit some Yugoslav pilots. The liaison officer comforted them that they would soon go back to Yugoslavia and would no longer have to put up with the English.

It became clear to me that, in spite of all assurances of friendship and co-operation at the highest level, there was a nasty tension between the Partisans and the British wherever they really had to work together. The main reason was presumably that the Communists considered the British their 'class enemies' and behaved accordingly, forever suspecting them of foul play. Naturally the British did not like this attitude, so there were continual clashes.

We spent the next three days waiting for trucks to take us from Naples to Gravina, the Yugoslav transit camp, and this gave us plenty of time for discussion. I heard a young lad who had been badly wounded in partisan fighting in Yugoslavia and now served as a messenger at the partisan office in Naples, declare that 'we were not just a National Liberation Army but a political army.' He might as well have said that 'we' were fighting for the Party rather than for the country. Such views augured badly for the Tito-Šubašić agreement and my black mood hardly improved when, after our arrival at Gravina, we were treated to a speech by a political Commissar garnished with words such as 'snotty-nosed King Peter' and 'lousy Royal Guard'. This did not look much like brotherly co-operation of all Yugoslavs in the fight against the enemy.

There was, of course, no question of my contacting Captain (by then Admiral) Kern or passing on the message from the British major in Naples about liaison officers to anybody else. The partisan officers, almost all without badges of rank in accordance with the fashion, distinguished themselves mostly by their boorishness and unpleasantness.

On 23 November 1944, after only one night in Gravina, we were taken by truck to the port of Bari to sail for Split. As a final assault on my morale and a clear demonstration that the Communists did not pay any attention to the Tito-Šubašić agreement, we had been given red stars to fix on our caps, though the agreement provided for national rather than communist emblems to be worn. I could not bring myself to attach the star to my headgear until somebody warned me that I should, unless I wanted trouble, which so perturbed me that I would have slipped away, given the chance. I did jump out of the lorry while it was waiting in front of the port entrance, but somebody called me back and then we went on board.

We were all loaded onto a small Yugoslav pre-war vessel which navigated along the coast to Monte Gargano, where we stayed at anchor overnight, and then crossed the Adriatic. My memories of Split were most pleasant and I was waiting impatiently to arrive there. But what a disappointment! No doubt it was foolish of me to expect it to be unaltered, but the change was shocking.

The shore was deserted, the streets empty. A few children stood on the pier, scrutinising the ship. The Paris of 1944 was certainly not the Paris of 1936, but it was full of life. Split was like a cemetery.

5

Enslavement by the Liberation Army

On land, we formed columns and watched in amazement as children threw themselves on a few biscuits a man happened to drop. It dawned upon us that Split was starving. There were only a few old women hanging around when we marched to the school where we were going to spend the night. Since no food was distributed, all we could do was go to sleep.

The next morning we were given a day off in town, so I started looking for my relative in Split, another naval captain from my home town married to a Dalmatian. I could not remember his address and started asking people, as Split was relatively small then. Somebody looking like a sailor gave me the address of the captain's father-in-law, a respected Split lawyer. 'But,' he said, 'I must warn you, one of the family was shot when the Communists came.' I found the address but the building had been hit in an Allied bombing raid. I learnt the new whereabouts of the family from neighbours.

Indeed, the old lawyer told me, his other son-in-law had been picked up with about 40 others and shot without any semblance of trial when partisan soldiers entered town in September 1944. The names of the victims had simply been pinned up. This son-in-law, a lawyer himself, had been a Yugoslav nationalist belonging to the Ljotić organisation, but not guilty of any kind of collaboration. At the time he was killed, his two sons were with the Partisans, and his daughter had enrolled with the Liberation Army as a nurse, hoping to save her father.

My relatives suggested that I rest and freshen up, which was to save me from taking part in a futile battle. For when I returned to the school where we were billeted, all I found there was my rucksack; all my comrades had left. As I learnt later, they were sent without training, and without any firm organisation, as the Fourth Overseas Brigade, to take part in the siege of Knin, where about 3000 Germans were besieged by a large number of Partisans, of whom about 8000 had been killed by the time the Germans received the order to withdraw, disentangled themselves and marched away.

I did not quite know what to do next – there were no established military authorities. By pure coincidence, I ran into my uncle Metod Pirc in the streets of Split that very afternoon. He was in a bad state because of an ear infection and had come to Split for an operation.

We had last met in the spring of 1943 in Ljubljana. When we had all left Kranj, Captain Metod Pirc had returned there with his wife and son and stayed with my grandmother in the family house. He had avoided being captured by either the Italians or the Germans and returned home from naval service, believing that he would be safe in our home town because he had never lived there since the First World War. But he soon became involved in the resistance and finally had to leave for his wife's home town of Karlovac in Croatia – under Italian occupation – to avoid persecution by the Nazis.

From there he joined the Partisans at the Italian capitulation and walked through Bosnia to Dalmatia. He visited Tito's headquarters on the way, had his rank recognised, converted into a colonel's, and he was sent to the coast, where he was supposedly to help with the organisation of a new navy. As a professional officer he was not entrusted with a command, but sent to a naval school on the island of Vis to teach. In the meantime this little outpost had become most important, since Tito took up residence there after the German parachutists' attack on his Bosnian hide-out.

In the summer of 1944, Captain, now Colonel, Metod Pirc developed a violent ear ache. No consultant was available, while ordinary physicians said they could not do much. Pirc wanted to go to Bari where there was a Yugoslav military hospital, but it was thought too dangerous to let him go to Italy because he might contact the Allies. By sheerest luck a Croat ear specialist from Šibenik arrived on Vis in time to carry out an emergency operation on Pirc, on a kitchen table by candlelight.

Pirc was then sent to Split, which had just been liberated, and was submitted to another surgical intervention though without much hope of saving his hearing. He did lose all hearing in one ear; but a worse danger threatened from an infection which was thought likely to yield only to the new drug, penicillin, and this was unobtainable in Split, at least for Pirc. Then I happened to hear that the physician who had treated my tuberculosis was in Bari in a high position with the Yugoslav Medical Corps. From him we soon obtained the penicillin, and Pirc was saved.

My previous consultant, who considered himself an old friend, wanted me to come over to Bari for a check-up, but it was absolutely impossible for me to return to Italy. The physician expressed his surprise and wrote that under no conditions would he allow me to join a military unit. 'Don't try to be a hero,' he wrote, 'you are intelligent enough to be of great help in other ways.' Frankly, I must admit that, had I gone to Italy, I would not have come back to Split. My eagerness to help in the war had evaporated after a few weeks under the Communists' combination of pettiness and murderousness.

In Split I met other old friends, including the senior student with whom I began my resistance career in 1941. He was arrested by the Italians and kept in a concentration camp until 1943 when he joined the Italian Partisans together with his brother. The brother was killed while my friend succeeded in crossing the battle-lines and going to Bari, whence he was sent to Split to help organise a brigade. He had in tow a young man, a former sailor who had left the Yugoslav Navy when the crews refused to hoist communist flags and join Tito. By the time I met him he bitterly regretted this decision.

Split continued to be an unpleasant place — there was not enough food and communist pettiness was at work. Everybody had to have a job. Although there was nothing to administer, a huge bureaucracy began developing whose members were given just enough food for themselves as their salary, while there was no food for families. People from the villages in the interior would bring food in dribs and drabs and people who had nothing else to eat would exchange their bed-linen and furniture for whatever there was. Scarcity of food was certainly no fault of the Communists — Dalmatia always had to obtain food from elsewhere. But we all knew that UNRRA — or the services preceding it — were in operation, and that Yugoslavia was not benefiting because the Communists would not allow the Western donors to inspect the distribution. Worse than that: while we Slovenes were being emphatically reminded almost daily to clear out of Dalmatia because we were eating their food, boatloads of civilian refugees, women and children, began arriving from Italy and from further afield. They had been taken away in 1943 to escape from the Germans and had been looked after by the Western Allies. The Communists were so eager to get them away from what they imagined to be Allied control, that they brought them home in positively indecent haste, although there was no means of subsistence.

The hatred displayed towards the British, and, to a somewhat lesser degree, towards the Americans, was hard to believe. In the middle of the harbour lay a British destroyer out-of-bounds to everybody. To the townspeople who must have remembered days of festivities before the war when the British Mediterranean fleet visited Yugoslav ports, it must have looked odd to see solitary British naval officers going for walks without anybody daring to smile at them, let alone address a word to them.

In this climate, I thought that the least I could do was to see a British liaison officer and tell him about the profound communist hatred of the Western Allies and the minimal chance that the provisions of the Tito-Šubašić agreement would ever be implemented. The former sailor, who spoke some English, already knew Captain Scott. We tried at first to get into the villa which housed the British mission unobserved, but in the end we simply walked past the partisan sentry.

The British officer did not seem surprised by my diagnosis of communist hatred and intentions, but he could not help me either when I said that I was so alarmed by partisan behaviour that I wanted to go back to Italy. When we talked about an alternative plan to go to Slovenia as soon as possible, Captain

Scott suggested we join Major Pearce, the new liaison officer for Slovenia, who would be travelling there in a jeep. It later turned out that Major Pearce was in company with the Reuters correspondent, Hubert Harrison, and could not take all three of us, while I would not go on my own. The British officers knew full well that it was dangerous for us to have contacts with them and helped us to get out of the villa through a side door.

We decided to set out on our own in mid-December, and asked for arms from the Partisan Town Command: my lot was an old Italian rifle. A boat took us to the badly bombed town of Zadar, whence we hitched a lift to Obrovac, but could get no further towards Topusko because the Germans, moving from Karlovac to Banja Luka, had cut the road normally used by the Partisans. The Germans had insufficient troops to keep it under permanent control but they could dispatch their supply column to Banjaluka at any time they chose.

During the two or three days' waiting, we listened to propaganda songs in rhyming couplets accompanying kolo dancing from 4p.m. till 11p.m.

> Oy, Comrade Tito, oy, Comrade Tito,
> White violet,
> You are followed by all the young.

or

> Oy, Communist Party, oy, Communist Party,
> Sweet scented flowers,
> You are followed by all our people.

By then it was decided it was useless to go on waiting, as the road was still blocked by the Germans and looked like remaining that way. Even Major Pearce and Hubert Harrison in their jeep had to come back to Obrovac. We all returned to Split.

There we soon found a Slovene partisan officer, a butcher's apprentice by trade, and the first member of the new Vth Overseas Brigade Command. A former Italian Carabiniere NCO was to be its Commander, with another butcher as deputy, and a blacksmith had been chosen as second political Commissar. My associate from 1941 became Chief of the propaganda section. Under him were several painters and a poet who were later to become well known. I was taken on as legal officer.

This team commanded the troops being shipped in from Italy and Britain, predominantly former Italian- and German-mobilised Slovenes who had either escaped over the lines or surrendered and then volunteered for Yugoslav units. They were well-trained soldiers who knew what to do almost without officers – there was only one officer among them.

When we had won the confidence of some of the better educated, they told us how reluctant they had been to join communist units. A few had even escaped from a camp in Britain and contacted a Slovene Catholic politician in exile there, but he told them that there was only one army they could serve in. So they came to Split to be put under the command of party members, regardless of their qualifications. Had the Yugoslav politicians in exile in London — and they were, after all, leading politicians from all the Yugoslav democratic parties — thought of organising one or two divisions under the command of proper officers, with British support, maybe the agreement between Tito and Šubašić would not have turned out to be simply a way of handing Yugoslavia over to Tito.

As legal officer, I visited the Military Tribunal in Split and sought guidance on the laws I was expected to apply. I was given just two typed sheets of paper, not specifying any crimes or punishments, only giving examples of each and concluding with 'etc.'. It was obvious to me that under such a code a death sentence could be passed on anybody. Little did I know that in the end such a mockery of law would be applied to me. Fortunately, I did not have to act under this code, since my only 'case' was a drunken elderly proletarian from Ljubljana. Under the protection of drink, this man told our commander exactly what he thought of him. I tried to calm him down, as it was my duty to do, but he just went on cursing the officer. I wrote a report on him which got him off lightly. I was relieved because I knew that things could turn much nastier.

In Split I also found a cousin of my father's, a former Yugoslav Naval NCO who had retired before the war and was living there with his wife. While I was in the town, he was called up and disappeared. Nobody could find out what happened until his wife was told that 'he had been sent to the 13th Battalion', which in communist language meant killed by the authorities. Why, we never learned. Possibly because he said an offending word to a former fellow-NCO who was now a high-ranking officer.

I spent most of my time in the propaganda section which was running courses in Slovene. Various foreigners of communist persuasion had rediscovered their long-forgotten Slovene origin after Tito's victories and now had, as it were, to learn their mother tongue. Some were children of Slovene emigrants to France, others Italian soldiers from Trieste.

The food that we, members of the Vth Overseas Brigade, got to survive on was limited: we had a daily ration of maize bread, the size of two rolls, with tea in the morning and a cup of maize soup for lunch and dinner. This compared favourably with what the civilians in employment were given, but not so favourably with the rations the staff officers could treat themselves to. I discovered this one day when I went into the brigade staff-room and found the table spread, not with maps or operation plans, but with loaves of white Canadian bread and tins of Spam. The officers looked embarrassed at first but then offered me a slice of Spam and a piece of bread.

At the beginning of 1945, cracks began showing in the Tito-Šubašić agreement. The quarrel was about who should be appointed regent until the promised plebiscite on the form of government. Tito succeeded in persuading Churchill to put pressure on King Peter and managed to have him accept three representatives with leanings to Communism. Nor were the feelings of royalists spared in Split. Columns of Partisans — among whom British reports said there were many royalists — could be heard daily marching and singing such anti-royalist songs as

Daj mi pušku od tri metra
da ubijem kralja Petra

(Give me a rifle three metres long to kill King Peter)

Fresh soldiers from overseas were still arriving in Split to join our brigade, while established units were being moved to villages around Biograd where the staff had gone. My worry was that the Vth Overseas Brigade would be used for other purposes and would not reach Slovenia before the end of the war, if then. I wanted to be there in time myself, because what I knew about the 'liberation' of Split made me fear for my father. The medical certificate I had received from the doctor in Bari made it easy for me to obtain a release from the Brigade.

Within a few days, I found the representative of the Slovene National Liberation Committee, a man whom I had known when still at home in Ljubljana. In fact I knew that he had been arrested and sentenced to death at the beginning of the Italian occupation, but had been reprieved, and had escaped from prison and joined the Liberation Army in 1943. He offered me a lift to Topusko from where I should be able to cross over into Slovenia.

On 2 February, I left Split for Biograd by boat in the company of Lieutenant Slamič, son of an industrialist who was in Split arranging supplies for the Slovene Partisans. He introduced me to a captain, a naval engineer, on his way to Slovenia en route for Trieste. He had joined the Partisans in 1943 and been sent to work in an Italian shipyard where they repaired small fishing boats armed with machine-guns for the Partisans. The British supplied all the materials, yet he too was warned off when he became friendly with the British Commander.

Before I left Biograd, my Italian rifle was replaced by a newly delivered British Sten-gun still wrapped in oiled paper. Travelling in lorries, lying on top of sacks and crates, we again reached Obrovac, but the road had been cut once more. It was while waiting around there that I saw German prisoners for the first time. They were hungry and dirty, running with lice, and it was said that several died each day. I was surprised to discover that I was sorry for them.

At Obrovac many of the Slovene party fell ill, so we returned to Biograd for a welcome disinfection and clean-up. This time round I was billeted on an elderly woman, in a room with a clean bed, and enjoyed warm hospitality when she discovered my views on the Communists. We would all listen to the BBC broadcasts, and learnt that King Peter had just withdrawn his support for Šubašić.

Leaving Biograd again we drove through desperately poor and war-torn territories before reaching a place named Slunj, where we were told food could be found. We were treated generously to bacon and 'rakija' (Yugoslav liquor), but salt was short. Salt in fact made up the larger part of the supplies for Slovenia transported on our lorries.

When we reached Topusko, a former spa and now the headquarters of the Croat Partisans, I almost immediately ran into an old friend, a lieutenant in the Royal Army, whom I had not seen for two years. He was now a major in the Liberation Army on his way to Belgrade with pupils for the Military School. His news was bad. Quite a few friends with whom we had spent a lot of the early summer of 1943, and especially the career officers, had joined the *Domobranci* and were, so to speak, on the other side. He revealed that his partisan unit had at some stage almost clashed with a *Domobranci* unit commanded by a friend and colleague. How disastrous and how stupid!

At Topusko, we were told by the commander of the Slovene transport base that a Slovene brigade should be coming for supplies, but that it would be delayed because the Germans were using the railway and road between Zagreb and Karlovac intensively, while the Partisans had to cross it to reach Topusko from Slovenia. The Slovene brigade had recently tried to come across but was forced back. Allied stores in Topusko were piling up with food and clothing for Slovenia since supplies were arriving faster than they could be sent on. We spent a good deal of time at the transport base, where they fed us and listened to what the Communists had to say. The Commissar who had come with our column from Dalmatia, a hairdresser by profession, had a lot to contribute although his basic philosophy could be summed up in the communist slogan: 'Everything must change, then things will be better.'

He took a sudden interest in me, and when he saw me glancing at a book and several sheets of paper he had on the table in front of him, he suggested I should read them. The sheets were a document intended for the use of political activists, the content some sort of elementary Marxism. First a bourgeois revolution was to be carried through under the leadership of the Party, then it would be turned into a dictatorship by the Party with the suppression of all liberties for the bourgeoisie. The Soviet Union Friendship Society had the function of selecting people ready to support these efforts. Land would be promised to the peasants so that they would side with the Communists, but later they would be persuaded to join co-operatives and pool their land. National liberation movements had to further communist ideas when a country fell under foreign domination, and their struggle was to be used to destroy all the pre-occupation domestic government institutions, administrative apparatus and law not destroyed by the occupation authorities, so as to make place for a communist take-over. These instructions were confirmed in a book entitled *The History of the All-Union Communist Party (Bolshevik)*. It explained the cunning and violence used by Lenin to emerge as the only victor in the Russian upheavals at the end of the First World War.

The last scales fell from my eyes — I understood the meaning of communist manoeuvres and tactics. It had been silly of us to expect common decency from Communists who believed that they were destined to save the world, and were therefore prepared to ride roughshod over everybody. There remained no hope that they would abide by the agreement between Tito and Šubašić unless they were forced to.

At the end of February, news came through that a Slovene brigade had finally crossed the railway line from Zagreb to Karlovac, bringing the wounded. It would be returning to Slovenia with provisions and the naval engineer and I could go with it. The brigade was north of Topusko, but by the time we joined it, its departure had been put off and we were billeted in a peasant house. I was amazed at the primitiveness of this Serb village in Croatia, only about forty kilometres from Zagreb. The wooden house in which we stayed consisted of a small kitchen and one room with a cowshed and barn outside. The floor was of mud and this log-cabin had to house a family of six or seven. An aged grandmother sat in the middle, spinning on an old wheel. The family offered us a bed to sleep in, but we felt it wiser to choose the table. For food we visited other peasant houses and were invariably given maize and milk which, in these conditions, seemed a delicious mix.

A final delay occurred because Germans and Ustashi came to confiscate cattle in a nearby village. I saw them driving cows down a road only a few hundred metres away causing great disturbance among the peasants, but although we had a Slovene and a Croat brigade in the immediate neighbourhood they did nothing, presumably because they did not wish to reveal their presence.

Late the next afternoon — in the first days of March 1945 — the column for Slovenia moved on. About two hundred Partisans of the Brigade, with the mules carrying salt in the middle, together with hangers-on like us and some civilians, advanced over marshy ground. At dusk we once lost contact with the head of the column because they were progressing too fast, which led to some discussion about who was responsible. 'Once we would shoot people like that,' somebody surmised. There were many stories around about how harsh partisan discipline used to be. Any man who merely took an apple from an orchard would be shot on the spot, or so the old Partisans proudly said. The same allegedly happened to men and women Partisans who fell in love and were found kissing. All this was not inconceivable if one knew that the communist leaders thought their creed entitled them to final judgement on everything.

We jumped over a stream one by one, crossed first the Zagreb–Karlovac railway and then the road, luckily without being spotted by any enemy. After being on the move for twelve hours we had covered perhaps 20 miles and were approaching a village when shots were heard. In the village two Partisans from our column were knocking on a door alleging that there had been rifle fire from the house. As a curiously pointless counter-measure, the Commander ordered the firing of a few mortar shells from the village square into the open fields. We took the road out of the village into a narrow valley, but after some 100 metres we left the valley and began a steep climb. The climb became a rush when machine-gun shots were heard from behind.

Nobody seemed quite clear what was going on. While the sun rose very red on the horizon, somebody was shouting unintelligible orders, and the column, badly disrupted, simply moved on over the crest of the hill. On the other side, all was quiet, but the Brigade failed to keep together. We had been almost 24 hours without proper rest and there were stragglers all along the road.

The naval engineer and I were walking together again and decided to go to a village we noticed high up on top of a hill. There a girl activist took us to her house and told us that groups of Germans and Ustashi sometimes came up to this place. The peasant houses in this region were built of bricks and divided into several rooms with wooden floors. The one into which we were shown had a crucifix in a corner. Just after we had settled down, somebody knocked and, to our relief, it was two men from our brigade. They had been in the rear of our column, and as they were leaving the village where shots had been fired, they had been hailed: 'Halt, who are you?' Somebody idiotically answered that they were Partisans, upon which the Germans and the Ustashi opened fire. About three or four of their comrades had been killed, but these two succeeded in running away and hiding. They watched as 10 to 20 Germans looked for them for a while, but eventually left on a truck with some five prisoners. One had been shot through his underarm and I did my best to bandage him after first applying plum brandy. To my amazement, I later heard that this inglorious clash was described as a partisan victory.

The next morning, the peasants gave us an ox-drawn wagon to carry the wounded man, who was in pain and feverish, to a partisan hospital. Right until we separated, he went on cursing the incompetence and the negligence of his so-called officers.

We were now in Slovenia and progress was smooth. The Slovenes being bent on efficiency, we were deloused and then slept in the drinking hall of an inn. The next day, the naval engineer and I walked a few more hours and reached

Črnomelj, a little provincial market town, the centre of the territory in partisan hands.

Again we were billeted at an inn where I spotted some familiar faces through the window. Recognising a group of professional people who had left Split just before the road to Topusko was cut, I learned they had arrived here a month or two before us, and were still hanging around in Črnomelj with nothing to do. It did not seem that I had missed much. This group of professionals, seven or eight of them, were people who had been in prison in Italy or were simply hiding there, awaiting the Allies. When they found themselves on the right side of the Italian front, they all volunteered for service under the Tito-Šubašić agreement and got to Slovenia. The Slovene Communists kept them billeted in a pub, supplied them with food and let them wait.

Among them was Ferdinand Majaron, President of the British-Yugoslav Association in Ljubljana before the war, who had been arrested by the Italians because of this post and had spent more than two years in an Italian prison. There was nothing for him to do. There was a director of a mining company who had travelled to Switzerland under the Italian occupation. His mission had been to report to London, via the Yugoslav Legation in Berne, on what was happening in Slovenia. Through the diplomats' bureaucratic negligence, the Italian intelligence had decoded the cables sent to London on his behalf, so that he was arrested on his return to Italy and sentenced to death, but reprieved. He was an officer in the reserve, but no employment could be found for him. Finally, there was one of my friends from Switzerland, Dr Milok, who was an Italian-trained artillery officer, but again without a job. He asked to be sent to a unit near his home town of Trieste, but the Communists would not have this. They feared that he would have political influence and would not allow him to go. His political influence would have stemmed from his pre-war, anti-Fascist activity, which had brought him the sentence of 30 years in prison.

The naval engineer and I wondered what would happen to us when we went to report our arrival to the headquarters for Slovenia the next day. We were both told to go to a transit room in a village some three miles north of Črnomelj and wait there for further instructions. The smallish transit room turned out to be inhabited by about 15 people sleeping all over the floor. I was to spend almost a month there, while the naval engineer left for Trieste within a fortnight. We were both closely questioned by the personnel section of the Slovene headquarters, and any foreign contacts seemed to be of particular interest to the investigators.

My companions in the transit room were a curious lot. The cook, a woman of no education and not much intelligence, was avidly reading a translation of the Soviet *History of the All-Union Communist Party (Bolshevik)* which I knew from Topusko and which was obviously an important instrument of communist instruction and indoctrination. She also attended a study circle organised by the communist cell of the unit guarding the headquarters. The 'guests' in the transit room were intelligent enough, but they had been so indoctrinated that it was difficult to talk normally to them. At that time Tito's rejection of UNRRA supplies was still an issue, and I was again told that there could be no question of supervision of the distribution by donors because such supervision would be a violation of Yugoslav sovereignty. The Communists were even drilled to say that we did not need anybody's aid, but that, of course, there was a moral obligation for the British and the Americans to help us because we fought so well; although it was also stressed that we were not fighting for them but for ourselves. In the end, Tito's government had to accept an agreement with UNRRA to avoid starvation, but obtained concessions on external supervision of distribution and on having a Soviet, Sergeychik, to head the UNRRA mission to Yugoslavia.

In March 1945, while the Communists passing in quick succession through the transit house were lecturing me on British-American treachery, some 50 Allied planes would appear over Črnomelj once or twice a week, each dropping 10 containers of military supplies. We were all in British battle-dress, ate food mostly supplied by the Allies and had arms dropped by them, yet the Communists incessantly sneered at Allied help and never stopped talking about Soviet aid, of which I never saw or heard a trace in Slovenia. Allegedly, Soviet planes always came by night. Everybody disparaged a small radio transmitter considered to be British and admired a bigger one, much superior and therefore obviously Soviet. When I finally had a chance to look at one of those, it did in fact have all instructions in Russian, but under a flap it said 'Made in USA'.

After two weeks of hanging around, I had orders from headquarters to translate a booklet about Italian and German small arms. My table was shared with young Partisans who amused themselves by taking apart and reassembling hand-grenades. My thoughts were on other things – the radio reported that a new coalition government had been formed in Belgrade. Since I knew from the same source that the Yalta conference had confirmed the Tito-Šubašić agreement I went on hoping that the Allies would enforce its terms.

The Allies were within a stone's throw. The Soviet mission had its seat in the middle of Črnomelj; the British and the Americans were confined to a small heavily guarded village outside. Sometimes Western liaison officers could be seen moving around, invariably accompanied by Partisans. A friend had already told me that he had been prevented from visiting a British sergeant on the Podzemelj airfield to borrow English books. I took heed and avoided any contact with the British mission, although I knew that my acquaintance from Split, Major Pearce, was in all probability there.

Then walking back from Črnomelj one day, I was offered a lift in a jeep with a British officer at the wheel, accompanied by a Partisan. Near my village, I asked the driver in English to stop for me to get out, which obviously surprised him, and brought me an invitation to come to see him at the mission. Turning to the Partisan, I enquired in Slovene whether such visits were allowed and was told: 'Of course, but you must first report to me.'

After deliberately waiting for quite a while, I went to the mission village but was stopped by a fierce-looking Commissar at the entrance. When I asked to see the Slovene liaison officer, I was told that he was not there. The second time I tried I was taken to see the officer in a peasant house and was sitting with him when Major Pearce happened to pass. He recognised me and waved a hand in my direction without any attempt to speak to me. The partisan officer invited me to lunch and generally tried to be pleasant, even offering me copies of *The Economist* and promising to lend me later Lippman's book on *US Foreign Policy* which he was reading. As I was leaving, he walked out with me to tell me that he would be pleased to see me again, but I would be well advised to avoid any contact with the British mission. Unlike the Partisans, ordinary people were far from showing them hostility — our landlady regaled us all with glowing reports about the British who had been billeted there before us.

On Easter Saturday 1945, I was in Črnomelj talking to the professional group there when one of them told me that he had been ordered to go to the Command of the Slovene artillery brigade to translate an instruction booklet for artillery from English. Apparently members of the British mission were due there within a few days to observe practice on the howitzers they had parachuted in. He suggested I should go with him to help with the translation and we set out on foot after I was granted permission to go.

The Commander of the artillery brigade of the VIIth Corps, as the unit was called, was a former lieutenant in the Yugoslav Royal Army, and his chief of staff was an elderly regular major. The political Commissar was an 18-year-old captain. Having attended a fortnight's course, the boy thought himself a greater expert than both the older officers but nobody dared tell him to shut up. The translating went smoothly, yet I wondered whether I would be allowed to meet the British when they came.

I needn't have wondered — the night before their visit was due, I was told to gather my translation material and my belongings and go to the headquarters of the VIIth Corps. This meant walking to Polane, a village of some 20 substantial houses surrounded by forest. It lay in a valley which, at its north-western end, some four kilometres away, opened towards the southern Slovene plain. A small town in the valley was still in German hands, or rather, in the hands of the Home Guards.

I stayed for four or five days, finishing the translation of artillery instructions. The commander was Major Miha, a regular officer, an ambitious man who had joined the Communist Party and kept talking about his proletarian origins. With him and other officers I frequently discussed the war, and one evening I spoke admiringly of the Allied equipment I had seen in

France. Later a friendly officer took me aside to warn me that it was risky to speak well of the Allies.

When I returned to Črnomelj, I was ordered to go back to Polane and stay with the artillery command. Observing the life of partisan troops from close up was no less than intriguing. The hierarchy showed in everything, especially food. There were three different kitchens: one for officers senior to major served several courses – soup, meat, two vegetables, salad and sweets; a second for staff members, to which I belonged, qualified for risotto or dumplings twice a day; the third for the ranks left men hungry. In pre-war Yugoslavia, the privileges of Army officers were a permanent target of communist criticism. Now everything had changed. Officers no longer had 'batmen', instead they had two or three 'couriers' each, doing the same jobs.

The staff of Corps Headquarters numbered about 500 and was responsible for only two divisions of some 800 men each, and each with its own divisional command. The divisions were supposed to block the passage through the valley south to Polane, but whenever one or two enemy tanks attacked, the divisions retreated into the hills on either side and the tanks could come straight at us unhindered. The Corps command subsequently moved to a village higher up on the road to Črnomelj. Even this move happened in a hurry – in the morning, I went with our howitzers to see them firing at a distant target; when I returned to Polane a few hours later, I found that everybody had left. The only people around were a peasant and a partisan soldier, the peasant shouting at the soldier for trying to carry off some of his chairs.

In the new village we were not safe either. At the first sound of rumbling, the headquarters packed up and retreated further. One day, as the partisan anti-tank gun was leading another escape, I saw the Vth Overseas Brigade with which I had been in Split arriving from the opposite direction. They still looked an efficient unit. They had come from Dalmatia as part of the newly formed IVth Army which was driving the remnants of war-weary German troops before them along the Adriatic coast. In no time the trained soldiers of the Vth Overseas Brigade had ambushed and destroyed the tank from which we had been escaping. Instead of earning any gratitude for this intervention, the Brigade was immediately disbanded – the men were dispatched in batches of about 20 to various other units. The Communists evidently considered this unit, which had come from abroad, politically dangerous.

At the end of April we began moving towards Ljubljana. On our way, I saw for the first time Italian units under Yugoslav command, belonging to the newly formed Garibaldi division. On 1 May, when we reached Brod, the motorised artillery of the IVth Partisan Army, equipped by the British, passed through on its way to Trieste. A battle between the armoured units of this Army and a German panzer division, withdrawing from Rijeka, had allegedly just taken place. It was at this time that the BBC broadcast the news of the surrender of the German Southern Armies to Field-Marshal Alexander.

While the motorised artillery moved west, we ourselves turned north. The villages on the way were deserted. Around here Maria Theresa had settled German peasants two centuries ago, but Hitler had made them all leave when the Italians occupied the regions. However, Chetniks must have been through recently, as some walls were covered with slogans in Cyrillic letters wishing King Peter a long life. At Kočevje, the castle in the middle of the town was in ruins and the population unwelcoming. They had had Partisans two years before, and regions liberated once before tended to be unenthusiastic about repeating the experience. This was *Domobranci* country.

Another little town, Ribnica, which the *Domobranci* had turned into a stronghold, was utterly laid waste. It was Sunday and I went to a smaller church outside the town, as the big one in the centre had been badly damaged. Although only a small part of the Ribnica population was still in the town, Mass was well attended and the churchgoers were manifestly surprised to see a man in partisan uniform amongst the worshippers.

The last stop was in a village on the approaches to Ljubljana where a copy of one of the newspapers printed in the city was circulating amid general merriment: it displayed a headline stating that a government had been formed by the *Domobranci:* for a fleeting moment I entertained the absurd wish that such a government could hold and prevent the Partisans from entering the Slovene capital.

But early on 9 May, we heard that the Partisans had entered. Members of the propaganda section set off on motor-cycles to take possession of the radio station. The artillery Commander left on horseback with some other officers. As the headquarters did not seem to be preparing for a move, I asked the deputy-Commander for permission to go to Ljubljana by myself. He said I should wait for another hour so that all the headquarters staff could enter the city together. Nothing happened for well over an hour, so I gave up waiting and went on my own in the company of Dr Zalokar who had arrived with the Overseas Brigade.

Public enthusiasm increased as we reached the suburbs. While communist Partisans frequently succeeded in occupying villages – for a while – Ljubljana had always remained firmly in the hands of their enemies, foreign or domestic. As a result the townspeople had no personal experience of partisan rule and still harboured illusions about what was coming.

A village 10 kilometres from Ljubljana displayed every sign of hostility – people were turning their backs on us and would not answer our greetings. But further on we met a peasant boy with an enormous red rosette in his buttonhole, who raised his fist in a salute. He seemed taken aback when – despite my uniform – I maliciously answered with the traditional Slovene greeting '*Bog daj!*' (God give a good day). In the streets of Ljubljana crowds hailed and threw flowers at every arriving Partisan. I was angry — I now realise quite unjustifiably. Why should people not rejoice at being freed after four years of foreign occupation? They were happy at the arrival of their liberators without knowing what kind of liberty we were bringing. They could not fail to be relieved when the last vestiges of German occupation disappeared. But the Allied victory in the foreign war was also a communist victory in the civil war.

Rushing in, I stopped at a corner barrow to buy flowers for my mother and paid with a hundred lire note — Italian money was still used. The seller had no change and wanted to give me the flowers for free, but I was already away. At home nobody was expecting me, believing that I was in Britain. Mother opened the door and did not recognise me as I stood there, dusty, sunburnt, a Sten-gun over my shoulder, clutching flowers.

Our joy was not unmixed. My mother's cousin was in the house and she was telling us that her brother was dead. As a youngster in 1943, he had joined the Partisans and was suspected by them of nationalism, even though his association with the Liberation Front was of long standing. He used to read Marxist literature and took part in clandestine activities, such as disarming Italian sentries in hit-and-run attacks. Though without fighting experience, he was sent into a shock battalion, was wounded in one of the first clashes and died of tetanus in an underground hospital. His younger sister had also been killed after she had followed his example and joined the Partisans as a nurse. Maybe an hour later, another cousin arrived weeping. Her father, an elderly regular officer, and her brother had been arrested as soon as the Partisans entered Ljubljana because the son was with the *Domobranci*. We never saw either of them again.

Settling down at home, I noticed British and American flags hanging from the windows and remarked: 'Aren't you afraid of being arrested?' My parents had heard rumours about partisan hostility to the Allies, but it was only I who warned them to be prepared for the worst. One valued friend asked me disappointedly whether I supported the Communists. She should have known better, but my uniform confused many. The Slovenes were no longer divided into the honest and dishonest but into political categories.

In the early afternoon we heard shouting in the streets and went downstairs to a comic sight. A procession of the senior officers of the VIIth Corps headquarters was making a ceremonial entry. They had been waiting all this time a few miles from Ljubljana for cars requisitioned in the city itself to assemble for their triumphal entry. The circus era had begun.

The next day I cycled off early in the morning to my home town of Kranj; as the war had officially ended on 8 May, we wrongly assumed Kranj had been freed at the same time as Ljubljana. About half-way, I caught sight of partisan troops resting in the shade, but a little further on, I met two partisan officers also on bicycles who said that there were no Partisans ahead and they did not know the whereabouts of the Germans and the *Domobranci*. Isolated shots were heard from different directions, so we three advanced cautiously through the forest where Germans had abandoned stores of piled-up ammunition. At one house we were told the Germans were still in Kranj.

By the time we arrived in the town, armed workers had appeared at the gates of their factories, organised by the Liberation Front. Some of them wanted to fire at us, mistaking us for Chetniks, but I was recognised. My Pirc grandmother was still there and overjoyed to see me back at Kranj after four years. I then toured the town greeting and kissing people whether I knew them or not. The pre-war Mayor of Kranj, looking grim, was waiting at the town hall. He was the father of Marko, the naval officer, who had joined the Partisans in 1943 and was shot as a suspected nationalist.

Among the places I visited was the printing office which, before the war, had belonged to my father and I was almost sorry to disappoint the printers who were expecting to receive proletarian Partisans rather than the proprietor's son.

On my way back to Ljubljana, I went to see my father's factory, and was taken aback when I found it in flames. During the last part of the war the buildings were used as a garage for tanks and ammunition stores, so the retiring Germans had set it on fire. Rounds of ammunition were still exploding, and I wondered how my father would take this news.

One of my first visits in Ljubljana was to Dr Nagode. I almost burst out laughing when I saw his house decorated with a red flag. He obviously thought it was more honourable to fly the Soviet flag than the Yugoslav tricolour with a red star. Several of my former *Pravda* group were assembled in Dr Nagode's study, wondering whether they should try to work with the Communists. 'You don't know yet what dirty tricks they can play,' I said, aware that I knew more than they did about the new régime.

Later in May, after the Allies had forced the Partisans to evacuate Trieste, Tito visited Ljubljana. Despite heavy rain, crowds enthusiastically greeted him. Many nationalists felt they had to support him and his Communists because they represented the only hope of Trieste and Carinthia's being liberated. Tito was reported to have vented his displeasure at the preponderance of Slovene flags over Yugoslav flags. I myself saw Tito once from a few steps away, as he was walking in the main park guarded by two lines of soldiers and wearing a richly decorated marshal's uniform.

At the end of May I was ordered to serve as interpreter with the Yugoslav troops occupying Austria under the supreme command of Marshal Tolbukhin, which took me to Yugoslav occupation headquarters at Leibnitz in Austrian Styria. The interpreter already there explained that there was nothing to do except dispatch a telegram to the Soviet headquarters once a day, always affirming that there had not been any change and that everything was all right.

Because there was no accommodation at the officers' mess, I found lodgings with an Austrian war widow who hoped that I would protect her from a Soviet soldier who was upsetting her by banging on her door every evening. In fact, as soon as I retired, the knocking started. My landlady summoned me and indeed there was a man in Soviet uniform to be seen through the glass in the upper part of the door. When I asked him in Russian what he wanted and for details of his unit he turned and fled. Many worse things were happening around us, of course, than banging on the door of a woman living alone.

One of the Soviet specialities was to rob people of cars; not just enemies, but their Yugoslav allies also. On my way to Leibnitz, for instance, I met a team of workers from a Slovene factory travelling to Austria by lorry, on their way to recover machinery confiscated by the Nazis and abandoned somewhere near the border in Austria. I chanced on them again later in a train. The Soviets, instead of helping them to repatriate their plant, had commandeered their truck and left them to walk home. Everybody was amazed by the behaviour of the brotherly Soviet people. They showed no solidarity with us that I could observe, or with each other, for that matter.

Having nothing to do in Leibnitz, I spent quite some time in the officers' mess going through the books in the library of the villa's owner, apparently a local industrialist who had clear sympathies with the Nazis and had fled from the Soviets and us. The shelves were choc-à-bloc with Nazi propaganda books – some expounding Nazi doctrine, hardly interesting after the Nazi defeat, others describing and criticising Communism. I spent hours reading and, I must admit, finding that most of their claims on Communism were credible in the light of my own experience. But all along I had the strange feeling that I was doing something wrong in handling books belonging to an unknown person.

I frequently wandered around the little town observing the wretched appearance of our troops. Many partisan officers exuded lack of education and ignorance of civilised behaviour, and I suspected that the defeated Austrians were laughing at us in private and would do it in public, had they not been afraid. Many an 'officer' had pearl-handled opera-glasses round his neck as if they were the best military binoculars, others were intent on showing their importance by drilling their underlings, often much wiser than themselves, in the streets.

As occupying troops we did not interfere much in everyday life. Former Nazis were made to clear the streets, supervised by other Austrians wearing red armbands inscribed 'Anti-Fascist'. Our propaganda units tried to attract the local population to performances in the town cinema, such as bad choir-singing directed by a man in an oversize uniform.

At some stage I was given leave to travel back to Ljubljana, where I knew I was expected to join the office of the Tanjug press agency. Its work was considered so important that a request for my demobilisation was issued by the

Communist Party organ *Ljudska Pravica*. The Colonel at Leibnitz agreed and at the end of June, I was out of the III Army.

Sitting in the train, I had a glimpse of how ordinary people fared. Patrols were checking on identity cards and various permits. A peasant was producing one paper after another until he finally said: 'Look here, this paper is even stamped by the Russian Gestapo.'

6

Opposition legal but not tolerated

The director of the press office in Ljubljana appointed me deputy head of its current news section, whose task was to translate Reuters and Tanjug's dispatches for use by newspapers and Slovene party leaders. It was expected that I would supplant Dr Majaron, the head. There was even some talk about my going to the United States later as press attaché. That was the nearest I have ever come to being offered advantages if I was willing to collaborate with the Communists.

I could not. I told Majaron that I had been given to understand that I would replace him. He did not know anything about a new job for him, though one had been mentioned to me. So I went back to the director of the press office and said that I did not want Majaron's post and some other colleagues who were approached did the same. We went on translating, but we all had black marks in some register somewhere.

Matters were made worse when the press office director got the impression that we, and especially I, did not attend political discussion meetings with due interest, and that we did not translate Kardelj's speeches with the required reverence and solemnity. At New Year 1946, a large proportion of us was dismissed with the explanation that there was not enough money to pay all of us. I half believed it, went skiing and then began working for a doctorate, switching later to public law.

My father was employed as an adviser in the Ministry of Industry, but we could not have survived on his salary or, for that matter, on his and mine combined. Fortunately there were still quite a few things of my father's one could sell for money. I sold the central heating equipment in the burnt-down factory and later a house in a Ljubljana suburb. We had bought it with the cash taken out of the factory safe when we left Kranj in 1941. That kept us all going.

Because I was in the daily news section, I became involved in some interesting outside work. One of my first jobs brought me together with the press office director and a young man whom I recognised as a junior fellow-student of law. He turned out to be Janko Smole, head of the agitation and propaganda section of the Central Committee of the Slovene Communist Party, who later advanced to the post of Finance Minister and chief negotiator with the International Monetary Fund. The three of us went to the temporary office of the British

Vice-Consul in Ljubljana, a Major Frank Waddams. We were supposed to interview him for the papers. The other two quite deliberately tried to push him off balance and I had to translate their impish questions. They insisted that the Consul should answer their question about what the British government intended to do about Trieste. The more the Consul underlined that he did not know, the louder the two officials claimed that this meant the British wanted to give Trieste to the Italians. I was relieved when the encounter ended because I saw that the British representative could not help getting angry. As we walked down the stairs, my two superiors were triumphant about the lesson they had imparted to the Englishman. I did not see what they had taught him, but was certain that this added to the unfavourable impression the Western foreigners had not just of communist Yugoslavs but of all of us.

When I next went with the press office director to have an interview, the boot was on the other foot. This time our interlocutors were members of the Soviet military mission, from whom we wanted to obtain a short biography of the Soviet Ambassador to Yugoslavia and his photograph. He was expected in Northern Slovenia to unveil a monument to the Soviet liberators who had passed through on their way to Austria from Hungary. The chief of the mission, Colonel Bogomolov, refused to tell us anything, while his press attaché, Major Zhukov, got quite nasty. He expressed a suspicion that the press office director and I must have collaborated with the Nazis, because we were unaware that Soviet papers would publish only pictures of Politburo members and certainly not of lower-ranking Ambassadors. 'Your press must become more party-like,' he said. He also took us to task because the Ljubljana papers were no longer sending the mission free copies. He wound up by expressing his anger at the frequent demonstrations in the streets of Ljubljana. 'Shout less and work more' – *'Menshe krichat, bolshe rabotat!'* he advised us. Privately I wondered what this meant and found it even more amazing when in his 1946 New Year's speech, Marshal Tito himself echoed this injunction. 'Less of all these celebrations and meetings, and more work!'

The press office director was visibly embarrassed and muttered, as we walked back to our offices, that the Russians could not understand what needed to be done to make the Soviets popular with our people. I was appalled by the general subservience to the Soviets and arrogance *vis-à-vis* the Western Allies and thought that this would have bad political, economic and military consequences for all of us.

It occurred to me that it would be an antidote if I went to the British Consul and told him that not everybody in Slovenia felt hostile towards the Western Allies, and I certainly did not. So I went to see the Briton, apologised for the interview in which I had unwillingly played the part of interpreter and warned him that the Communists hated the British. He was visibly astonished, not knowing what to make of all this, but invited me to come back and have tea with him. I became an occasional visitor to his office, where we talked at great length about many things, primarily developments in Yugoslavia. He confided in me that he used to be sympathetic to the Partisans, but that his work as liaison officer with the IVth Army had quickly disillusioned him. 'They just deceive people,' he would say. We went for walks and eventually I took him to my grandmother's house in Kranj.

While I was working at the press office I met other foreigners. There was a group of war correspondents from Moscow who toured Yugoslavia: three Russians – a general and two majors – two British – the Reuters and the *Daily Worker* correspondents – assorted Americans, including Anna Louise Strong, the old admirer of Chinese Communists, a few Frenchmen and a pretty Czech woman journalist.

We were told to show them 'ruins and only ruins' so as to impress on them how much our country had suffered. They were taken by bus to Žužemberg, a little town with a castle in the middle, half destroyed in the battles between the *Domobranci* and the Partisans and bombed at their request by the Allied air forces. Everybody was duly impressed, and to impress them even more a press conference was organised in the presence of numerous local people. The chairman of the local committee embarked on a speech of regurgitated slogans, but was stopped by the correspondents who said they would rather ask questions. The unhappy history of Žužemberk unfolded before us – I was interpreting – and local people thought it advisable to blame everything on *Domobranci*. While translating their outpourings I was wondering how many among them had relations in the *Domobranci* ranks and how many *Domobranci* actually came from this town, which was known for its anti-communist feelings.

My thoughts were interrupted when a girl got up and radically changed the topic. She opened by saying that she was from the town of Gorica under Anglo-American occupation, but had to leave because her Slovene teachers' college had been closed down by the occupying authorities. She closed her eyes and declaimed at length about the wicked British and Americans. The correspondents were very interested and thought the girl intelligent. In contrast, I had my doubts, not just about the girl's intelligence but about the intelligence of those directing Yugoslav policy on Trieste and the surrounding territory. In fact I wondered how this girl from Gorica had so handily cropped up in Žužemberk at the other end of Slovenia. It was not inconceivable that she had been sent here to show 'Yugoslav' spite for the Western Allies. The Slovenes in territories under British-American control were ordered by the Communists not to send their children to Slovene schools opened by the Allies, although everybody there had been dreaming about schools in Slovene all the time these were prohibited under Italian Fascism. Peasants whose buildings were damaged during partisan operations were ordered not to allow Allied troops to repair them.

While we were wandering around together, I talked to several of the visiting journalists. The Reuters man was extremely pessimistic — he thought that Yugoslavia was the key to Greece and that both had been lost for the West. In his view the Soviet Union had made a great deal of progress and had eliminated all classes except for the leaders and the people — one more move and there would be a classless society. After leaving Yugoslavia, this same Reuters correspondent wrote a special Sunday feature under the heading 'The lost kingdom of King Peter' as if this was the issue at stake. He eulogised the land reform, a preposterous piece of communist dogmatism in a country of smallholders such as Yugoslavia. There had already been one land reform in 1918 and no land, or hardly any, remained to be distributed. This much was admitted by Kidrič, the economic dictator, himself at the Vth Party Congress in 1948. An American correspondent questioned me closely on my salary and prices in Slovenia. I did not know all the answers, which alerted me to the need to follow events closely if one wished to argue with foreign newspapermen.

When I said in his presence that there was a communist dictatorship in Yugoslavia, the *Daily Worker* correspondent Gibbons protested vehemently. Later, when the same group of war correspondents were received by Tito, this man asked him: 'What does the Marshal think of the version spread by some foreign circles that the Yugoslav government is communist?' Tito's reply was cunning: 'I cannot imagine how they have come to this conclusion. It is generally known that this is a People's Front government which includes all democratic forces in the country including all direct democratic forces whose aim is to create the Yugoslavia we are creating now.' Gibbons continued: 'Can one speak of socialisation measures?' Tito answered: 'Up till now, we have taken no steps which could be so interpreted. No collectivisation has taken place and private property is respected ... We have confiscated exclusively the property of our people's enemies, but that has happened in other countries too.' In fact, full-scale socialisation and collectivisation was to take place a little more than a year later, in 1946–8.

Before the journalists departed, they were given a dinner in Ljubljana's leading hotel. The large dining-room was empty except for us and two young Soviet pilots sitting at a table apart. I wondered why the press office director and I were the only natives. The director made a speech which I translated into English and which was answered by the American National Broadcasting Corporation man in immaculate Russian. He went overboard with his praise of the Soviet Union and the prospects young people had there. When the American finished, the two Soviet Air Force officers stood up and one of them asked the journalist with the rank of general for permission to speak. The silence that followed was broken by one of the Soviet majors: 'Is this the way to behave in the presence of Comrade General?' The young man said: 'I have asked Comrade General for permission to speak as I should like to point out that one should always speak the truth.' He seemed to take exception to the American's predictions of a bright future for Soviet youth. Strange. The journalists also thought so.

Strange too was the tale my father had to tell after he had been to Vienna on official business in the summer of 1945. The official business was to take several truck-loads of German occupation money there and spend it on anything that could be bought. The officials were issued with travel permits on behalf of the Slovene Ministry of Industry, countersigned without much ado by the British Consul, while the Soviet mission refused to co-operate in this or any other way.

The Soviet soldiery behaved savagely not just after the invasion of Austria but even months later. Rapes of women in the ruins by Soviet soldiers were apparently a normal occurrence in August 1945. What had befallen the Austrian Germans could best be gauged by the fact that even the Yugoslav officials were apt to be ordered out of their cars by Soviet officers. They were lucky if they got a less good vehicle in exchange.

It was appalling that precisely these arrogant and unpleasant Soviets were worshipped by our own communist bosses, while Westerners were exposed to continuous abuse. I discussed these attitudes, misguided in our view, with Dr Nagode and other political associates. We were all anxious to prevent the identification of Yugoslavia with the Communists in Western eyes, especially as we felt strongly that the Communists were quite capable of provoking a war. We also thought that it was our patriotic duty to organise an opposition and participate in the forthcoming elections. As a first move, we contacted France Snoj who had served as a Slovene Catholic Party minister in several pre-war and war-time London Yugoslav governments, but had come back to Yugoslavia towards the end of the war in the wake of the agreement between Tito and Šubašić. In 1945 he was a member of the Slovene government but, of course, had no real say in anything. Mr Snoj thought that elections would bring a change and that the Communists would have to soften their line. In my opinion this was the last thing the Communists were going to do, and I went to see him and explain my views.

People who were as ruthless as the communist leaders and who did so many terrible things to gain control would hardly allow a democratic election to interfere with them. In the eyes of outsiders, everything in Yugoslavia was entirely normal and the rare foreign visitors laughed at silly stories about people hanging from lamp-posts, allegedly spread by Yugoslav anti-Communists who had fled the country. In reality, although nobody was hanging from lamp-posts, people were being killed in large numbers.

In Slovenia, just as in Split, people had been taken away by the hundred from their homes all over the region, never to be seen again. Among them were petty collaborators, but also people whose only fault was that some Communist disliked them. I knew that some 300 people in my home town were taken by truck to a forest nearby and shot one by one. We were told about it by old truck drivers who used to work for our factory and one of our relations was among the victims. Milovan Djilas states in his memoirs that the Secret Police were given authority by the Communist Party to kill people until the end of 1945.

Worse massacres were perpetrated by the Communists on those who fought against them during the war. The Slovene *Domobranci* were escaping from the Communists in their thousands, followed by their families and other civilians. They took refuge in Carinthia, under British occupation, but the British authorities handed them back to the Communists. We knew that they were assembled at the Catholic high school of St Vid. One afternoon in the early summer of 1945, I was at the central Post Office in Ljubljana, still wearing British battle-dress and a partisan cap, when Marija came straight up to me saying: 'Jože is at St Vid, please save him.' Jože was Marija's fiancé and I used to see a lot of them in 1943. After I had left for Switzerland he joined the *Domobranci* and was now in danger of being killed. I was confused, because Marija obviously thought that I could intervene for him on account of my uniform, whereas I could not do a thing. Jože and 12,000 others, including friends of mine among them, were taken to different places and 'liquidated' *en masse*. There was not even a semblance of a trial.

The defeated Croat troops, mostly mobilised peasants, met a similar fate. They tried to escape through Slovenia and Austria, but were unable to get through and had to surrender. Those who were not killed immediately were marched back and massacred on the way. I heard that 60,000 to 80,000 Croats were killed in this way in Slovenia. Their corpses were ploughed up from their shallow burial grounds in several places.

All these killings added up to a truly horrifying total. One cannot know precisely, but one can assume that some 300,000 perished (that was the figure rumoured). None of them was tried, nor were the courts involved in any way.

In the autumn of 1945, Slovenia was given its first taste of communist administration of justice. The Director of the Jesenice Steelworks was sentenced to death because he had persuaded the Partisans not to blow up this factory – while Tito praised the workers for preserving the works so that they could contribute to post-war recovery. Others were convicted simply because their banks or other enterprises did not close down during the occupation. Collective responsibility was introduced, making all members of administrative boards liable for what their firms did during the war. Needless to say, the businesses themselves were confiscated.

All the personal belongings of the condemned were taken away and distributed among the communist hierarchy. The best villas in Ljubljana went to communist leaders. Anything the Gestapo had confiscated was considered German property. I know of at least two cases when Jewish property was treated as German to provide a reason for confiscating it. Kidrič, later the

Yugoslav economic dictator, was given the villa of the Jewish family of Ebenspanger while the remaining members of the family, Mrs and Miss Ebenspanger, had to make do with one room somewhere else.

It soon became clear how unimportant it was where people had been or what they had done during the war. The main requirement was unreserved support for the communist régime. Even former Nazi collaborators could obtain minor posts in the administration if they had changed sides in time and started praising the wise communist leadership. In contrast, many Partisans had difficulties. The head of the propaganda section of the Vth Overseas Brigade ended up in prison, having been denounced by somebody. Similarly, the man who went to Switzerland and was arrested by the Italians upon his return, on suspicion of communicating with the government in exile in London, was in prison again for the same reason.

Relations with individual Communists became difficult for ordinary people – they always assumed a menacing attitude in discussion. They believed that Marx had revealed the final truth about everything to them and that anybody contradicting them was despicable. As a kind of vent for their suppressed feelings, Slovenes were writing anonymous letters to the British Consul and pushing them through his door when they thought they were unobserved. Frank Waddams showed me some of these letters of complaint about the communist régime, and particularly about the communist massacre of the *Domobranci*. Some letter-writers wanted to return to Austrian rule, claiming that Slovenia had become communist only because of its integration into the Balkans as part of Yugoslavia. They forgot that Slovene Communists had played a leading role in the victory of their party in Yugoslavia. They ignored the fact that Austria had chosen Hitler, that the Nazi terror in Yugoslavia had been mostly the doing of Austrian Germans and that it had driven people to the other extreme.

At the end of September 1945, I was summoned to the government palace in Ljubljana. I was to interpret a conversation between the Vice-Chairman of the Slovene government and the British Consul, who was becoming ever more incensed by the petty troubles various communist authorities were making for him, especially after the Consulate had moved to a villa. The Vice-Chairman regretted the worries the Consul was having, but said the Slovene government had nothing to do with them, and that the political police were under direct orders from the Defence Ministry in Belgrade. He promised to pass on the complaints, and also to mention in his report that the Consul was receiving letters on the *Domobranci* massacre.

I happened to meet the Consul on the stairs on his way out. He invited me to have a whisky at his office and then asked me point-blank whether I was an agent of the Secret Police. My face must have convinced him that he was wrong, so he said: 'Well, my boy, you are playing a dangerous game. Here I take you for an OZNA agent, while the police presumably also think you are a spy.'

However, the police did not seem worried about me. Even when a man in uniform once stopped me in the street and asked for my identity card – I had come from the Consulate about 20 minutes earlier – he seemed satisfied with my press office card.

September 1945 saw the end of independent politicians' participation in Tito's government. The former members of the various governments in exile resigned: first the Serb, Milan Grol, then the Croats, Ivan Šubašić and Juraj Šutej. Resignation was the only way for them to protest against the behaviour of communist leaders who promised all freedoms under the sun and granted none.

It became clear that any remaining hope of free elections was an illusion. The development was the sadder because the Allied governments had sponsored the negotiations between Tito and Šubašić. Tito himself had boasted that he had met Churchill on 16 June 1944 about speeding up the formation of a unified government. But while there was no sign of the West reminding Tito of his obligations under the Tito-Šubašić agreement, they seemed to be directing their newly-found anti-communist policy against the State of Yugoslavia, and this was most alarming to all of us.

The circle around Dr Nagode had by now been reduced to six or seven people. Still, we felt it our duty to prevent the identification of Yugoslavia with Communism. When discussing a programme for a political group, without which there could be no political action, I pressed for a return to Christian morals, to a minimum of good faith which would exclude murder, lies and robbery from politics. This may sound abstract, but it was very appropriate at a time when Yugoslav Communists were using to the full 'Leninist morals', involving deceit and violence in the service of the 'final truth' of Marxism.

In his dealings with the democratic opposition, Tito proved himself a consummate master of Marxist-Leninist tactics. In an interview with the press on 11 November 1945, he claimed that Grol's opposition paper could not be published because the printers would not print it. But soon afterwards in his answer to the British MP, Arthur Lewis, he said that it had to be confiscated because it tried to spread dissension and mistrust of the Army. According to Tito, its editors wanted to publish something outrageous, so that the paper would have to be prohibited; then this would be used as evidence that there was no democracy in Yugoslavia. Finally, Tito accused the opposition of not actually wanting to publish 'constructive' newspapers, and only claiming that there was no paper to print them on. Needless to say, the Titoists in turn complained bitterly when the Allied authorities in Trieste refused to supply them with newsprint available from Yugoslavia; while the opposition in Yugoslavia had no other source. I myself arrived in Belgrade on the very day when the 'public' (that is, Secret Police agents) were attacking the street vendors of Grol's *Demokratija,* which was a great success. Bundles of papers were drenched in petrol and burnt.

A political friend who had gone to Belgrade before me had given me an introduction to Milan Grol, now opposition leader, so I went to see him. It was the end of October and my friends in Ljubljana wanted to know whether he had any intention of participating in the forthcoming elections. He looked at me: 'You see what is happening in the streets. Any activity is impossible. Everything depends on relations between the great powers.' I was aware that this answer was the only possible one there, exactly as we had found in Ljubljana. Our discussions with some remnants of Christian Socialists and Social Democrats had petered out because we all felt that we were surrounded by terror. And indeed, before long any attempt at establishing contact with other people interested in political activity was branded (by the Communist Police) as the organisation of a spy ring.

The result of the elections on 11 November 1945 was, of course, a victory of the communist-controlled People's Front, which won over 90% of the votes cast. An opposition without newspapers or any possibility of organising itself was doomed from the beginning, even without the possibility of intimidation during elections and fraud.

The Communists went on and on about how the opposition had no positive programme, and Tito himself said in an interview with a Polish journalist: 'Our opposition has not produced one single idea which would be better than what is already in the programme of the People's Front.' He would say so, would he not? But he also drew the conclusion that the opposition was no opposition at all but the old camp of people's enemies who wanted to turn the clock back.

This was the keynote of all pronouncements: only the Communist Party had a programme and could show the way forward – everybody else was against the best interests of the country. This conceit went so far that the Communist Party refused to register as required by its own law on political activity, because it considered itself something special. Yet Tito became incensed when the two main opposition parties, the Serbian Democratic Party and the Croat Peasant Party, refused to register either, so long as the Communist Party did not.

The Western press wrote little about communist chicaneries, and its comments on the Yugoslav elections were sparse and sceptical. Some papers approved of them, others were not much interested. Anybody who opposed Tito was still taken to have been a collaborator during the war and many people philosophised about a different Eastern concept of democracy. Some visiting British MPs made nauseating comments and one of them, J.F.F. Platts-Mills, wondered why the editor of *Demokratija,* the paper suppressed by the Communists, had not been imprisoned as he would certainly have been in Britain.

Under these circumstances, I was strongly tempted to go abroad. The French offered scholarships and so did the British, but their distribution was in the hands of the Yugoslav authorities, which meant the Communists. The British scholarships were not taken up at all, the French were predominantly given to communist activists whose main interest in France was to participate in communist upheavals there. The French scholarships were later discontinued because of this. I was told I could not be given a scholarship because my family was still rich enough to pay for my studies abroad. So I applied for a passport to go and study abroad without the scholarship — and I was turned down.

When asked about sending students to Britain by a visiting British MP, Mrs Leah Manning, Tito talked at great length about the lack of finance, as if the Communists had not simply ignored the offer of 10 British scholarships. What is more, no lack of finance prevented the Communists from sending numerous students to the Soviet Union. These students found life there so difficult that one, a friend who knew my opposition to Communism, wrote that he could now appreciate my 'modern ideas'. A closer acquaintance with the 'fatherland of workers' undermined most people's faith in Communists and their ideas.

At the end of 1945, Yugoslavia moved formally another few steps nearer the Soviet model. On 29 November, the newly elected parliament proclaimed a republic and then the 'discussion' of the blueprint for the new constitution began. In all main features the proposals followed the so-called Stalin constitution of the Soviet Union. From what we heard, the Western press did not have much to say about these further steps towards totalitarianism, except perhaps trivialities, such as that King Peter had thereby lost his wealth in Yugoslavia.

The debate by the 'great mass of the people' was a sham. Thousands of meetings were held and thousands of telegrams and letters containing amendments sent to Belgrade. The submissions were full of platitudes and I never heard any substantial criticism. Such criticism would have been difficult, even if anybody had had the courage to express it, because the draft constitution promised every human right imaginable. The acid test was of course the interpretation of these freedoms in practice. But if anyone had accused the Communists of robbing Yugoslavia of freedom of speech, for instance, they would have flatly denied it. They would have pointed to the so-called 'wall newspapers' which, according to them, permitted the 'great mass of the people' to express their opinion as nowhere else in the world. These 'wall newspapers' were full of naïveties. In the centre of Ljubljana, a 'wall newspaper' hanging in the window of the café 'Emona' proclaimed that in India there were two British police officers to terrorise every Indian native, while nobody would dare to add that such terror was extraordinary since there were only about 50 million British and about 400 million Indians.

Similarly, at innumerable 'meetings', citizens freely criticised and denounced neighbours for their opulent living or for the number of rooms in their flats, but would not dare say anything critical about the higher echelons of the government. They could also mention the shortage of food or clothing, but hardly question whether this shortage was due to the Marxist policies. The Communists did admit to many failures but explained them away by the presence in the State apparatus of reactionaries who had infiltrated it to commit sabotage. In public, Kardelj stated that the new Yugoslavia would preserve the rule of law so that every act of a State organ would be based on law. Yet at about the same time Ivan Maček, the chief of the Slovene Political Police, told the prisoners in Ljubljana that in Yugoslavia laws became obsolete very quickly and were sometimes obsolete by the very moment of promulgation. The discussions at the meetings of the press office employees, under the chairmanship of the director, were at times ridiculous. Once I was foolish enough to laugh out loud and was later told that the director had noted my laughter. During these meetings I learnt that the Germans had done so much evil because they were a capitalist nation and therefore wanted to possess the means of production and force other people to work for them. When there was a complaint about food in the press office canteen, the director blamed UNRRA for not giving us sufficient provisions.

My friends and I were firmly convinced that only an all-Yugoslav opposition had any chance, if a chance there was, to exert a moderating influence. In January 1946 I again went to see ex-Minister Grol. He repeatedly said that we Slovenes should contact the democratic leaders in Croatia and stressed: 'We are in full agreement with the opposition leaders in Croatia and it is irrelevant whether you Slovenes keep links with us in Belgrade or with them in Zagreb.'

This time I also visited Professor Dragoljub Jovanović, the leader of the left-wing Serbian agricultural party. A friend had contacted him before, but I was in no hurry to see him because I disapproved of his behaviour during the election campaign. At that time he was still a faithful ally of the Communists in the People's Front and was ridiculing the independent opposition in the hope that the Communists would accept him as a full partner. However, as early as during the preparations for the elections, Tito began threatening the waverers within the People's Front and telling them they would share the fate of the opposition. At the beginning of 1946 Professor Jovanović was Vice-Chairman of the National Assembly, but was nonetheless in bad odour with the Communists; so much so that I had to contact him in a roundabout, half-secret way. He received me very cordially and I told him about our fears that a new war might break out, and about our special fears for the future of Yugoslavia in this event, since it would find us on the wrong side. The Professor thought our fears exaggerated and blamed them on the tension of being in the immediate neighbourhood of Trieste. He thought his strength lay in the Communists' need of him 'because they were limping along on one leg'. They had the support of the workers but not of the peasants whom he represented. Possible partners and allies in Slovenia were of considerable interest to him. Professor Jovanović explained that the ideals of his peasant party lay not in the West, but in the East with Tolstoy and Gandhi. Our discussion had to cease because a French newspaper correspondent was waiting for him but he invited me to come again.

I had another talk with Jovanović in March 1946. His evaluation of the political situation had not changed, but now he had the impression that the peasant party was stronger than ever because the bulk of the Serb people had shifted their support from Grol's democratic party to his, since Grol was far too passive and people preferred an active policy.

Jovanović read me some passages from his programme out of a book first published during King Alexander's dictatorship but confiscated. With a great deal of effort the Professor had succeeded in obtaining permission to have his work reprinted under Tito. I was to distribute his book in Slovenia, and he sent me some copies which I sold to friends. When touching on my law studies, he suggested that my doctoral thesis should be on 'Unity and Separation of Power', showing how the unity of power under Louis XIV had been abolished by the French revolution and now we were returning to Louis' unity under the Communists.

The next day he met me at the parliament building and gave me a gallery ticket so that I could hear Tito's speech on foreign policy. In the event no such speech was delivered and I sat through an ordinary day in the parliament of the new Yugoslavia. The business in hand was a bill extending military service to two, three and four years from the pre-war nine months, eighteen months and two years. If anything required discussion, it was this change but the *rapporteur* just briefly recommended the bill as one of the great achievements of our people and claimed that our youth should be proud to serve in such a glorious army. A deputy belonging to Jovanović's peasant party had the courage to suggest an amendment giving financial support to the families who normally lived on the earnings of the recruits. Hardly had he finished when a communist deputy in full general's uniform jumped up and shouted abuse, accusing everybody entertaining any doubts about measures taken by the people's authority of impertinence if not treachery. Upon which the Act was unanimously adopted.

The People's Assembly depressed me deeply by this ridiculous 'discussion', but the new Act also worried me personally, because under its provision I would have one more year to serve after my service with the Partisans was taken into account. Six years earlier, I had been depressed by my inability to serve in the army; now matters were different. The new army was officered by the fiercest Communists and unbearable for a man of average intelligence. Moreover, the ideas for which it stood were directly opposed to my own beliefs. That night I hardly slept and by the morning I had decided that I would escape rather than serve the Communists.

Before leaving Belgrade, I went, at Professor Jovanović's invitation, to a meeting of the local branch of his party. On the agenda was a disputation between him and his rival, Kirilo Savić, more pro-communist than he was and a member of Tito's government. Interest was so great that the small hall was packed, and people were standing outside. I could not hear the debate, but the issue was clear – the Communists were using Savić to get rid of Jovanović, who had by then served his purpose. Later Savić's friends outvoted him in the agricultural party with the help of the Communists, who seemed to have infiltrated all other parties. Kirilo Savić himself was soon ousted from the government.

Back in Ljubljana, there had also been changes. Although Frank Waddams had been joined by his wife Elizabeth and baby son Alan, he was recalled to London and replaced as Consul by Leonard Scopes, a regular member of the Foreign Office. Scopes and his wife arrived in November but the Waddams family were unable to leave till after Christmas. The communist authorities would not give them an exit visa, one can only imagine so that they should have yet another reason for remembering Ljubljana as a nightmare.

After the Waddams' departure, I thought I would stop my visits to the Consulate. It was only too clear that the communist authorities frowned on foreign contacts and that such contacts were dangerous, though (in my worst dreams) I could not have imagined what was eventually to befall me. Moreover, I understood that the Consul could not enlighten me, even if he wanted to, on Western intentions towards Yugoslavia. But Frank Waddams had become a friend and I went to see him every now and then simply because I felt like talking to him.

My political associates thought that what I had found out from the two Consuls about Western attitudes amounted to very little, so they sent somebody else to see the new one. He was supposed to inform him about cultural conditions and prisoners in Yugoslavia. He was also to ask him to forward a letter to a prominent Slovene exile in London in the hope that this man would be able to enlighten us about Western intentions. The British Embassy in Belgrade hesitated for a long time before it finally forwarded the letter, but we never had a reply.

In the whole of January 1946 I did not go to the British Consulate once. But then I began feeling a terrible coward, especially as Scopes and his wife seemed nice and interesting people, intriguingly having spent some time in Japan and Mozambique. Surely my talking to them could not cause any harm to anybody so I visited them again and was invited to dinner. Soon I was involved in a social circle comprising the British Consul and his wife, my university teacher Boris Furlan and his wife, the British press attaché Captain John Gibbs and his Slovene secretary Tatjana, and occasionally the French Consul Gabriel Heuman and the American Red Cross representative Jake Hoptner. We used to meet, talk about politics among other things, and play bridge. I soon dropped out of the bridge because I was no good at it.

To my mind, these social contacts could almost have been considered useful to Yugoslavia, compared with the deliberate rudeness with which the Communists treated foreign representatives. At an official dinner the Consul was seated next to the Chairman of the Slovene Academy of Sciences, the father of the communist leader Kidrič, who idly chatted about the iniquities of British rule in India — which the British were about to leave anyway. Mrs Scopes sat next to a Slovene novelist who had spent the war in London as a BBC announcer in Slovene, but he only opened his mouth to tell her: 'These days we only talk about Trieste in our country!' Then he sank into a sulky silence.

I often wondered whether the Communists seriously thought such behaviour would advance the Yugoslav territorial claims on Trieste at the Paris Peace Conference. They pursued their campaign relentlessly. In the 1946 First of May procession, an enormous mock Moscow–Trieste railway ticket was carried along by the demonstrators, as if to underline that giving Trieste to Yugoslavia meant giving it also to the Soviet Union. After the procession came to an end, detachments were sent to the British Consulate where they shouted against the British imperialists. The Consul sat on the window-sill, drank beer and laughed, which was described as particularly offensive in various wall newspapers.

The Yugoslav delegation at the Peace Conference in Paris did not behave any more intelligently. Under Kardelj's leadership, they vigorously defended the claims of defeated Bulgaria against allied Greece and yet were shocked when the Western Allies in turn sided with Italy in some of its disputes with Yugoslavia. The Communists' explanation was that Bulgaria, being communist, was a democratic country, while Greece was fascist. If, in the end, the bulk of the Croat and Slovene ethnic area previously under Italy was incorporated in Yugoslavia this must have happened in spite rather than because of communist 'diplomacy' and been due to the incredible patience displayed by the Western negotiators.

In June 1946 a victory parade was held in London, but the Yugoslav government refused to send any troops, following the example of the Soviet Union. After the Paris Peace Conference, the British Consul was no longer invited to any official function.

In this climate, anybody politically conscious must have been asking himself where all this was leading. There were some sinister signs. A Slovene woman married to a well-to-do Belgian came to thank Tito for what he had done for her native country. But listening to her own acquaintances, she soon became aware of the true nature of Tito's régime, of its terrorism and mismanagement, and she also met my political associates. After attending a lunch given by the fellow-travelling writer Josip Vidmar, then President of Slovenia, she told them that her host had talked volubly about how there would soon be a revolution in Belgium and in other Western countries. The Yugoslav Army would go to the help of proletarian revolutionaries, and governments of the same hue as in Yugoslavia would soon emerge.

This was bad enough, but in the summer of 1946, General Franjo Pirc (not a relative), who had just relinquished his command of the Yugoslav Air Force, told my uncle, Captain Metod Pirc, that he was certain Tito was preparing for war. It was the personal opinion of a high commander and confirmed by the military training organised for young people, when they were sent in masses to do 'voluntary' work on railways, roads and administrative buildings, with the explanation that they had to get ready to assist the oppressed Western European peoples in their struggle for liberty.

While this kind of warlike policy was being pursued, nobody in Yugoslavia could publish any dissenting views. In the West, despite communist belligerence, many people seemed to be indulging in pacifist illusions. Dr Nagode remembered that, at a pre-war anti-Hitler meeting in France, the veteran French politician Edouard Herriot, correctly recognising the dangers, had said: *'Il y a pire que la guerre.'* Dr Nagode therefore wrote to Herriot, who also happened to be the Chairman of the French League for Human Rights, reminding him of this assessment and warning against softness *via-à-vis* the aggressiveness of the Communists. In fact, Western reactions seemed subdued – there was Churchill's speech in Fulton, but it remained almost an isolated occurrence. There was some stirring criticism, especially in the United States, after the execution of General Mihailović, Tito's rival war leader. This was the death of the man who was no match for communist cunning. He and his followers had been trapped between Hitler and Tito, yet the disgust aroused led to no change in policy towards his executioners.

In spite of the Yugoslav Communists' offensive behaviour, the Western assistance channelled through UNRRA continued to pour into the country. The Yugoslav government thanked the Soviet Union and praised its unselfish aid which, as they themselves later admitted, was non-existent. Some of the UNRRA inspectors sent to Yugoslavia whom I met were left-wingers, and full of admiration for the communist use of the supplies, while I was sceptical. My doubts were justified by subsequent demonstrable waste of economic resources. In 1946 the Communists themselves supplied some evidence of inefficient use of UNRRA deliveries. Yugoslavia had received, for instance, some 10,000 Army surplus lorries. The number of skilled drivers available was insufficient and the training of new ones was so badly handled that a considerable proportion of the lorries finished up in ditches or became unserviceable. A scapegoat was promptly found in the leading staff members of the State Road Transport enterprises. In each republic, a group was put on trial and harsh sentences were meted out, including death sentences. I myself went to see the proceedings in Ljubljana and was shocked by their peremptoriness.

My own father became involved in UNRRA operations. The communist authorities sent him to the United States as an experienced cotton expert to negotiate the free deliveries of cotton and re-conditioned textile machinery. He was far from enthusiastic about going to America because he felt tired and was put off by the casual communist approach both to the dealings with UNRRA and to his own journey. There were several false starts, such as when he was rushed to Belgrade without enough time even to collect his luggage, only to be told that his departure had been postponed, and when the Secretary of the US National Cotton Council came to Belgrade to discuss deliveries, none of those in charge would meet him, because he was an 'imperialist'. When the unfortunate secretary eventually left Belgrade without seeing anyone, my father was ordered by telephone to intercept him at Ljubljana railway station and try to transact the business with him there.

In the end, my father did leave and toured the United States, discussing cotton deliveries and ending up in Washington in late August 1946. There he had an appointment with the Chief of the Economic Division of the State Department, about securing additional supplies for Yugoslavia. He waited for a long time in the ante-room but was told that Mr Clayton could not receive him. What had happened?

A little earlier, a Yugoslav communist fighter plane had intercepted a US passenger plane flying from Vienna to Udine when it tried to take a short-cut over the north-western corner of Yugoslavia. The pilot was preparing to land near my home town of Kranj when the fighter opened fire. The Yugoslav Embassy in Washington did not bother to inform my father of the event — perhaps they thought that it was perfectly all right to shoot down planes while asking for cotton or other favours. What was even more surprising was the fact that Yugoslavia was given the cotton a little later in spite of this communist impertinence.

Maybe the legal points of the case were not entirely clear, but the political question was, why was this incident staged and who gained anything from it? The communist authorities claimed that Allied planes flying a few miles over Upper Carniola were spying, but spying on what? Having flown in masses over Yugoslavia during the war, up to a little more than a year ago the Allies had all the maps and data they needed. What is more, in those days we had all been enthusiastic at seeing little dots appear in the sky or hearing their buzz. Resistance prisoners in Ljubljana jail sang and shouted, full of hope every time Allied planes flew over the town. The shooting down of American planes (another was shot down a few days later over the Lake of Bled, observed by Tito) could be explained only by the megalomania of the communist leaders, who had lost all sense of proportion and wanted to teach the United States a lesson. It was all very sad and dangerous.

During August 1946 I kept away from the British Consulate — Leonard Scopes was absent on leave, while I was passing through another bout of caution. But then I spotted a car in the Consulate courtyard with a placard announcing its route: 'London–Athens'. Curiosity prevailed and in I went.

The Acting Consul, Ted Kay, introduced me to the owner, Captain Francis Noel-Baker, a young Labour MP. I was distracted from him by the presence of the American military vice-attaché from Zagreb, who was in Ljubljana because of the plane incident. His indignation was such that I thought I at least ought to make a gesture of good will. I impetuously offered to help find a wounded Turkish passenger by enquiring from the local doctor. Nothing came of it, as the doctor had not been near the plane. The only outcome was to give the Communists more material against me.

Noel-Baker was in Slovenia on less pressing business – accompanied by a friend, he was on the way to Greece to observe the forthcoming elections. When he noticed that I was not a follower of Tito, he said he was glad that I could talk to him on neutral ground – I was amazed that he could consider a British Consulate neutral ground; surely most Communists would consider it an enemy fortress. I was no less surprised when he warned me about the viewpoint of British Labour. 'We are not in favour of the kind of political régime you have in Yugoslavia,' he said, 'but an economic system like yours is indeed our aim.' Then he and his friend left in a hurry for Bled where they hoped to interview Marshal Tito.

When I explained to Dr Nagode how indignant the American attaché had been, he asked me to write a letter regretting the incident and took it himself to Ted Kay with the request that it be forwarded to the American Ambassador in Belgrade. It said that while the Yugoslav State might be held responsible for the material damage inflicted, the Yugoslav people should not be blamed for the actions of a group of people who had usurped power in the country.

Perhaps the Communists' lack of concern for human life was not to be wondered at, since they showed so little respect for it in Yugoslavia. During 1946, four people I knew fairly well were killed by the Communist Police without a trial of any sort. To describe just one of these: the brother of a university friend came to Yugoslavia in 1944 or 1945 with a British military mission but, being a Slovene, he then joined the Partisans. When the hostilities were over, he was hospitalised for some reason, and in 1946 he simply disappeared from the hospital without trace.

Confronted with such violence, one felt ashamed, but also frightened. In my case, shame was probably the stronger emotion, so that I welcomed an involvement in the attempts at bringing together an all-Yugoslav opposition. In the spring of 1946 in Belgrade, I ran into the Slovene politican France Snoj. In the 1945 federal elections he had been elected member of the House of Nationalities on the common Liberation Front list but was as opposed to the Communists as ever. He told me about attempts at organising a peasant group in the federal parliament, but he particularly wanted to establish contact with the democratic politicians in Zagreb, and asked me to go there. The man to see there was Dr Jančiković, a lawyer.

He told me that a draft statement to be signed by all opposition leaders had just been sent to Ljubljana. It demanded free elections in accordance with the agreement between Tito and Šubašić. Dr Jančiković sent me on to the leading Croat Peasant Party man in Zagreb, Dr Šutej, who, in a long talk, optimistically suggested that the proposed statement might have a considerable influence on further developments. Thus encouraged, I returned about a week later to tell him that of the Slovenes, Snoj and Furlan and perhaps some others were willing to sign. 'Now all depends on Belgrade,' was Dr Šutej's reply, but I never found out what happened there. This initiative at any rate seems to have petered out.

In the autumn of 1946, elections were to take place for the People's Assemblies of the six constituent republics. This made some of us think about possible participation, although personally I was firmly convinced that the Communists would not allow anybody else to stand. To clarify the prospects, I went to see Dr Šutej in the late summer. The scene had changed. While the Croat leader had thought that he was closely watched in the past, now a police car with four men stood in front of his house. They did not bother people entering or leaving the house, but would trail Dr Šutej when he came out. It was hardly surprising that he told me there was no hope of any independent candidates' taking part in the election. Yet he thought that financial straits would soon force the communist government to be more prudent. How wrong he was.

In the elections, 98% of votes were cast for the People's Front candidates, but a change since the 1945 elections was noticeable. Then there was still a great deal of enthusiasm, now there was none. Our daily help, who used to be a fervent activist during the war and later concealed the Secretary of the Slovene government in her flat, said to my mother: 'The Communists do nothing but lie!'

Despite discontent amongst the population, a feeling of impotence prevailed, a feeling that there was nothing one could do about the Communists: there was something final about their rule. The BBC broadcasts, to which we had listened with so much hope during the war, became ever more non-committal. If only we knew, we would say, what the West was up to. Both Dr Nagode and I were of the view that our meetings no longer made any sense. There was no ray of hope anywhere in spite of the Zürich speech by Churchill about the need to unite Europe. Yet one evening in October, I went again to talk to Dr Nagode out of desperation. He took me to his study and showed me a letter that one of our women associates, an elderly teacher, had received from Austria. The sender was a *Domobranci* officer to whom she had written as she thought him a patriot. He said he could not answer all her questions about Western attitudes and policy, but would contact somebody else who could.

On about New Year's Day 1947, Dr Nagode gave me a wad of mail from Austria to read. Our woman associate was now in contact with Mihailović's Colonel Glušič, head of some kind of National Committee in Salzburg. He was one of the officers arrested in Ljubljana in December 1944 by the Gestapo for conspiring against the Germans, sent to Dachau and liberated by the advancing Americans. Colonel Glušič comforted us, saying we should not think the West had forgotten us. 'On the contrary,' he wrote. He enclosed the draft of a constitution which dealt at length with the organisation of Armed Forces, to consist of Slovene, Croat and Serb Armies commanded by their own local officers. A questionnaire was included with requests for information about military matters. I took these papers home and kept them for a few days in my drawer. They were elaborated with great care, but I found them one-sided and even naïve and not at all what we had hoped for. We certainly had no intention of collecting military information.

It all suddenly made me shudder. I had a premonition of sitting behind the iron grating of a prison window, but shook off this feeling as incredible. However, I had had the same sensation once before when I read about the trial of the old Serb politician Miša Trifunović, a former member of the Yugoslav government in exile who had returned home to Belgrade after the war. He had been given a severe sentence for having kept up relations with foreigners and his son-in-law had been sentenced to death at the same trial.

Then something went wrong with the messenger from Colonel Glušič. He was unpunctual and unreliable. I thought that the link should be suspended forthwith; Dr Nagode accepted my opinion, and I never heard of any mail from Austria again. With the advantage of hindsight, it is obvious that the Secret Police had played a trick on us, supplying a messenger to Austria to manoeuvre us into an awkward corner.

Maybe I did not watch what was happening with sufficient care, as I was very busy. In February I was to sit the oral examination for my doctorate in public law. When it came, I had a very good day and passed *summa cum laude*. The Chairman of the Examination Commission of five professors was the Dean of the Law Faculty, Professor Furlan. I almost missed this examination because a few months earlier I had been called up to complete my military service. My first reaction was to escape abroad, but my father insisted that I should apply for the postponement to which I was entitled till the completion of my studies. The application was granted although the recruitment officer had taken some persuading. Immediately after my examination, I embarked on writing a thesis on the Nuremberg trials.

Also in the autumn of 1946, I applied for the post of assistant at the University. Professor Furlan was sympathetic but urged me not to mention his interest in my appointment because it could only harm me. In the end no assistants were appointed because the Party was not willing to confirm those selected by the University.

The consultant who treated me for tuberculosis thought that I would do better to try to become a diplomat. He had considerable influence because of his war service. Several times he suggested that I should be employed in the foreign service to Jože Brilej, Chief of Personnel at the Foreign Ministry and later Ambassador to Great Britain and the United Nations. However, his interventions did not help, and he was wondering why. Finally Brilej told the doctor: 'There is no place in our diplomatic service for a friend of the British Consul.'

In December 1946, my consultant protector advised me how to repair the damage I had done myself by visiting the British Consulate. 'You should "legalise" your relations with foreigners,' he said, and noticing my reaction, added: 'It is no use getting angry. I know perfectly well you do not intend to do any harm to our country, but you should go to the Ministry of Internal Affairs and tell them that you see the British Consul occasionally. They will most probably ask you to write reports on your meetings, just as they ask everybody who meets foreigners.'

I told the British Consul about this conversation, and then I went to see Boris Trampuž, an old acquaintance. In 1946 he was *Chef de Cabinet* to the Minister of Internal Affairs, Boris Kraigher. I telephoned him and was told to come to his office during working hours; he sounded very official. After listening to me he said: 'I cannot see what your doctor means. In our country everybody is free to see as much of foreigners as he wants and I am certain there is nothing illegal about your visits to the British Consul.' I found that reassuring and left for Planica, the ski resort, where I spent a few days in the same hotel as the British Consul and his wife, the Director of the French Institute in Ljubljana and his wife, the British press attaché in Ljubljana and the representative of the American Red Cross. There were plenty of Secret Police men among the guests but after my visit to the *Chef de Cabinet* I felt safer. It turned out that Professor Furlan was also told by Josip Vidmar that his relations with the British Consul were too friendly and that he should stop seeing him. He stopped his visits, but then he felt ashamed and saw the Consul again.

There was some hopeful news. I was not able to reach the Croat opposition leader, Dr Šutej, when last in Zagreb in January 1947, but I understood that there had been talks between another member of the Croat Peasant Party, Ivan Šubašić (of the Tito-Šubašić agreement), and the Croat communist boss, Bakarić. What was this supposed to mean? As it turned out, it did not mean anything unless it was intended to mislead.

The population in Slovenia was becoming restive – almost two years after the war, instead of becoming easier, life had become more difficult. In April 1947 a strike broke out in Jugobruna, the textile factory in Kranj. When the Slovene Prime Minister went to calm the workers, the angry weavers, mainly women, refused to let him speak, complaining that they could not live on their wages. The money was insufficient even to buy shoes for coming to work in winter. They were at length persuaded to return to work by various promises. The communist reaction was: 'Those lazy dogs do not want to work' and gradually most of the workers who had participated in the strike lost their jobs, and some disappeared altogether.

The former workers from my father's factory would stop my mother in the street and ask: 'Madame, when will you be rebuilding your factory? It was so much nicer to work for you than it is now.' But there was no hope of private initiative being given any scope. On the contrary, on 6 December 1946, all factories except small workshops were taken over by the Ministry of Industry among great celebrations and the former owners were turned out.

The First Five-Year Plan was launched in the spring of 1947. Professor Dragoljub Jovanović, as an economist, analysed it in parliament and made the economic dictator Kidrič so angry that he was speechless for several moments when he came to the rostrum to answer Jovanović.

At the University of Ljubljana, the Communists wanted to oust a number of professors. From the Law Faculty they sought to remove Professor Pitamic, a former Ambassador in Washington and author of a *Treatise on the State* published there, and Professor Ogris, an economist with several books on economic policy to his credit. The former was a practising Catholic and the latter a liberal, which the Communists abominated, and both were men of great personal integrity. Professor Furlan was angered by communist plotting, as he was telling me when I accompanied him on his way to the opening of the exhibition to mark the tenth anniversary of the Communist Party in Slovenia. He had to attend as Dean of the Law Faculty.

'This is a scandal,' he was saying. 'They could wait till the two old men die or retire. I shall tell the British Consul about it. You should tell him too, as you will probably see him before me. The world should know how our most respected people are treated.' We were walking through the Tivoli Park and out of the corner of my eye I spotted the President of Slovenia, Josip Vidmar, the fellow-travelling former liberal literary critic. He was catching up with us, and I wanted to warn Professor Furlan, but could not because Vidmar was within earshot. So Professor Furlan went on audibly cursing the Communists until Vidmar was level with us. They shook hands because they knew each other well and Professor Furlan introduced me to the President. 'Oh, I see,' the latter smiled, 'so those who wish to commit suicide are now killing others as well.' Later I wondered what these cryptic words were supposed to mean but was not unduly worried. Everything seemed to be all right. Among my friends, Dr Nagode had just got a good job at the Institute of Geology, and Svato, another associate, had also found congenial employment.

7

A trial on Stalin's orders

On the eve of Tito's birthday, Saturday 24 May 1947, I was arrested in front of our apartment house on my way home from an evening with my girlfriend, Katja. I was ordered to sit between two Secret Policemen in a car and taken to the former Psychiatric Department of Ljubljana hospital, turned into a jail by the Gestapo and used for the same purpose by the Communists.

There they searched me and locked me up in cell No. 48. Then I was hurriedly taken to a largish room with some half a dozen people waiting for me. Presiding over the session was a man in the uniform of a colonel of the communist Secret Police, whom I later identified as Mitja Ribičič, chief of the political police investigators. They wanted to know with whom I had associated over the past two years. I gave some sixty names, including university professors and the British and French Consuls.

'Who will believe that all these people were your associates?' Ribičič looked at me sideways. Then he went on: 'And who were your girlfriends?' Everybody knew Katja. Ribičič further enquired whether my relations with a certain married woman were sexual or political. For her sake, I assented to the former.

After a pause, the Colonel said sharply: 'What about the wife of the British Consul? Was she not your mistress?' I jumped. 'Don't get excited, Mr Sirc. Don't you remember the evening when the Consul was out? For a while you sat in the drawing room, then you both went to the bar next door, she poured drinks and you drank to your love.' Amazingly, he was describing exactly what happened apart from the 'toast to our love'. The maid must have been sending very detailed reports.

'Is the Consul's wife his wife at all?' Ribičič asked gleefully. 'But they have two children', I answered indignantly. 'Oh, have they? Anything can be arranged to catch a fellow like you.' We passed on to my last meeting with the Consul, when we drove with his wife, the two children and an UNRRA secretary, to the mountains above Jesenice. 'What did you do there?' the Colonel insisted. 'We picked narcissi and had a picnic,' I said, upon which everybody in the room roared with laughter. 'What did you discuss with the Consul?' I could not remember, it was not anything important. 'Now, really, Mr Sirc, you must tell us the truth.'

He went on and on for hours. To cut short the niggling interrogation, I eventually said that we had talked about the factories along the road, which I thought was safe since the newspapers were overflowing with reports on them. The subject was dropped but the final judgement stated that I had 'collected and transmitted ... data ... on Litostroj in Ljubljana, on the Hydro-power station at Jesenice ...'

Ribičič told me what a pity it was I did not tell him the truth from the very beginning because he could have let me go immediately and nobody would even have known I had been arrested. 'Everything depends on how people behave,' he informed me, the implication being that the more subservient anybody was to the interrogators and the more readily he admitted to what they wanted him to admit, the more lenient was the treatment. Such statements were a psychological trick to soften up those under interrogation. The prisoners summed it up in the joke: 'Whoever is ready to admit his crime will not be punished for half of his misdeeds, but for the remainder his punishment will be doubled.'

To round it off, he asked again why we had established contact with Austria, so I told him that we wanted to be well informed on what went on abroad. 'Weren't our papers good enough for you?' Ribičič asked sarcastically and I replied, I thought very bravely, that they were not. I went on to say that we were afraid the Communists' one-sided policy would bring the wrath of the West on us. When he began to dictate my statement, I requested that I do it myself. He made a disparaging gesture and walked out, leaving me to do it.

Taken back to my cell in broad daylight, I lay down wearily on the camp bed. The door flew open and the guard started shouting that I was not to lie down during the day. So I sat on the bed again, and again he did not approve. I was given a backless chair to sit on but told not to lean against the wall.

Interrogations by a number of policemen followed, branding me a friend of foreign imperialists. I was in a fighting mood and retorted that imperialism was a thing of the past. But my fighting spirit soon subsided after I had been repeatedly hauled up as soon as I fell asleep and dragged, dishevelled, in front of an interrogator.

I was taken to task because I used to visit Tatjana, the Slovene press secretary of the British press attaché, and helped her with filling in BBC audience research questionnaires. 'Don't you know that Tatjana is a British spy?' the interrogator remarked with a malevolent smile. 'If I knew her, I would be scared stiff.'

On Monday night, Ribičič was waiting for me in a room grotesquely draped in red curtains. Again I told him that we had been trying to organise an opposition and participate in elections as guaranteed by Marshal Tito in his agreement with the Yugoslav government in exile in London. I deliberately stressed our contacts with democratic political leaders in Belgrade and Zagreb. At that Ribičič began remonstrating, pulling at the red curtains as he shouted: 'What elections, what opposition! You are all bandits!'

My stomach shrank and a lump formed in my throat. Any reader who has by now recognised the true nature of Tito's régime will expect that a brilliant career was awaiting a Secret Policeman of the Ribičič brand. And indeed, he became Federal Prime Minister and Vice-President of Yugoslavia in the early 1970s. In the 1980s, he was 'elected' Slovene member of the Praesidium of the Yugoslav League of Communists.

At my first meeting with Ambrož, real name Švent, who was to become my principal interrogator, I was treated to a communist homily. I was a spoilt capitalist brat who knew nothing about the harsh realities of life. He himself was a land surveyor before the war and earned only 800 dinars per month. I quickly calculated that this was much more than the Communists were currently paying to over half the employed university graduates.

By then Ambrož was singing the praises of the communist régime and suddenly rounded on me: 'And you really believed that you could overthrow us with the help of a few old women and Nagode?' He wondered why we were not afraid of them and why we did not panic when they arrested our colleague, the old school-mistress, a week or so earlier than the rest. I said: 'Why should we have? The only awkward thing, the connection with Austria, had been dropped a long time ago.'

'Ah, but if everything was legal, why were your meetings secret?' I said: 'Why should we have publicised them? Although criminal prosecution was out of the question, the Secret Police could have made life difficult for us in other ways.' Ambrož warned me that my ideas about law were all wrong because I had studied law before and during the war, while now the legal approach was entirely different. Humble confession was the best response.

Without a doubt, the approach was different! While our criminal law professors had taught that prisoners under interrogation must be given enough rest, the Communist Police were out to tire me. They had me spend all day long on a backless chair, then the minute I lay down and fell asleep at night, they woke me. I had not been given a chance to rest properly for at least a month, and was becoming confused.

The accusations were puzzling, to say the least. Ambrož knew, presumably from one of the typists in the news agency where I worked in 1945, that I had sometimes taken home teleprinter tapes, and he manoeuvred me into admitting that I had once shown the British Consul a speech by the British Foreign Minister, Bevin. To my consternation, Ambrož called this spying and the later judgement read: '... he committed thefts of Tanjug dispatches at his office and handed them over to a member of a foreign mission....'

The interrogator tried hard to make me say that our group had had an intelligence unit during the war and that we were in receipt of money from some doubtful source. He claimed that a thick file of paper lying in front of him contained all the data on this score. I soon noticed that the paper was blank. I was also aware that the group never had any money to speak of. I could only say that a friend of Dr Nagode's had tried to collect intelligence at some stage, but was arrested by the Italians and died soon after in Italian captivity.

Another ploy used by the interrogators was to make prisoners feel uncomfortable by besmirching those close to them. With me, they tried claiming that my girlfriend, Katja, had had love affairs with Italian officers during the fascist occupation. 'But she was hardly twelve,' I said. 'And with whom did her father collaborate?' Ambrož insisted. 'He had to escape to Switzerland because he is Jewish and Katja was arrested twice by the Nazis at the age of fourteen,' I retorted. 'What did she know about your criminal activity?' was the next question. When I was being interrogated about her, Katja had actually just been arrested by the Communists who tried to make her talk by describing to her my real and alleged love affairs.

The protocols of my interrogation were always written by Ambrož, who tended to embellish them in his own way. I objected ever more feebly. Then one night I broke my spectacles in a dark toilet. Presumably the authorities wanted to make life difficult for me by not procuring another pair, while I used my lack of glasses as grounds for refusing to sign the minutes of interrogation, saying that I had difficulty in reading them. This refusal turned out to be to my own detriment.

A few days later, although still without glasses, I was asked to sign the accumulated minutes. When I protested, pressure was put on me and I finally signed, though I could not possibly have read everything properly. My resistance was weakened because, as a student of law, I knew of a legal principle called the principle of oral trial, which requires all evidence to be corroborated by examination in Court. I did not realise as yet that communist judges did not pay any attention to such achievements of bourgeois civilisation.

From passing remarks about the search for another pair of glasses, it became clear to me that, after my arrest, our flat had been sealed and my mother had nowhere to go. I felt horrible, but worse was to come. One night towards the end of my first week in prison, I was left in bed longer than usual before the night interrogation. Unable to fall asleep, I was tossing and turning restlessly, when I heard voices from the corridor. I thought I recognised the voice of my uncle, Captain Metod Pirc, followed by the voice of Professor Furlan, but to this day I do not know whether it was a trick of my imagination or whether it was really they. At any rate, they were arrested about a week after the rest of us.

By then my interrogators had turned to cotton textiles, the subject of my father's work. I thought it would be unconvincing if I claimed that I knew nothing about it, so I raked my memory for something to tell them. I came up with the information that the United States were to supply Yugoslavia with 20,000 tons of cotton on behalf of UNRRA. I had learnt this when I was interpreting a conversation between my father and Mr Read Dunn, the representative of the National Cotton Council of America. As I related earlier, this talk took place in the Orient-Simplon Express at Ljubljana station.

Like everybody else in my home town, I was aware that some textile factories there were also processing Soviet cotton, and also that workers were dissatisfied with the new inexperienced management. In one factory they even petitioned the authorities for the former owner to be brought back. I knew little else since I had my own work to do at the University and my father had no time to discuss anything with me. He went to the ministry at seven in the morning, came home for a quick lunch and returned to his office only to come back late in the evening, too tired to talk about textiles.

While searching our flat the police also found the application from a factory for coke, the by-laws of the Soviet-Yugoslav Chamber of Commerce, a report on the shortage of knitting needles and the minutes of a consultation with spinning experts. These documents must have been left behind by my father between his frantic journeys up and down the country.

Somewhat earlier, a new man had appeared on my prison horizon. He was the head of the Communist Police in Slovenia, Niko Šilih, a slim and ascetic-looking man. Šilih intervened in person in the textile interrogation by suggesting that the papers found at our home were clear evidence that my father had regularly brought the official mail from his department for me to read and report to the British Consul. 'And', Šilih shouted, 'on the night when you were arrested, you were on your way to your father at the ministry to be handed new spying material.' 'No,' I said, 'I simply could not have been, because my father was in Warsaw with the Yugoslav trade delegation.' All my arguments were useless and the final judgement read that I had collected and passed on (without stating to whom) data on the situation in the textile industry.

After about ten days, Ambrož changed tack. I had to stand four yards from his desk and he heaped on me accusations that I was lying. After so many nights without sleep, I was no longer certain whether I was speaking the truth or not. It still had not dawned upon me that I was confronted with pure malice. Strangers would come in, listen for a while and leave, exclaiming it was obvious I was a dangerous spy.

Then a sympathetic interrogator appeared. He seemed to know Katja. 'What a pity you interfered with our business instead of sticking to courting her,' he said. 'Now you will not see her for a while.' He reduced me to tears. I kept telling myself that I was hysterical but was unable to stop. Back with Ambrož, I was told he would no longer interrogate me because I was obstinate. To my utter amazement, I fell onto my knees and begged: 'Please, carry on, please!'

To shorten the long days in the cell and also to make a good impression, I asked for some Marxist literature to read. At this stage I began to wonder whether Marxism was not the best philosophy after all. What if the Communists were right?

I received no food parcels and no mail, though they were provided for in prison regulations, and I worried about what had happened to my mother. Once, when I heard a woman sobbing somewhere in the building, I imagined it was she. As I found out later, she was arrested and interrogated for one night. One morning I overheard a chillingly familiar sound. It sounded just like my father coughing and then somebody was cleaning his teeth in the bathroom making exactly the noises I used to hear coming from our bathroom at home. My knees trembled. Then I brushed it all aside, telling myself that there was no reason why my father should have been arrested.

But signs of his presence in prison multiplied. Eventually, Ambrož produced a letter I had written to my father in Warsaw just before my arrest and that they must have taken out of his wallet or briefcase. 'Why did you write to your father that there had been a strike in Kranj?' The court considered this letter as evidence that I had been reporting everything to my father, which implied to them that he must also have known about the activities of the Nagode group.

A special interrogator came to grill me on Professor Furlan, who, he claimed, was a senior agent in the British Intelligence Service. About a week before our arrest, Professor Furlan's wife had died and I was now told she had been killed by him with the connivance of the British Consul because she knew too much about their crimes.

This accusation made me so obviously indignant, in spite of my sleeplessness, that they did not press it. The interrogator switched to a series of questions put to us by the American Red Cross representative Jake Hoptner, who was writing a dissertation on Yugoslavia. I thought the questions were innocuous, as they dealt with the history of the Liberation Front and the implementation of the Tito-Šubašič agreement, but was told that even giving Hoptner the *Official Gazette* with this agreement printed in it was a terrible crime. I did not realise then that Professor Furlan had refused to talk at all. He had lived in Trieste under Fascism and was well acquainted with the way totalitarian police and courts functioned, so he had claimed he was too old and could not remember anything.

How right he was, since everything one said was turned into a crime. The Hoptner questions contributed a sentence to the judgement according to which I had compiled 'false reports on nationalisation and other affairs of general importance to the State'.

Suddenly I was confronted with the accusation that I was an Italian spy. Ambrož showed me a letter I had written to my father from Italy in July 1942 and which they had found in a drawer in our flat. It was carefully folded so that I could read only one sentence which said that I would send the names to the Italian Major D'Amato later. He inferred that I was spying for the Major amongst Slovene students in Italy. It came slowly back to me that what D'Amato wanted was the names of Carabinieri officers in Perugia, so that he could recommend me to them in case persecution of Slovene students spread there. Although this may have been clear from the rest of the letter, Ambrož dismissed it with 'anybody can claim that'. In another move I was given to understand that the British Consul was about to leave Ljubljana. And again Ambrož pressed me to tell the truth about everything and threatened me with a secret military tribunal. He mentioned the names of two men I knew had disappeared in 1946 and were apparently killed by the Secret Police, nobody quite knew why. His malicious comment was: 'If I were answering questions in the way you do, I would see the noose dangling in front of me right now.'

In the third week after my arrest there came a gala session. I was brought into a room where there were at least five people, among them Šilih and Ribičič, and ordered to sit in the middle. Then they started firing questions at me. Šilih was lying across a table and eventually whispered: 'Wherever we scratch, it's always you we find under the surface. Who was in contact with the Consuls? You. Who paid visits to Jovanović, the bandit in Belgrade? You. Who wrote to Carinthia? You. Tell me: Are you an agent of IS?'

'What is IS?', I asked in my naïveté, never having heard of this abbreviation.

'Intelligence Service,' somebody interpreted from the background.

'Oh, the Intelligence Service, yes, I have heard of it, but I have never had anything to do with it.'

Šilih slid off the table, paced up and down for a while and then came up close to me, uttering in a low wicked voice: 'You are a master spy!'

'Oh, no!' I shuddered, 'If you believe that, I am lost.'

'No, you aren't', Šilih retorted. 'Tell us everything and you will be safe. Who are the members of the English spy network in Ljubljana?'

'I don't know.'

Šilih called the guard and ordered him to take me to my cell.

By that time I was allowed to sleep on Saturdays and Sundays, but the light was constantly left on so that I was very restless. One night I woke with a start: somebody was sitting on my bed. Šilih's pale face was looking down at me and he said slowly: 'Well, Sirc, how do you feel now that we are going to hang you? You had better tell us everything.' Upon which he got up and walked out. There was a repeat performance some days later.

The interrogation returned to normal, that is, to fabricating crimes out of my explanations of what I had done. My quest for the wounded passenger from the US plane shot down over Yugoslavia was turned into military espionage; Dr Nagode's and my bewilderment over the collaboration of some Slovenes with the Italians at the end of 1942, into our approval of this collaboration.

When asked what, in my opinion, was my worst crime, I answered that I considered the only awkward thing to be our contact with émigrés in Austria.

'By no means', they said, 'those contacts were of no importance. The real criminal activity consisted in your visiting the British Consulate.'

They wanted me to give my own legal definition of what I had been doing. In fact, they wanted me to say that I had been a spy, and they added that self-criticism was the best way of atoning for my mistakes. The little legal training I had led me to insist that it was up to the Court to interpret the legal qualifications of a crime, but that I could not imagine how anybody could claim that discussing matters printed in newspapers was spying.

'How wrong you are, Mr Sirc,' Ambrož retorted. 'It was like that in the old days, but now everything is different. A schoolmaster was sentenced to ten years in prison for having made cuttings from newspapers for the Germans during the war.'

Just before the end of June, I was marched to a largish room where some six people were waiting for me. I knew none of them, but subsequently I identified Viktor Avbelj, the chief Public Prosecutor of the People's Republic of Slovenia, and his two deputies, Martin Žalik and Marjan Simčič-Marko, who all appeared at the trial later. After a few introductory questions about the émigrés in Austria and the British Consul who, they repeated, had fled to California, the interrogation was taken over by a man who had been sitting quietly by the window. He raised his left hand and introduced himself: 'Ljubo, listen to me now. When you are in trouble, you will remember me, the man with two fingers missing who came to talk to you in Serbo-Croat, or rather, in Montenegrin. I want to help you but if you are not prepared to accept my advice, you will have to fend for yourself.'

Much later I discovered that this was Colonel Grkić of the Serbian Secret Police. After a while, everybody else got up and left the room so that he and I remained alone. He came nearer to me and said: 'Again, Ljubo, I am warning you, be reasonable. Tell us everything or you will die.' I muttered that I had already told them whatever I knew, but he went on: 'My only interest is Dragoljub Jovanović. I want to free the Serbian people of this impostor — I want to crush him and you must help me.'

When he noticed that I was startled, he continued: 'You will have to choose. Either you help me or else . . . you ought to know that Jovanović had contacts with the well-known English spy Seton-Watson.' Then he altered his tone: 'Don't be alarmed. If you help us, you may get away with only three years in prison. Of course, you will be sentenced to many more years, but we shan't forget you.'

Grkić comfortingly told me that, after the sentence, I could volunteer to work on the construction of one of the new railway lines, become a shock worker and be set free as a useful member of communist society. 'But, you haven't much time,' he added, 'make up your mind!'

He rang the bell, whereupon Simčič came back and they both advised me to be sensible. Grkić wanted me to write another detailed account of my meetings with Jovanović and promised that I would see him again before the trial began.

He had obviously expected that his blowing hot and cold would make me write a piece as incriminating for Jovanović as I could manage, but I simply repeated what I had been saying all along without changing a word. The same day, a Secret Policeman from Zagreb also questioned me about my encounters with the Croat ex-Minister Šutej and his friend, Dr Jančiković.

After these two interviews, the interrogations stopped. I was no longer woken up immediately after I had fallen asleep in the evening, and I was left alone night after night. This lull I found far more worrying than the, by then familiar, continued interrogation. What did it mean − did it mean that they had given me up for good?

Even though it was midsummer, the radiators in the cell were on full blast and there was constantly that most terrible light above the door shining into my eyes. Whenever I turned away from the light, the guard came running in and told me to lie facing the door. When I bound a handkerchief around my eyes so as to get some rest, it made me sweat profusely. If only they would start interrogating me again, I thought, turning over and over on my camp bed. What was happening to my father and mother, I wondered. Was our flat still sealed off? For a fortnight I saw nobody except the guard.

It was a relief when Ambrož summoned me again and announced that we were going to be tried in public. This was good news, for I thought that the public trial would be an opportunity to defend myself and explain what had in fact happened. I asked Ambrož what was going to happen to my father, and when he told me that he would also be on trial, I asked: 'What on earth for?'

'Nothing very serious', Ambrož said. 'And do behave yourself in Court. In the old days it was worthwhile defending oneself, but now the best thing is to admit to everything. This makes a far better impression on the Court. I shall not interrogate you many more times, so, please, make up your mind and tell me everything when we meet next time. The Prosecutor will not question you at all, so this will be the last chance for you to confess to your crimes.'

At that time people outside thought the trial would be on a small scale and that my father would be released. But the two leading Slovene Communists, Kidrič and Kardelj, defeated these expectations by insisting that there should be a proper trial with exemplary punishments. For some reason, Kidrič considered Dr Nagode his personal rival and wanted to get rid of him. The Slovene Minister for Industry, Franc Leskošek, a leading Communist himself, interceded on my father's behalf, but Kidrič, a much more powerful man, turned his requests down by accusing my father of 'having betrayed the Five-Year Plan' of which Kidrič was the author, although nobody quite knew how. Some people from our home town, envious of my father's past fortune, also seem to have pressed for him to be tried and punished for having exploited the working people.

One morning, about 20 July, the door of my cell opened and in stepped a slim man in civilian clothes. I noticed that he had a golden front tooth which later led me to think that he was most probably Major Ronko of the Secret Police.

After the usual preliminary questions he said, leaning against the door: 'Remember, the fate of both you and your father depends on whether you tell us everything.' And then he walked out.

This was a very good introduction to my last questioning by Ambrož that same evening. 'I shall not be seeing you again, Mr Sirc,' Ambrož opened the interrogation, 'so a complete confession is the best thing.'

'Yes, I am aware of that.'

'All right then, what about the Italian officer who rented the two rooms at your aunt's? Did you supply him with the names of your fellow-students in Perugia?'

'No, I did not,' I said firmly.

'Think carefully, Mr Sirc. The officer was staying at your aunt's flat. We could ask some very awkward questions about that.'

Naturally, I did not want my aunt to get mixed up with this terrible business too. So I admitted to having sent the names of three of my good friends, adding 'so that he might protect them as well'. I even thought I could remember that one of my friends had come to Perugia on a pass provided by the Italian officer in question.

'Very well,' Ambrož looked up, 'what about you father's papers that we found in your flat? Did you see any of them?'

I admitted to having seen the document about the shortage of knitting needles, most probably because I subconsciously thought this was the best choice. Since I had been told once by an UNRRA representative that a Mr Liepschitz was looking in Belgium for knitting needles for Yugoslavia, I thought this could not have been a very great secret. Ambrož then insisted that I had told everything about the knitting needles to the British Consul who, in turn, had promised to warn me if I should be in danger of arrest and provide me with a passport to escape.

'How could he have obtained a passport for me?' I asked.

'Oh, really,' Ambrož acted as if my question quite astonished him, 'every British Consulate is a forgery workshop.'

'But the British Consul did not promise me anything.' I tried to be firm.

'Now let us be sensible, Mr Sirc, let us strike a bargain. Give way a little more!' After a while, I 'confessed' that the British Consul had promised to warn me and help me to escape. By then, I had not the slightest illusion that they were in any way interested in the truth.

Niko Šilih came in and said, after listening for a while: 'I see, you have finally come to an arrangement. Very nice indeed.'

'What about the Consul's wife? Was she your mistress?' Ambrož tried again.

On 24 July, I was handed the indictment, a neatly bound booklet of 31 pages with a supplement of eight pages.

I looked first at what there was about my father: there were only four lines. In them it said he had co-operated with the indicted organisation by handing me data on industrial enterprises obtained in his employment at the Ministry of Industry. This did not sound very bad and I thought it would not be difficult to refute it.

But my own name was splashed over every single page. It was placed second on a list of 14 defendants. Was the frequency of my name due to my prominent position in the trial, or was it a consequence of my having talked too much? What a terrible question.

The same evening I was ordered to roll my belongings into a blanket and climb into a Black Maria with compartments just big enough for one person on each side. I could hardly squeeze myself in. I could not see anything, but I thought I could hear my father climb in. As the Black Maria drove to the Court Palace, I managed to catch a few odd glimpses of the town through the ventilation slits.

The van seemed to pass through an entrance. I was told to get out into a poorly lit courtyard. After I had been through the admission routine I was conducted to cell number 101 in the so-called 'nave'. I recognised that much from the stories told me by Katja, who was imprisoned there during the war for being half-Jewish and released on payment of a fine.

The light was left on, which made me sleep badly, and as I woke up repeatedly I noticed what I thought were bugs crawling along the wall. But my spirits revived when I had a good breakfast next morning (we were given a prison infirmary breakfast) and was handed a parcel from home.

In the afternoon I was taken to meet my officially appointed lawyer in the presence of a Secret Policeman. The lawyer, Mr Čobal, was dressed all in black but had a kindly face. I wanted a copy of the 'Act on the Security of the People and the State' to which the indictment referred, but he did not have one and, anyway, he said, it was all high treason. Hardly had we settled this when a telephone rang and Čobal told me he had to go. A black mood descended on me; I did not feel it was worth preparing for the trial. I wrote to my mother and Katja instead, warning them not to attend. That frame of mind was too sombre for the liking of the Secret Police, so Ambrož and another man came to pep me up with a talk marked by overflowing benevolence.

We were kept one to a cell, with every other cell empty, as I found out by peering through the cracks in the door. The normal occupants had been moved out and crowded into other cells, up to ten in a cell intended for one. Secret Policemen were doing the rounds, looking through the peep-holes at regular intervals. The courtyards on both sides of the prison were heavily guarded and, although the building was in the middle of Ljubljana, passers-by were not allowed to walk on the pavements outside the prison wall. Maybe all this fuss was necessary for the communist bosses to persuade themselves that we were very dangerous. On the whole, we were treated with mildness, permitted to lie down and fed infirmary food. On Thursday 27 July 1947, I heard Ljubljana Radio from the house opposite. It was announcing that the trial of the following spies and conspirators would open on the following Tuesday:

Črtomir Nagode, Civil Engineer, born 1903; Ljubo Sirc, lawyer, 1920; Leon Kavčnik, university professor, 1897; Boris Furlan, university professor, 1894; Zoran Hribar, professor, 1889; Angela Vode, schoolmistress, 1892; Metod Kumelj, schoolmaster, 1900; Pavla Hočevar, schoolmistress, 1889; Svatopluk Zupan, lawyer, 1919; Bogdan Stare, surveyor, 1907; Metod Pirc, naval captain, 1896; Vid Lajovic, employee, 1913; Franjo Sirc, Commercial School graduate, 1891; and Elizabeta Hribar, sculptor, 1913.

We were well groomed for the great occasion. Our suits and ties were pressed, our linen laundered and my spectacles turned up. Everybody had a wash. I was taken to the showers by an OZNA man, Slovenko. He was short and fat with bloodshot eyes, and wore a Browning, without its holster, stuck in his belt. The look of him was enough to account for my immediate dislike, though I did not know then that he had allegedly volunteered to assist in executions.

On the Tuesday morning, amid shouting and confusion, we were marched out of our cells, one by one, and stood in a line in the corridor. My guard led me behind Dr Nagode, who tried to shake hands with me but was prevented by the guards placed between. 'Who would have expected this?' He shook his head. 'What a humiliation!' All the defendants looked like shadows of their former selves, thin and worried. Captain Pirc's eyes were deeply sunken. My father refused to look at me. He was obviously convinced that his arrest was my fault. What else could he have thought?

We were marched through the wing connecting the prison building with the Courts and down to the ground floor to the big courtroom. We passed through corridors crowded with people staring at us. I noticed some familiar faces. No wonder, since the entire staff of the Tanjug agency seemed to be there. Various doors bore the inscriptions 'Press', 'Typists', 'Duplicating'. Everything was thoroughly organised.

As we were standing in the glassed-over passage leading to the defendants' entrance, a soldier between every two of us, the Secret Policeman Colonel Ribičič passed by and gave everybody another warning look, as if to say: 'Now behave yourselves!' When we were conducted into the big courtroom, I could see that the first row of the section for the public was taken up by all the secret policemen whose acquaintance I had already made during the interrogation. Behind them was a dense crowd. Tickets had been given to one relative of each defendant and to reliable party people from various enterprises. In addition, there were loudspeakers all over Ljubljana and the trial was being transmitted almost in full by the radio.

We were seated on two benches one behind the other and told that we were allowed neither to speak to each other nor to turn round towards the public. The soldiers accompanying us in the courtroom were placed on both flanks so as to intervene in case anybody tried to disobey. On our left were the lawyers, already in their places and busying themselves, while on the right were the seats for the public prosecutor and his aide. Behind them were the stenographers. One of these, who had worked with me at Tanjug and later resumed his post of district judge, sat at the judges' desk as a special court stenographer. He looked past me. When I referred to him as a witness to the fact that I could not have taken any secret documents from the Tanjug agency, because there were none, he said when we were next marched past him in the corridor: 'And this scoundrel dares to mention my name!'

I also knew all the other shorthand writers. I tried to catch the eye of at least one, but they all looked away; I learned later, though, that they were not unsympathetic towards me. The only man who waved a friendly hand at me was Dr Žirovnik, our relative, who was counsel for the defence for my uncle and my father. I was grateful for his kind gesture, because I felt entirely abandoned. I also overheard him explaining to my counsel who I was and who my grandfather was. I had last been in this courtroom six years earlier when Dr Žirovnik's daughter was sentenced to eight years' imprisonment by an Italian Military Tribunal because of her collaboration with the Liberation Front.

Then we had to rise for the entry of the Court. After some formalities, the Chairman of the Senate of three Judges invited the Public Prosecutor of the People's Republic of Slovenia to read his indictment. To create the right atmosphere, the judges and prosecutors addressed each other as 'Comrade', while the defence counsels were called 'Gentlemen', but in a tone one would use when saying 'You bandits'.

The Prosecutor read out that we were members of an anti-people's organisation which had intended to overthrow by force the existing constitutional order of the Federal People's Republic of Yugoslavia, to endanger its external security and to abolish the basic democratic, national and economic achievement of the liberation struggle.

He went on for hours, accusing us of the most horrible crimes fabricated out of our confessions on matters which had little to do with these crimes. There followed a special section for each defendant. In my case it was a repetition of the main indictment.

In his substantiation, the Public Prosecutor of the People's Republic of Slovenia, Viktor Avbelj, said that each defendant (as a member of our spy organisation) was responsible for all the enumerated crimes. Our feeble attempts to contact people in various parts of Slovenia, since you can hardly carry out political work without such contacts, became an intelligence network. The illegal names, cyphers and confidential messengers we used so as not to be detected by the occupation authorities were presented as monstrous. While the post-war 'network' was described as elaborate and dangerous, it was said that, during the war, *Pravda* had not been a political group with a basis among the people, but a 'small circle of people plotting and spying'.

Avbelj wound up: 'As national outcasts, as servants of foreign nations, they used the most hideous criminal means in their treacherous struggle against the people's rule and our State.' He asked that all defendants be heavily punished according to the seriousness of their guilt. Our working people could not allow the sabotage of their Five-Year plan and of their wish to live in peace and co-existence with other States. He sat down to tumultuous applause.

The presiding judge ordered everybody except Mrs Hočevar out — she was to be heard first. As I was led out, I caught a glimpse of my mother, very small and frail, sitting far away. I could not see Katja, but Ambrož, who visited me in my cell, told me that she had been there.

He was very friendly, trying to keep my spirits up, but I was at a disadvantage, wearing only my underpants because the August weather in 1947 was boiling. I made a movement to put on my jacket, but he stopped me. He wondered what I thought of the presiding judge and I muttered some approval. At that time, I did not know that the judge had been a member of the German-organised groups fighting the Partisans in Styria during the war and was therefore a pliable tool in communist hands. I knew, though, that judges were regularly told by the party bosses what sentences to pass.

By Thursday, 31 July, I again felt miserable and worried and went to my straw bed early. Suddenly, I woke and saw, standing at my bedside, the Secret Policeman Colonel Grkić from Belgrade. 'I promised to come before your Court interrogation,' he said. I got up and he led me downstairs. I did not know what time it was, but it must have been very late because everything was so quiet. We went to an office, and sat down on a large red sofa. Through the window, I could occasionally see the sleepy people of Ljubljana going home.

'You look fine,' he said, 'are you all right?' 'Yes,' I said sheepishly.

'Tomorrow, as a matter of fact today,' (he looked at his watch) 'the Court will be examining you,' he continued. 'That is why I have come.' I remained silent.

'You remember that we spoke about Dragoljub Jovanović?' he asked. 'Yes, I remember.'

'I have read what you wrote about your visits to him. That is very nice, but it is not enough. The Public Prosecutor is going to ask you four questions about Dragoljub Jovanović.' 'All right!' I said.

'He is going to ask you whether he was informed about the activity of your group in Ljubljana.' I replied that of course he was informed since we were trying to create a united opposition.

'Never mind the opposition! He is then going to ask you whether he was interested in the political situation in Slovenia.' 'Interested? There can be no doubt about it. How could he not be interested, if he was a politician?'

'The prosecutor is further going to ask you whether you told Dragoljub Jovanović that you knew the British Consul,' Grkić went on and raised his third finger. I protested: 'I never told him.'

Grkić jumped: 'Ljubo, you are playing with your life!' and then after a pause: 'The fourth question is going to be whether Dragoljub Jovanović knew about your connection with Carinthia.'

'Goodness gracious, how could he have known about that, when I last visited him in April 1946 and only learnt about the connection with Carinthia in September myself.'

'All right, get hanged!' 'But it's absurd!' He went on quickly, decisively: 'Well, he will ask you whether Dragoljub Jovanović was interested in the activity of Yugoslav émigrés.' After a moment of silence, he stressed: 'Now let me make it entirely clear: Don't think that the Court decides anything, everything is decided by the Party. If you do what I've asked you, you won't get sentenced to death. Otherwise you will.'

I could not understand exactly what it was he wanted and I said neither yes nor no. The four questions seemed harmless to me. He insisted further: 'Now, it is understandable that it is difficult for you to speak in public. Therefore we shall help you.' I was astonished at all this fuss.

'We shall use the outburst by one of the defendants yesterday as a pretext for excluding the other defendants from future hearings, that means also yours. Furthermore', he was again raising his fingers one after another, 'the radio will be switched off during your hearing. And the admission tickets will be controlled again. Only our most reliable people will be present.'

'Yes, but my relatives will be there too,' I said without any special purpose.

'All right, if you do not want to co-operate, get hanged, but don't forget that your behaviour during the trial is the most important thing.'

We were moving towards the door. As always, I started begging for my father: 'Please, leave my father alone. He is an old man and has done nothing.'

'This is politically impossible. He will be convicted, but, of course, he will be released from prison soon. As a matter of fact, he behaved very well in Court. He confessed to everything.'

'He could not have confessed to anything, because he has not done anything.'

'Do you want to see the shorthand minutes?' I gave up.

He shook hands and said: 'And behave well in Court. Don't be as foolish as Kavčnik, who defended himself like an ass. He will get his deserts!

'Take him back to the cell,' he ordered. I was so tired that I fell asleep immediately in spite of the interview.

After a few hours I was woken up again. The court proceedings were to start at 7 a.m. because of the heat. They groomed me once more and I was led down by a guard to the glass corridor leading to the courtroom.

Through the closed door I could hear the Public Prosecutor propose to the judges that from then on the defendants should be questioned in the absence of their co-defendants because their presence could have an unfavourable influence on the one under interrogation. Everything seemed to be developing according to my night visitor's programme. I noticed him in the front row when the door opened.

Almost immediately, the presiding judge asked: 'Do you acknowledge the accuracy of your statements during the investigations?' I had not the courage to say 'No!' I was trapped. Violating the rule that the Court itself should interrogate every defendant, the Court freely used the minutes, drafted by Secret Police, to substantiate the judgement.

'Do you plead guilty?' was the next question.

'I plead guilty, but I have not always been aware of my guilt.' This answer represented the policy I unconsciously adopted during the trial. I used to admit things in the first clause of a sentence and deny them in the second.

As I am writing these pages, I have in front of me the reports of our trial in the newspaper *Slovenski Poročevalec*, then published in Ljubljana, which my mother kept for me. Apparently they differed from what was actually said in Court. Newspapers were even at variance with each other, although the coverage was very extensive. The report about my interrogation took up one-and-a-half pages of six full columns, in a large newspaper. The headings were sensational. The issue with my interrogation had the caption 'The fourth day of the Ljubljana Supreme Court trial of Nagode's spy ring – the defendants Ljubo Sirc and Angela Vode stated that they sent messages to foreign spies in order to provoke a foreign intervention in Yugoslavia.'

The section on me had the sub-title 'Defendant Ljubo Sirc pleads guilty'. Some of the sub-headings ran: 'Defendant Sirc gave a member of a foreign mission in Yugoslavia political and confidential economic data'; 'Nagode's spy ring had contacts with Jovanović, Jančiković, Grol and Šutej'; 'The spy group discussed messages from abroad so as to co-ordinate their activity with émigrés in Carinthia'; 'Nagode's group received orders from the spy centre 101 in Austria'; 'A member of a foreign mission took people over the border in his car'.

The technique of the presiding judge and the Public Prosecutor was very simple. They asked questions which I could answer only briefly in one sentence. As soon as I tried to explain anything, I was stopped and told that I should keep to what I had been asked. 'You will have an opportunity to explain things later,' said the presiding judge, but this opportunity never seemed to arrive and finally I was sentenced without having ever explained anything.

For instance, the Prosecutor asked me what kind of messages we had sent abroad: political, economic or military. I said primarily political, sometimes also economic. (All this according to *Slovenski Poročevalec*.)

Prosecutor: 'And military messages?'

Sirc: 'I could not say that we did.'

Prosecutor: 'Do you remember that your organisation was given the task of finding out what the situation was on the Yugoslav-Greek border?' He simply jumped from report to task without mentioning whether either was carried out or not.

Sirc: 'Yes, I remember.'

Prosecutor: 'Was this a report of an economic character?'

Sirc: 'No, it was a report of a military character.'

The Prosecutor did not mention the fact that in 1946 there was a United Nations Fact-Finding Commission officially inquiring into the situation on the Greek Northern frontier.

Then I was asked whether I remembered an event in Upper Carinthia – or as *Slovenski Poročevalec* puts it: 'a report which informed foreign countries about an event in Upper Carinthia', and it goes on: 'Sirc remembered this and stated that they (his spy group) had made reports about the shooting down of the (American) aircraft.' No hint was given that I had only tried to find out where the wounded passenger of this plane had disappeared to, and that even in this I had been unsuccessful. And so forth.

After a while we came to the four questions prepared by Colonel Grkić. I cannot now recall exactly what I said, but I remember that I was very pleased with myself because in my own opinion I managed to answer these questions in such a way that I could not possibly have done any harm to Dragoljub Jovanović.

During the interval that followed, while I was standing with my guard in the glass corridor, Colonel Grkić came and shook my hand. 'Very good,' he said. 'Please, leave my father alone,' I said, 'and don't confiscate his flat.'

'That is an impossible request.'

After the interval, the Prosecutor was trying to make me admit that, together with Professor Furlan, I had informed the British Consul about the meetings of the students' organisation at the University and given him false reports about Yugoslav parliamentary elections.

Then followed the accusation that I had given the Italian Major D'Amato names of three students at the University in Perugia who were hiding from the occupying forces. This was ridiculous, since the three were my good friends, and they could not have been hiding because they were registered with the University secretariat. What is more, one of them regularly visited her brother in Siena prison, which she could hardly do in secret. But no matter, anything was good enough to slander the opposition. In the same vein, I was linked with the Hitler SS because in Perugia I had met Rudi, a German friend from my time in the Austrian sanatorium.

It also seemed to be very damaging for both of us that the Slovene politician, France Snoj, had given me a copy of a speech made by Dragoljub Jovanović in full National Assembly during the Five-Year Plan debate, and that he had brought to Ljubljana Jovanović's book, legally published in Belgrade. Much head shaking about the wickedness of imperialist spies was provoked by my statement that Professor Furlan knew the recently-appointed American Ambassador to Belgrade.

How thorough the court proceedings were is shown by the following statement by the presiding judge: 'You are accused of helping Nagode's group use dirty tricks in order to besmirch our highest dignitaries, and the group is also accused of taking decisions to get rid of some of them. You also prepared your own draft constitution, took part in meetings, collected various data and wrongly interpreted a talk between the representative of our government and the representative of a foreign state.'

To this odd assortment of accusations, I only replied: 'Concerning the talk, I remember only that a few sharp words were exchanged.' Together with what was in the Secret Police minutes this answer was deemed to substantiate the accusation that I had intentionally misinterpreted a conversation between the Vice-Chairman of the Slovene government and the British Consul. The Vice-Chairman later told a relation that he knew full well that I had not misinterpreted anything but did not dare come forward and say so.

Even the *Slovenski Poročevalec* reported that I denied having ever obtained any data on the textile industry from my father, but this did no good to my father or to me. The defence counsels said nothing. And so I was led away after three and a half hours. On my way out I caught a glimpse of my mother and Katja. Katja smiled at me and pursed her lips in a kiss.

The next afternoon it was time for me to meet Professor Furlan in Court. After I had said in his presence that our views of communist rule were similar, partly negative and critical, the atmosphere started warming up and I felt almost defiant. Then we were back to the questions given us by the representative of the American Red Cross, Jake Hoptner. What were they all about, how were they answered? We repeated that they were about land reform, elections and nationalisation.

While the questions and the answers to them, which were found in our flats, were being read out, Professor Furlan made a sign to the presiding judge indicating that he would like to sit down. The judge nodded his assent, and I sat down next to him. This, I was later told, was considered an affront to the Secret Police.

The answers turned out to be very much to the point and contained some valid accusations against the communist way of conducting the liberation struggle. Professor Furlan and I could not help laughing at the accuracy of some points, and I had the feeling that the selected public behind us was laughing also. Even the presiding judge laughed out loud once – the Public Prosecutor's voice trembled with anger. The report was referred to in the sentence and qualified as 'containing spying data about the political and economic situation in the State and as describing the situation as if terror and lawlessness reigned'.

When we were led back to our cells, one behind the other, Professor Furlan obviously had the same feeling as I did, that we had given a good account of ourselves. He asked the guard whether he could shake hands with me, but the guard jumped in between us.

Ambrož came and told me that the former Minister Snoj would join our group as a co-defendant and that it would take three days to prepare his indictment. On 7 August we all trooped down to the big courtroom and learnt that France Snoj had passed information to us, members of the indicted political organisation. He had gathered the information from his party friends from pre-war Yugoslavia; this was spying. It sounded particularly bad that he had translated Orwell's *Animal Farm*, an article by the Croat journalist Bogdan Radica from the *Reader's Digest*, and Ambassador Bullitt's 'slanderous article' on the Soviet Union from *Life* magazine. Because Snoj was a former Minister of Motor Transport, everything he did was 'an abuse of his official post'.

There followed a session *in camera*. In my view, the closeted proceedings were a pretence, staged to make people believe that the most sacred state secrets were involved. In reality I personally was only asked to confirm that I knew a number of British, American and French people who had come to Ljubljana since 1945. Further, the Prosecutor asked whether I knew that Captain Gibbs, the British press attaché in Ljubljana, was a member of the Intelligence Service. I did not, and most probably he did not either.

At this point the presiding judge wanted to conclude my interrogation, when suddenly my father's defending counsel asked to be allowed to speak and turned to me with the question whether I had in fact been stealing documents from my father's office. The Prosecutor was furious. I could not understand why the counsel raised the question, since I had made statements to the contrary in open court. Only later, reading the *Slovenski Poročevalec*, did it occur to me that the presiding judge and the Public Prosecutor were misleading my father, saying I had admitted passing on information received from him. Instead of allowing me to explain, the prosecutor shouted that it was no small thing to give information on the Slovene textile industry to a foreign mission and called me a 'traitor' and a 'spy' till I almost trembled at my own alleged guilt.

On 8 August, the Court turned to written evidence. Any documents Dr Nagode and I suggested were immediately turned down but a letter of Professor Kavčnik's to the communist Vice-Premier was read out so that Kavčnik could be taken to task for addressing a letter to a man in such a lofty position. During an interval, my defence counsel came to ask why I was not defending myself, since he could not do a thing to help. 'You are your own stage-director,' he put it. Nothing could have been more discouraging.

While our proposals for evidence were being refused one after another, the Public Prosecutor had a field day submitting various private letters and diaries in which the defendants had written nasty things about each other, although this could not be relevant to the matter in hand; unless it proved that the defendants were not as closely knit a group as the indictment claimed.

Then came a moment of light relief which would have been hilarious had we not been in such desperate trouble. It was announced that a secret intelligence report on Professor Furlan would be read by one of the assessors. I could not believe my ears when he seriously read out that Professor Furlan had been born on a stormy night in Trieste and went on in the same vein including a statement that he was known as a sought-after adviser to amorous people. By then everybody was laughing, fully aware that the report had been written at some jolly party in New York when people were slightly tipsy, but the assessor resolutely plodded on. The presiding judge was making desperate signs to him to stop, and finally snatched the paper from his hands. The day was rounded off with an announcement that the Court had received many letters and resolutions in which trade-unions and other mass organisations demanded extreme punishment.

On 9 August, the prosecutor alleged that the Catholic Bishop of Ljubljana had links with members of our group. Later on we heard that the Yugoslav Vice-Premier, Kardelj, had addressed a meeting in Ljubljana with the object of blackening our characters and setting the audience against the bishop. They had marched to the bishop's palace, but dispersed when his secretary told them that the bishop was absent.

The final speech by the Public Prosecutor first praised the war effort of the Yugoslav population and maintained that our group used all criminal means available to subvert the achievements of this sacrifice. He dismissed our claims that we were organising a legal political opposition and described it all as spying and treason. We wanted to sell Yugoslavia's independence to Britain and the United States, as shamelessly as we had collaborated with the enemy during the war. The language did not contain words strong enough to convey the baseness of the defendants. We spoke about the gratitude Yugoslavia owed to the West for its help, but in reality the West would never be able to reward us sufficiently for our sacrifices. Anybody who helped the Partisans abroad, as professor Furlan had, or joined them in the country like Captain Pirc, did it only to work the better against them.

The Prosecutor's speech culminated in the assertion that it could not be true that we had views and opinions on how to organise our State, differing from what was provided for in 'our' Constitution. He asked: 'Have the defendants any ideas of their own? Since when have spies had an ideology?' In the view of communist devotees only their own ideas are ideas at all, everything else is invalid. He ended up by saying that we were in the dock because our moral corruption was such that we refused to become free citizens of free Yugoslavia.

This speech was received with frantic applause.

Under the circumstances, the defence had a thankless task. My defending counsel only mumbled that I was highly strung because of having suffered from tuberculosis and had been misled by the co-defendant Dr Nagode. I felt very uncomfortable about this kind of defence, the more so as it seemed that Dr Nagode found it offensive.

The two lawyers defending Professor Furlan showed their mettle. The older counsel defended all of us, and I was deeply grateful to him. He was, I heard, a freemason and thought it his duty to defend his fellow-mason Furlan. The second counsel, who had served with the Partisans, even ventured to say: 'Dr Furlan's name will remain without doubt written in golden letters in the history of our national liberation struggle. No truthful man will be able to deny Furlan's great services.'

The Public Prosecutor jumped up, red with anger, and started criticising both the defendants and the counsels. When he finally stopped, nobody moved or said a word. The newspapers took up the attack on the lawyers and accused them of acting against our people's sense of justice.

During his reply to the defence, the Public Prosecutor also produced a letter written by Dr Nagode to his mother which his counsel had tried to smuggle to her. It was the letter of a man who was certain to die — as he was told he would — but the Prosecutor presented it as a sign of Dr Nagode's obduracy. Such a chilling atmosphere was created that when the defendants were called upon to make their final pleas, they all spoke briefly.

We had to wait three days for the sentence. I remained suspended between hope and the worst misgivings. I worried so much about my father that even the policemen thought they had to console me.

While I was still distraught, I was interrogated by two young men about Tatjana, the Slovene secretary to the British press attaché. They claimed that Tatjana admitted she had known everything about Dr Nagode's group and asked me to explain what the source of her knowledge was. I repeated that I had no idea.

On Tuesday morning we waited for a long time in the glass corridor to be led into the Court. Thoughts chased through my head: 'Maybe I shall be sentenced to ten years and my father will be free.' This seemed much too optimistic.

In the presence of the judges, I heard almost immediately that my father had been convicted along with the rest. My head began spinning and I sat in a daze, hardly hearing the dreary list of our alleged crimes, which was a word-by-word repetition of the indictment. My drifting was cut short by the sound of clapping when Dr Nagode was sentenced to death by shooting. One of the assessors gesticulated to the public with an expression of disgust at the applause.

Then followed my own death sentence – I could not have cared less. When the presiding judge read that Professor Kavčnik was sentenced to 16 years, somebody shouted: 'That is not enough.' Professor Furlan was sentenced to death; and so it went on. The prosecutors and the judges were in such a hurry that one of the accused was also sentenced for the alleged crimes of his brother who had escaped abroad because they could not tell them apart. The substantiation of the judgement ended in abuse: we did not deserve to be called intellectuals; ours were the ambitions of diseased minds.

When we were led out, I could not see either my mother or Katja. They had left for Belgrade to plead for my life. They succeeded in seeing some fellow-travellers in important posts who said they could not help because everything was in the hands of the Communists themselves.

On the afternoon of the judgement, my counsel came to see me in the presence of a Secret Policeman. He asked me whether I would allow him to apply for pardon. I almost laughed. Was he crazy? Did he expect me to want to die because of all this communist nonsense? I suddenly felt free to speak and started pouring out explanations of what had happened in reality. 'Why did you not explain this before?' he asked. I said I had but nobody would listen.

Back in my cell, I wrote a postcard to Katja and asked her to forget me. Then some kind of torpor overtook me. Slovenko, the police NCO, came to see me and asked: 'Did you expect a bullet?' The question was so brutal that it amused me.

After dark I was taken back to the OZNA central prison. No light was on, which was a relief, but I still kept turning over and over in my bed. The guards looked into the cell at regular intervals. I had a sudden desire to be comforted by somebody. Although ashamed of the comedy, I began moving about nervously on purpose. The NCO on duty opened the little window in the door and tried to soothe me: 'Don't be so restless and try to get some sleep.' I slept fitfully; the night seemed endless. At long last, it was daylight.

The OZNA Lieutenant, Milan, the first to talk to me at some length, was eager to know how I felt. We also talked about my father. 'You must realise he is not guilty at all,' I maintained. 'So he is in prison only because of you?' he asked. 'Yes, only because of me,' I repeated. 'Well, he will not have particularly pleasant memories of you when you are dead,' Milan kindly remarked and walked out.

During my worst moments, I leaned against the wall and imagined a firing squad in front of me, but instantly dismissed the idea. I never quite believed that they would kill me – it seemed too absurd.

The second night I slept well. However, somebody woke me up at an indeterminate hour. It was Major Ronko, who came to ask me whether I considered the judgement fair. This was, as it were, the beginning of 'communist re-education'. The first step in this direction is for the subject to admit that the sentence passed on him is the fairest sentence ever pronounced. 'Yes, very fair,' I said, 'except where my father is concerned.' 'Why so?' he protested. 'Do you think that our courts are not impartial?'

'By no means' I tried to correct myself, 'they are very fair, but maybe the Court did not know all the details about my father's case.' We left our conversation at that.

Then I was honoured by a personal visit from the OZNA Chief, Šilih. He grinned: 'Aha, Sirc, you tried to outwit us, but we forestalled you. The only purpose of Šubašić's agreement with us was to get us out of power. Churchill believes himself to be very astute, but we are more astute than he is. As for you, Sirc,' Šilih continued, 'you showed some sense as long as you were with the Partisans – I assure you you were being closely watched. However, later you ran berserk.'

After some four or five days, the guard took me to an interrogation room. To my utter amazement, my mother and Katja were sitting there on a sofa. A few steps away, Lieutenant Milan was leaning against a desk. 'You have fifteen minutes,' he stated brusquely. I sat opposite the sofa and held Katja's hand. 'I'm so sorry,' I began speaking in confusion, 'I've spoiled everything, I've brought harm to everybody.'

'You must not let this worry you,' my mother said, 'it's not your fault.' I sobbed as tears began rolling down my face, 'Oh yes, it is my fault, I feel terribly guilty.'

They looked puzzled, not understanding that I was speaking about the guilt I felt towards them and towards my father, whom I had ruined because I had tried to oppose a régime which had turned out to be far too strong.

'Stop, fifteen minutes,' Lieutenant Milan announced in triumph. We went to the door. At the threshold, my mother turned and kissed me. 'You kiss him, too', she said to Katja. We kissed and I could feel her young body through her summer frock. The guard led me away. My mother could not help crying. 'What are you bawling about?' was Lieutenant Milan's comment. 'One man more or less makes no difference.' I could not entirely blame Milan. He was young and had a leg amputated in the war.

Some nights later I was taken to a long room and ordered to sit on a chair in the middle, while a strong light was directed at me from a table at the far end. This arrangement reminded me of Wild West films in which the sheriff sits behind a lamp interrogating bandits. Somebody from behind the lamp said: 'Why don't you shave?' 'How can I?' I replied, 'I depend on the barber and he only comes once a week.' The voice went on: 'You must shave so as to look decent. You should have made a fuss and asked for the barber.'

My eyes became accustomed to the light and I saw that in front of the two uniformed men sitting behind the lamp there lay a pile of white paper, on which one of them was doodling bottles. I later discerned that these two men were Ribičič and Šilih. 'Why were you afraid of Furlan and why didn't you speak out when you came face to face with him?' one of them asked. I insisted I was not afraid of Furlan. 'You were. Why were you afraid of him?' I shrugged my shoulders. 'Tell us, Sirc, were you afraid of him because he's a senior IS agent?' Patiently, I replied: 'I don't know whether Furlan is an agent or not, but even if he were, what could he do to me now that I am in prison?' They were determined to resist my logic: 'Don't rush things! You won't always be in prison. And the English are capable of anything. For instance: a car can simply run you over in the street.' I thought they were crazy. 'By the way, Sirc, tell us something about the English spy network in Ljubljana.' This time I exploded. 'Oh for heaven's sake, I don't know anything about any networks!' The guard took me back to my cell.

Some days later, the guard opened the door and brought a typewriter; Major Ronko followed him carrying a bulky blue volume. 'You will translate this,' he said. 'But translate everything exactly! Make six copies and one on thin paper for me! If you translate everything exactly, you will get better food.'

'Thank you. Could I have a bath?' 'Of course, you will have a bath twice a week instead of once.' 'Thank you!'

I looked through the book. It was the Canadian Blue Book about Gouzenko, a Soviet cypher clerk who asked for asylum in Canada. I eagerly took up work and translated 17 pages on the first day, glad to discover that the Canadian Royal Commission knew exactly what Communism was and how the Communists operated. Noticing that the book had over 700 pages, I also thought to myself they were obviously not intending to shoot me for quite a while yet.

After another few days I was woken up at about five o'clock in the morning and led to a room bright with early morning sunshine. Ribičič sat at the desk, Ronko at his side. 'The Praesidium has commuted your sentence to twenty years' forced labour,' Ribičič began. I thanked him but asked: 'What about my father?' My tormentor replied: 'Oh, he is enjoying good health. He is in the court prison. He is not yet entitled to submit an application for pardon.' I persisted, insisting that my father had done nothing at all. Ribičič explained: 'Well, if he is not guilty of what we have accused him, he certainly must be guilty of something else. Some re-education will do him no harm.'

I preferred not to ask any more questions. Soon afterwards I received a postcard from my mother telling me that she was breathing more easily since my pardon. It must have been around 22 August 1947, the date on which Reuters published the news of Furlan's and my reprieve.

Again at dawn, I had an interview with Šilih who invited me to sit down at a table with him, offered me plums and treated me to a lecture on freedom. 'It is a great pity,' he said regretfully, 'that you, a capable man, are in prison now that we have full freedom in our country.' When he saw my astonished face, he explained: 'Of course, one has to know what freedom is. Freedom is the recognition of necessity.' This was taken from Engels' philosophy. In communist jargon, it is historical necessity that puts the Communists in power. 'So, Sirc,' Šilih concluded his short lesson, 'behave well and we shall release you sooner or later and give you a job.'

For the time being I worked in my cell, translating. Ronko visited me from time to time and was astonished that I was translating without a dictionary, but I had not been given one. 'Are you really translating everything correctly?' he asked suspiciously. 'Of course I am.' His distrust of everybody and everything came to the fore. 'You're not hiding anything from us?'

I assured him: 'If I have intentionally mistranslated anything, you can shoot me.' He seemed very pleased: 'Fine, that is how I like you to talk.' Then he had another attack of generosity: 'Have you been given better food?' When I answered 'No,' he replied: 'You will get it. And would you like to have more baths? You will have them.' I did not get better food and I did not have any baths at all. When I asked Lieutenant Milan about it, he said the bathroom was out of order.

I also enquired from Milan whether I could get some of my things from the flat: some underwear and a pair of trousers. I did not really need them, but I wanted to see what had happened to our flat, because this was still not quite clear to me. 'You must ask your mother for all that,' he replied. I was happy with his answer, because I thought that perhaps they had at least given her some things.

In reality, they had emptied the flat and distributed the contents among themselves. My mother saw a woman wearing her shoes in the street. The wife of a Secret Policeman, who came from a well-to-do family, was seen wearing a scarf of my mother's. My parents' bedspread was in some basement flat: my mother saw it through the window. She was also told that her linen with its embroidered monograms was hanging out in people's back yards. My father's suits were sent, neatly packed in sacks, to the prison tailor's workshop. Papers with the measurements of their new owners – no doubt Secret Policemen – were attached to them. The tailors knew whose suits they had been because our tailor always sewed the customer's name in the pockets.

I finished the translation of the Canadian Blue Book, but nothing happened. They seemed to have forgotten me. Not only did I not get any better food and had no baths, but I was also deprived of the visit to which I was entitled in September. When my mother and Katja duly came to see me, they were told that it was not known where I was.

I was, however, given the parcel permitted for the month. One night, the guard came for me and accompanied me to a room where the barber officer handed me my parcel. I found everything smashed to pieces and thrown back into the box; still I was happy. The night distribution of parcels was normal. The Secret Police simply loved to 'work' at night. Other prisoners reported that they had had baths at midnight and were taken to exercise in the courtyard by moonlight.

Short walks of some ten minutes every second or third day were the only change in the monotony of my solitary life, interrupting my pacing up and down the cell. Another interference from the outside world was a column of ants which found their way into my room and attacked the sweets in my parcel.

October was advancing quickly; so I began to worry about missing the October visit as well, when one morning the door opened and I was ordered to get ready. After the obligatory wait in the room under the stairs, I was given back what I had been wearing when arrested. In addition, I was handed my briefcase and an empty notebook, which they themselves had obviously brought from our flat after searching it. In bright autumn sunshine, I climbed into a Black Maria waiting outside the main entrance.

8

Wisdom from the solitary

The Black Maria took me back to the court jail where I once again went through the usual admission procedure and was then locked up in the so-called transition cell. I spent the afternoon climbing up to the window and watching the amazing variety of prisoners exercising in the courtyard.

I was about to lie down on my bunk for the night, when the guard suddenly came for me and led me through badly lit corridors up to the third floor. He unbolted a door and, as it opened, a heap of shoes fell out. The floor was covered with sleeping people – and they had nowhere to put their footwear. A prisoner (he was the 'senior' of the room) jumped over them to the door and said: 'Mr Guard, there is really no room for another man!' The guard made no reply and pushed me in.

A narrow 'path' down the middle of the room between human bodies was the access to the lavatory, a wooden compartment with a container, too small and overflowing at night. I prepared to lie down along the 'path' but a number of people protested that this would hinder the night traffic. Then one of them jumped up and exclaimed: 'Hello, Ljubo!' It turned out that several prisoners knew me, but I still had to lie in the middle.

The next day, a Saturday, was spent chatting. The ones who had come from labour camps said they had been made to work very hard there. There were forty-four people in the room, built for six to eight. I was the forty-fifth. The prison building was supposed to hold about a hundred people but it had never been used to full capacity in pre-war Yugoslavia or even while Slovenia belonged to Austria. Now, it contained about 1300 prisoners.

Most prisoners optimistically hoped the West would soon strike at the Communists and talked about upheavals everywhere in communist countries, even in the Ukraine. Yet the Communists had struck back: in Bulgaria, the opposition leaders Petkov and Lulchev had just been hanged; in Romania, the old politicians Maniu and Bratianu had been sentenced to long terms of imprisonment; in Hungary, the Premier and Small-holders' Party leader, Ferenc Nagy, had left for Switzerland and refused to return. His party, incidentally, had obtained 60% of the votes in the last free elections ever held in Hungary. Only Czechoslovakia remained a half-way democracy.

As for Yugoslavia, in Belgrade Dragoljub Jovanović had been sentenced to nine years' imprisonment, primarily for an article he had written in a London newspaper *The Times*. In Zagreb, Dr Jančiković and his co-defendants had been accused, with the usual communist imagination, of trying to poison everyone at a certain students' meeting. There seemed not the slightest doubt that a concerted action against any political opposition, probably orchestrated from Moscow, was under way in communist-dominated Europe.

In the afternoon, the guard gave me a parcel with some food, and a few clothes somebody must have donated, because I had never seen them before. Later on, the room 'senior' found a comfortable place for me along the wall. At about ten o'clock at night I heard a crowd passing by, singing Italian songs. 'What is that?' I asked. 'Don't you know', somebody said, 'that Ljubljana is full of Italian Communists being trained to take over in Italy?' On Sunday there was no walk; we were given a mess-tin of goulash at mid-day, but, to offset this, there was no supper. We had to kill time as best we could. A prisoner who had been in Russia during the war dragged me into a corner and began talking about his experiences. He said we should be careful, because any unfriendly remark about the Soviet Union was severely punished. He whispered about the almost incredible wretchedness of the Russian population, the peasantry in particular. There was such a lack of consumer goods that everybody had taken to stealing. Ripening crops had to be protected by armed guards overlooking the fields from high towers. He and his friends attended several popular dances when everything not tied down was stolen. A pocket-mirror seemed to be something near to a miracle for the Russians. In face of these shortages, enormous quantities of goods were being wasted. Railway engines were heated with wood cut along the way. If nothing else was to hand, the sleepers stacked ready for track repairs were burned. Leaving this enticing picture of the country which was supposed to serve as a model for Yugoslavia, we joined in the general pastime: playing children's games.

On Monday afternoon, the guard opened the door, called out my name and added: 'With all belongings!' I shook some hands before the guard took me one floor down into a single cell which I had all to myself. My three-day stay with other prisoners may have been an administrative error, since from now I was to be alone for more than two years; but I may have been put into a crowded room for a few days so that I should feel the solitude all the more keenly. My new cell was just under the room I had come from and I could hear them all up there laughing.

Only now did I have the time to take in what my room-mates had told me: that Professor Furlan had been reprieved along with me, while Dr Nagode's death sentence had been confirmed. They thought that in fact he was probably not shot, but hidden away somewhere. Such rumours about people sentenced to death sprang up among prisoners from time to time, but they were not true.

The days dragged on interminably. I did not know what to do with myself, nor had I the energy to try doing anything. It was autumn and the sun was very low, its weak rays moving along the walls. My autumnal thoughts turned to the future. Even if I came out within a foreseeable time, I would remain an untouchable under the communist régime. What could I do? I would have to go abroad. And what would I do there? Who wants lawyers or economists? It was a pity I was not a dentist. I decided that next time I saw Katja I would tell her to study something very practical.

One morning, when the guard was distributing coffee and bread, he said: *'Na bob!'* (Have a doughnut!), and instead of the customary larger loaf gave me something more the size of a bun. It occurred to me that the communist economy must be in sharp decline if we were to be fed on 150 grams (just over five ounces) of maize bread a day. And indeed, this minute amount was to be our ration for a full seven years, until 1954, except that those working got double portions.

A man came to question me about my property as it was to be confiscated. Trying to be kind, he told me to write home for paper and books. He was Stane Kersnik, an assistant to the prison governor. Before the war he had been the owner of a bicycle workshop. After having fought with the Partisans, he began re-educating political prisoners. At the beginning he was very friendly towards me, then he began to hate me bitterly, I do not know why. That day, he told me I might go to bed at four in the afternoon if I wanted to, so from then on I spent all my evenings in bed. I was never taken out for exercise: they had obviously forgotten me.

On the last Sunday in October 1947, my mother and Katja came to visit me. They were not allowed either to kiss me or to shake my hand. Katja held a red rose in her hand. Later she wrote: 'Do not think that I was trying to play the lady with that rose. The rose was for you, but I forgot to give it to you in my excitement.' Anyway, the guard would have prevented her. At a nearby table my co-defendant Vid had his parents visiting him and said, in a specially loud voice so that we could hear: 'Father Sirc is very well. He is in very good spirits.'

I asked about Tatjana and was told she was in prison. On the way back to my cell I kept wondering whether it was my fault. I must have been clumsy during my interrogation, although I could not remember when. Nevertheless, the interrogator had apparently told Tatjana that she must know all about Nagode's group — that I had said so. She was not even angry with me, because she thought I had managed to save my life this way. In spite of all the good reasons I had for believing that Tatjana's arrest was not my fault, I had a guilty conscience and began repeating to myself: 'Coward! Ljubo, you are a coward!' It was a great relief when Katja sent me a postcard a few days later, saying Tatjana was home and sent her best wishes. They had released her when she promised to 'co-operate' with OZNA. Of course, she did nothing of the sort but went straight to Zagreb to Captain Gibbs, her fiancé. They went to the registry office to marry, and Tatjana was invited into the registrar's office, while Captain Gibbs was made to wait outside. Once inside, she was arrested and taken off to prison again through another door.

In November, my mother came alone. Katja was not allowed to visit me but had to wait outside. I was not to talk to her again until I was released from prison seven years later, though I saw her a few times standing in the corridor. Once she was even daring enough to come into the room where I was talking to my mother and said something — to the horror of the watching guard.

Between the two visits, I had again been taken to the Secret Police prison and ordered to translate a report by the Judge-Advocate Department of the US Army Headquarters in Europe. It was about the Nuremberg side-trial of Dr Schilling, a Nazi doctor who experimented on prisoners.

As soon as I returned to the Court Prison which had just been renamed the Home for Penal Re-education, an OZNA man brought me some more material for translation. I figured out that he was the man who had asked me for my identity papers once when I was leaving the British Consulate. Much later I found out that he was Dr Damjan, a graduate in law, who had acted as military prosecutor against General Rupnik, the German-appointed chief of Carniola during the war. We naturally started discussing my trial, about which I was feeling more aggressive the more time I had to think about it. I complained about my father's treatment. Dr Damjan listened for a while, then he said: 'Even if what you say is true, what can we do? My father was killed by the Germans.' Because the Germans persecuted the fathers of OZNA people, OZNA had to persecute my father.

On my second return to the court jail, I was taken to cell No. 104, an unpleasant one. Some of the window panes were missing as a result of an ammunition explosion soon after the war, and had been patched up with pasteboard. I tried to remove the lower half of the window to let in some light, but it was too cold. I was sitting in a corner half asleep, when the door opened and Kersnik, the assistant governor, came in and asked why I was not reading. Within half an hour, the guard took me to cell No. 136 on the second floor, a real paradise. The windows were complete and a chimney in the wall kept me warm.

Furthermore, I had just had some books from my mother and Katja, including *History of Europe in the 19th Century* by Benedetto Croce and *Theoretische Sozialoekonomie* by the Swedish economist, Gustav Cassel. I jumped on them and the time flew by. I was almost sorry every time I had to abandon my reading for ten-minute walks, but I was rarely disturbed in other ways. Once or twice the prison governor, a staunch proletarian, came in, but did not seem very interested in me.

A major disturbance was created on Christmas Day. After taking power the Communists had abolished all holidays except their own. Early in the morning, the guards searched our rooms to see whether there was anything we could celebrate Christmas with: a candle, a pine bough, or a crib – which is particularly popular in our country. From me they took a plastic spoon and fork that had come in a parcel. However, a few hours later one of them brought them back and seemed to be ashamed of himself.

When all was calm again, I returned to my thoughts. Even at night, my brain went on working. One evening I lay in bed unable to sleep, and found myself trying to figure out why my sentence was unjust, although it may have been in accordance with Yugoslav communist law; and why I believed the Nuremberg judgement was just, even though there had previously been no established international law on war crimes. I recalled discussing the Nuremberg sentences with Professor Furlan, who had taught philosophy of law and belonged to the so-called positivist school. In his view, killing the defeated was common practice and therefore all right. To me, this reasoning was unacceptable (and it must eventually have become so to Professor Furlan, who turned into a practising Christian after his release from prison). Surely one cannot argue that some people have a right to punish others simply because they are stronger. Suddenly it dawned on me, almost as a revelation, that there must be some higher law, a law based on the nature of things, if one could speak of a law at all. From then on, I spent hours trying to prove to myself that it was so, using arguments that could convince others and also serve as a solid base for my dissertation when I got some paper. When I got paper, I wrote it all down. The prison officials left me alone because they knew that I was writing about the Nuremberg trials of which they were in favour, but they did not realise that I was supporting the Nuremberg judgement with arguments directed against themselves. The final conclusion I reached, while still in prison, was that the Nuremberg trials were merely the first step and that Stalin and his like ought to be tried as well.

The communist economy was another puzzle. Quite soon after the war, everybody realised that something was wrong with it. At the end of the war it was still possible to buy things in the shops, but then stocks ran out in spite of UNRRA supplies. Even in prison one could see that the economic situation was deteriorating. In the autumn of 1947, prisoners could buy fruit or gherkins, but soon there was nothing left except cigarettes. I learnt from my visitors that it was impossible to find a tooth-brush or a comb in the town. Before my arrest I had asked various economists for an explanation, but nobody could give a consistent, general answer.

In cell No. 136 I read Cassel, and soon realised that the Communists were sinning against elementary economic principles, not against capitalist rules but against those of common sense. I started suspecting this much earlier, having read, in Switzerland, the textbook by the German anti-Nazi refugee, Wilhelm Roepke. Having destroyed the price mechanism, they could not measure the cheapest way of doing things; instead of combining much manpower, which is abundant in Yugoslavia, with little capital and land, which are both scarce, they did exactly the opposite; instead of building up the industries which were essential to meet the demand for the most elementary consumer goods, they invested in heavy industry which they would not be able to cope with technically and which might never bear fruit; at the same time, they neglected existing industries; they abolished the market mechanism and fixed prices, and without prices to match demand and supply there was soon nothing to be found in the shops.

Most people hated reading the communist papers, while I lovingly scrutinised them every morning. Every copy was yet more proof of what terrible economic mistakes the Communists were making. I read every word, and to me they confirmed that a communist economy would never work. Marx and Engels came next, and every page of their lengthy works contained a message: that my tormentors were wrong. I started writing down my thoughts in a state of constant spiritual excitement. My mother was taken aback when I enthusiastically told her at one visit: 'This is the real university.'

Poor creature, how could she understand such exhilaration? Her life was much worse than mine. She had to find food for parcels for my father and me, and also for my uncle, since my aunt had had to take a job. Finding food was difficult, though luckily many relatives and other people, especially peasants, were very helpful. My mother learned how to ride a bike and went round the villages, until she fell off and came to see me with her broken arm in plaster.

I often wondered where she found the money, but did not dare ask for fear that the supervising guard would hear and she would have difficulties afterwards. In fact the director of a bank had been decent enough to have a pre-war account in her name paid out to her, and several people, whose names I cherish, offered to help her with money. Meanwhile the food in the jail had become so bad that I really do not know how we would have managed without parcels.

Of course, I also had spells of utter despair, but my enthusiasm for my theories was such that it helped me to recover. Just when I was wondering whether there was any sense in the course of action which had landed my father and me in jail, I came upon a book on psychology by Wilhelm Jerusalem. He wrote of the importance of expressing one's thoughts and of the way people were prepared to make great sacrifices in order to satisfy their need for expression.

OZNA men would come to see me and question me on all sorts of subjects. One of them enquired what I thought of the communist economy in Yugoslavia. 'Not much,' I replied. 'Do you think that we shall not fulfil our Five-Year Plan?' he continued. 'I don't doubt that you will,' I said, 'but that is the trouble – because the plan is wrong and will bring a lowering of standards.' Clearly he was astonished by this answer and began muttering something about how 'the people' decide everything in our country. 'You know as well as I do,' I hammered on, 'that the people have no say at all. They can look into each other's cooking pots and denounce those who eat too many beans to OZNA, but they can scarcely do anything else.' He said nothing. I was in an aggressive mood and proud of my courage. At that point I did not realise that for every such answer I was given a black mark somewhere in a file.

My feeling was that most of the prison staff were impressed by the books and newspapers I had in my cell. I do not know what they thought I was doing, but nobody ever touched either my books or my manuscripts and they treated me with some sort of respect. I noticed, for instance, that an NCO of whom most prisoners were terrified left out my cell when he was searching all the rest, throwing prisoners' belongings all over their beds and the floor. Soon I saw why. One day he asked me to do his mathematics homework. Many guards were attending quick secondary school courses but were not, it would seem, doing very well!

Eventually, it became clear why I was given all the translation work for OZNA. On 19 April 1948, I could not believe my eyes: the newspapers carried an announcement of the forthcoming trial of a group of well-known Communists on charges that they were agents of the Gestapo. Among them was a surveyor, Stane Oswald, a close collaborator of the economic dictator Kidrič who went to Belgrade as his *Chef de Cabinet*; further, a schoolmaster, Mirko Košir, who had taught me physics at school and was dismissed for being an active Communist, was among them too. It was rumoured that he had been Secretary-General of the Communist Party of Slovenia before Tito took over in the underground.

While I was puzzling over this announcement, the guard came for me and led me to see Ambrož, whom I had not met since my trial. After enquiries about my health, he asked what I thought about the morning's news.

'I am stupefied and do not believe Oswald and Košir have done anything.'

'Oh, Sirc, Sirc, you haven't changed. You will see what the defendant Stepišnik will declare in court.' 'I do not believe a word of such statements.'

'Why not?' 'You and I know best how you extort them.'

'Sirc, don't exaggerate ...' He seemed uncertain, and astonished at what he must have considered my incurable impertinence. To change the subject, I asked him whether this Stepišnik was the Yugoslav champion hammer thrower and regretted that a hero of my youth was in deep trouble. Ambrož asked whether I was receiving books and when I told him I was not given the last batch, he said he would see that I got them.

The new prison governor was a former timber worker and not excessively intelligent. His hobby was lecturing prisoners on the evolution of man from monkey. His explanation of Socialism was: 'Socialism is when everybody has his own car. I for instance have already got one.' But his own socialist car proved fatal for him when a military lorry hit him and killed him on the spot. This governor Sevšek would not give me the books Katja had brought and was especially suspicious of the German original of Hegel's *Logik*.

He had me brought down to his office and asked why I needed Hegel in German. I explained: 'Hegel was one of Marx's favourite authors and I should like to see what he says.' He concluded: 'You see, Sirc, I followed your trial closely and I know that you used books as ciphers. I shall have to think about it.' I certainly would not have got the books if Ambrož had not told him to give them to me.

The trial of Oswald, Diehl (another communist official) and their co-defendants was worse than anything one could have imagined. All the defendants had been in Dachau concentration camp during the war. The Public Prosecutor deduced from this that they were obviously Gestapo agents sent to Dachau for re-education. Some of them certainly seemed to have had some privileges in the camp, but this could easily be explained by the instructions of the communist parties that their members should do anything to preserve themselves and survive for the greater glory of Communism. Some passages of the indictment were directly copied from the US Judge-Advocate Department's report I had translated a few months before. The result of this trial was that ten staunch Communists, among them two Austrians, Martin Presterl and Paul Gaser, were sentenced to death and hanged. My former teacher, Košir, was sentenced to ten years and died in prison.

A general hunt for people who had been in Dachau followed and many unfortunate enough to have been sent there by the Gestapo were put in prison. Next to be hunted as suspects were Communists who had fought as volunteers in the Spanish civil war.

I never had the slightest doubt that the trial of Oswald and Košir was staged, but for a long time I was unable to understand what was behind it. The first explanation that sprang to mind was that the two Austrian Communists had come to see their former Dachau mates in Slovenia and that the Secret Police thought they were recruiting for the Soviet secret service. But as the years passed, people came up with the contrary interpretation: that the Yugoslav Communists were trying to placate Stalin, as he was suspicious of anybody the Nazis either captured in war or imprisoned for political reasons. Everybody sentenced in those so-called Dachau trials was rehabilitated in the 1970s but the mystery remained as to why all these people had been persecuted in the first place.

The next cell I was moved to, in May 1948, was so dirty that I had the impression fleas were jumping around my feet. I wanted to scrub the floor, but by then floor brushes had vanished in Yugoslavia. For more than a year we could not wash the floors properly. On inspecting the walls, I discovered that two people sentenced to death had been there before me and had written their addresses on the walls asking other prisoners to let their relatives know. I memorised the addresses but later heard that the two men had been reprieved.

One afternoon, somebody began knocking on the wall. Eventually, I started reciting the letters of the alphabet along with every series of knocks. I heard: 'W-H-O A-R-E Y-O-U'? of course in Slovene. 'S-I-R-C', I knocked. Whoever was on the other side seemed to know my name, because he excitedly bumped against the wall several times.

This time-consuming conversation could take place because we were in the so-called death wing of the prison. The entrance was under special lock and key so we could hear the guard well in advance if he came in.

My knocking partner was a 'C-O-M-M-U-N-I-S-T A-N-D S-P-A-N-I-S-H V-O-L-U-N-T-E-E-R'. I asked him why he was in prison. Back came the answer: 'G-E-S-T-A-P-O S-P-Y'.

After much knocking to and fro, I learned that everything he had done had been twisted to mean exactly its opposite. Because he had been an illegal Communist before the war, he was accused of being 'an agent of the Yugoslav Royal Police'. By OZNA logic, there could be no doubt that he really was a Gestapo spy, because he had been sent to Dachau. In fact, he was a brother-in-law of one of Oswald's co-defendants.

A few weeks later I was moved to cell No. 102 on the first floor in the so-called 'nave'. The continual changing of cells was a part of the communist re-education policy. No one was permitted to settle down. Exceptionally, I was to remain in No. 102 for more than a year.

It was in this cell that one morning toward the end of June 1948, I glanced at the Slovene daily the guard had handed me round the door, and rubbed my eyes. What was this? The All-Union Communist Party (of Bolsheviks) was criticising the Communist Party of Yugoslavia. I rubbed my eyes again. Good gracious, for whatever reason? The Yugoslav Communists had been the most faithful of allies to the Soviet Union. They had extolled Stalin and everything around him to the skies. I read the letter from the Soviet leaders to the Yugoslav leaders and the Resolution of the Cominform. Some of the criticisms of the Yugoslav Party were quite unfounded, while some could just as well have applied to the Soviet Communists themselves. (Thus they accused the Yugoslav Secret Police of 'Turkish' methods, as if the NKVD or MVD were angels personified.)

The door opened again. The guard had come back to ask me what I thought. We both wondered what could be happening, then the guard said: 'Everybody will have to give in a little, then we shall be friends again.' I did not think this was possible, but he turned out to be quite right, as events after Stalin's death were to show. He became extremely friendly towards me. When my cell was whitewashed and my things had to be moved out and back in again I did not have to lift a finger, because the guard brought the so-called 'house-workers' (prisoners detailed to do the cleaning) and they did everything for me. I could see what the guard was thinking: Sirc is a political prisoner and if Tito should suddenly go to hell, he may be able to help me out of trouble one day.

All things considered, I felt in wonderful spirits. During the whitewashing I was taken down to the cellar and shut in some kind of storehouse. There I sat on a heap of tyres and looked through the window at other prisoners walking in the courtyard. Half of Ljubljana seemed to be in prison. Among them, I saw a sixteen-year-old boy from the neighbourhood of our former flat. This influx of people put me in a good mood — one might well ask why. It was the effect of prison psychology. The prisoners' slogan was: The worse things get, the closer the end must be.

That summer I discovered a clue to the motives behind the Soviet-Yugoslav dispute in an almanac devoted to the reformer of the Serbo-Croat language, Vuk Stefanović Karadžić. Vuk had fled to Zemun (then in Austria) to escape persecution by the Serbian Prince Milos, and wrote him a letter from there in 1832. In it Vuk was giving the view of one Serbian official on why the prince was persecuting another one, Mileta. It was 'simply in order to blacken Mileta's name and lessen his merits. Our prince does not want anyone in Serbia but himself to have merit or honour or good name.' That was it: Stalin was an oriental despot who could not stand Tito because Tito lifted his head a tiny bit above the crowd, even though he was far from challenging Stalin. Tito's very eagerness and extreme devotion to him angered Stalin, so that he wanted to destroy him and would of course not shrink from using any means at his disposal.

My puzzling over Stalin and Tito was disturbed by a prisoner in the neighbouring cell who behaved most oddly. I could hardly figure out what he was trying to tell me with his knocking, he was so nervous and upset. Finally he killed himself by cutting the veins between his legs with a razor. He was one of the military medics whom the Commissar in a hospital had accused, out of the blue, of murdering the soldiers who happened to die.

All of a sudden my supply of books dried up. When my mother brought *A Treatise on Money* by Keynes she was told angrily by Kersnik that such books were not suitable for me and that I should read Marx. Kersnik would have been even more angry, had he known that I was actually reading Marx and laughing at his nonsense. *Anti-Dühring* by Engels was even worse.

Most books in the prison library were not even up to the standard of Marx and Engels but dreary communist tracts. I was lucky in that the librarian always tried to find the most interesting books for me. Once he gave me Galsworthy's *Forsyte Saga* in a Slovene translation, which I gobbled up within two days. The librarian was a Communist, but why he was in prison I cannot remember. He was released about a year later, and went on to organise an armed band in favour of Stalin and even enrolled some guards from our prison. They were all captured and in 1950 I met some of them in the prison at Maribor.

I kept on fighting for my books; but I received no answer to my requests although the new prison by-laws permitted books from outside. When I quoted the appropriate article, the answer came back: 'You are a prisoner and thus you have no rights and must not refer to any articles.' I then wrote another request quoting even more articles, whereupon the guard took away the copy of the prison regulations he had given me a few weeks earlier — so that I should know my rights.

I carried on with my writing: about the Nuremberg trials; about the failure of the communist economy in Yugoslavia; and the beginning of these memoirs. I was afraid somebody might come and look at my manuscripts, but nobody did. To prevent the guards, at least, from understanding what I was writing, I wrote in English and noted many things in shorthand. I was in fact allowed to write freely for about one year out of the seven and a half. For this there were good precedents: the Yugoslav communist leader Pijade had translated Marx's *Das Kapital* and painted pictures while imprisoned, though the Communists never tired of describing the conditions in pre-war prisons as most awful. The chief ideologist Kardelj had written his *History of the Development of the Slovene National Question*, a Marxian analysis, while he was in prison. When books and paper stopped coming in, I quickly ran out of paper. I did what I could, trying to erase what I had already written and re-writing smaller to allow extra room for new material.

When I was not writing, I thought or daydreamed. I often imagined myself walking through shady woods. Every morning I did keep-fit exercises. I recited all the poems I could remember, such as Pushkin's 'Ya Vas Lyubyl' (I have loved you ...), I learnt passages from Dante's *Divine Comedy* which I happened to have with me. The medieval verses consoled me when I felt dejected and laden with guilt over my father's fate. Did I have to get involved in political events at the peril of my family?

> .... né la pietà
> del vecchio padre, né 'l debito amore
> lo qual dovea Penelope far lieta,
> vincer poter dentro a me l'ardore
> ch'i' ebbi a divenir del mondo esperto,
> e de li vizi umani e del valore;
> ma misi me per l'alto mare aperto
> sol con un legno...

Ulysses told Dante, when they met in hell, that neither the filial respect for his father, nor his love for Penelope could keep him from wanting to learn about the world and about human vice and human courage. So he set out on his last voyage in a wooden ship.

When the boat reached the Pillars of Hercules, which the ancients believed was the end of the world, Ulysses was tempted to venture past the limits of the known and appealed to the ship's company:

Considerate la vostra semenza:
fatti non foste a viver come bruti,
ma per seguir
virtute e conoscenza.

'Do not forget your human origin,' he said, 'you have not been created to vegetate but to pursue virtue and knowledge.' I felt the same way, I was also caught up in a storm. Ulysses' ship turned round and round three times; the fourth time the stern rose out of the water and the sea closed over the ship.

... infin che 'l mar fu sopra noi richiuso.

For how long was I to remain submerged? Mostly such thoughts were interrupted by the sound of keys unlocking doors, a sound which still rings in my ears and still makes my heart beat faster.

One day I saw a vision. Taking out my refuse container, I saw a door on the other side of the 'nave' open and out came a beautiful girl with black hair in a white blouse and blue shorts. I believe her name was Mafalda and she was one of the numerous Italians – men and women – whom the Communists had caught either in Slovenia or in Trieste. Who knows why Mafalda was in prison for so long? By then she must have been inside for more than three years.

These Italians were exchanged soon afterwards for Yugoslav prisoners in Italy, mainly criminals. We heard them leaving one night, *'Addio, addio!'* On their way home they paraded through the border town of Gorica we were told, each displaying our meagre daily bread ration on a stick.

In the autumn of 1948, the Vth Congress of the Communist Party of Yugoslavia introduced the wildest social changes yet, so as to prove that the Yugoslav Party were as good Communists as the rest, if not better. Kidrič acknowledged that the communist land reform had not changed anything and that Yugoslavia was still a country of smallholders. (I had been condemned about a year earlier for claiming something very similar.) This was read as the signal for the forced collectivisation which was to bring agriculture and the food supply to near-collapse. Kidrič stated that the highly developed pre-war agricultural co-operatives were capitalist and had to be destroyed. State co-operatives on the Soviet model were introduced instead.

Politically, the Party felt it had to rebut the Stalinists' accusations that it had let itself be submerged in the Liberation Front and had ceased to be a Marxist-Leninist party. So it admitted that the Liberation Front had never been other than a 'transmission belt' for the true 'hegemon' of the National Liberation Struggle – itself. The agreement between Tito and Šubašić on a democratic régime was said to have been tactics, while the dictatorship of the Party had always been the aim.

I became involved in a lively 'conversation' with a new prisoner next door later that year. He told me he was a former *Domobranci* officer who had come back from Austria to size up the situation, but was caught. Strangely enough, he wanted to know whether I had ever worked for the *Abwehr* which, as he told me, was the German counter-intelligence service. We both became fed up with the tiresome knocking and he explained that if I pressed my forehead against the same brick as he did, we could hear each other clearly. This made our conversation so much easier that I talked to him about my political and economic views, what OZNA did to me during the investigation and so on. He asked me whether I hated OZNA very much. I said that I did not and that I rather pitied them because they were such wretched people. I would rather be their advocate than their judge, I insisted.

He tried to get into contact with people on all sides. He knocked on the wall of cell No. 104, but said the men there were not interesting. Eventually he succeeded in establishing contact with the cell immediately above his. There were several women in that cell. One of them was particularly courageous and began sending down letters in a match box hanging on a thread. She was Simona, the sister-in-law of Vito Zupan, a partisan author whom I was to meet later in my prison career.

I, in turn, established contact with a woman prisoner in No. 101, Kristina. To my amazement she told me that she was a relative of Mrs Dobbeler, a Slovene married in Belgium. Mrs Dobbeler was the woman who came to Yugoslavia in 1946 to thank Tito for what he had done for us Slovenes, but became disillusioned and got in touch with our co-defendant Mrs Hočevar. Apparently she came on a visit again just before our trial – she could not have had a guilty conscience – and had been arrested for spying and sentenced to death. My neighbour Kristina was given ten years for knowing her. One day she was taken out of her cell and came back, frightened; she begged me not to knock any more because the prison authorities knew we were in contact. After some prompting she told me she had been interrogated by a very handsome man, Franjo Turk-Gorazd, the same man as had questioned Katja and ended up as secretary to the Slovene government.

'It is such a pity he is an OZNA scoundrel, he is so handsome,' poor Kristina sighed. Soon afterwards she disappeared from No. 101.

This interlude did not stop my exchanges with the man in No. 103 until a few others joined him, apparently because they were all to leave for another prison. One of them told me through the bricks that my former interlocutor – this happened while he was out of No. 103 for some reason – was not a captured *Domobranci* officer at all, but an OZNA man who had murdered his wife and was now working his way back into the service.

Early in 1949, an OZNA captain came to interrogate me about two professors at the Law Faculty and about the former *Chef de Cabinet* of the Minister of the Interior. The first two were known Communists so I guessed they were in prison on suspicion of Stalinism. I knew little else about them, as we had not taken to each other. I told him that I had last seen the *Chef de Cabinet* when I went to tell him about my visits to the British Consulate, and that on that occasion he had said there could not be anything illegal about them. 'Who is he to state such a thing?' the OZNA captain said, 'we shall have to teach him a lesson.'

He then began asking my opinion of the economy. I told him frankly that I thought one could not expect much of an economy guided according to Marxism, which was a ridiculous doctrine. 'What?' he jumped. 'Do you want us to direct our economy according to your Churchill?' I retorted that Churchill at least did not pretend to be always right, upon which the captain quoted the splendid things the Russians had achieved by following Marxism.

'We'd better drop the discussion about the Russians,' I warned him. 'You can read in our own newspapers what a mess they have made for the last twenty years or so.'

This challenge prompted my OZNA man to exclaim: 'I shall never believe anything bad about the Russians.'

Nonetheless, the newspapers were by then full of horror stories about the Soviet system our rulers had been faithfully copying since coming to power. Yet all the 'mistakes' of the Soviet régime were presented as merely accidental. In 1949 they still refrained from criticising the Soviet economic system designed by the 'great Stalin', and his picture was still hanging in the large hall of Maribor prison when I arrived there in May 1950. Our Communists kept claiming that they were the most faithful pupils of Marx, Engels, Lenin and Stalin. The most tragi-comic episode of the attempts to prove their loyalty was the 'St Bartholomew's night of pigs' sometime in the autumn of 1948. The economic dictator Kidrič decided that he would break the capitalist spirit of the peasants and that pig-breeding would be taken over by the Ministry of Trade. Centres for the confiscation of pigs were established all over the country – in secret of course. Then, one night, Communist Party members and militia men invaded all the farms and took away most of the pigs; they put them in open pens, exposed to rain and bad weather, and fed them badly. To no sensible person's surprise, they began dying by the thousand, with the result that Yugoslavia, always an exporter of pigs, had to import pigs and fat. Subsequently we had the pleasure of welcoming several directors of government pig farms to our prison!

The exclamation of the OZNA captain, 'I shall never believe anything bad about the Russians', was typical of the attitude of most Communists, leaders included. Having swallowed Soviet propaganda they felt like angels expelled from the Red Paradise. Tito could hardly tell his followers that the dispute stemmed from Stalin's belief that he, Tito, was too big for his boots. Nor could he put it to them that the rift would endure because he was not ready to sacrifice his head for the unity of Communism. So the propaganda machine had to circulate stories about how Stalin was badly informed, and how the main culprit was Yudkin, the editor of the Cominform magazine *For Peace and People's Democracy*. The Yugoslav leaders only thought of inventing a different ideology, called Titoism by the West, in 1950. Had Stalin not underestimated Tito's popularity and had he struck immediately, he could easily have overthrown the Titoist régime before Titoism was born.

The OZNA captain, not knowing any better reply to my mention of 'Russian mistakes', tried to humiliate me: 'It is stupid to argue with you. All you know is how to sit in your car and drive around.' When I said my family did not possess a car, he accused me of never having worked and said that my father had not worked either, because directing a factory was no work at all.

So I said: 'Maybe it is not, but if you believe that it is work persecuting people as you and your OZNA comrades do, you are very wrong.'

He gasped and began stammering something about having been a Partisan during the war.

I patted him on the shoulder. He jumped: 'Don't touch me!'

I said: 'I congratulate you on having been a Partisan. It was very nice of you to fight against the enemy. However, I still have to say that what you have been doing since the war is very evil.' This was the end of our interview.

The winter of 1948–9 was very cold. There was no heating in the prison. It was difficult to read or write even with gloves on and I had nothing much to read except newspapers and an Italian book on statistics by Boldrini. It was lucky that I had this book crammed full of mathematics, at which I had never been very good, to keep myself busy. It was already spring when the prison governor finally made up his mind to hand over to me *A Treatise on Money* by Keynes.

'Where does your mother get the money from to send you such parcels?' enquired the militia NCO who was new to our floor. 'Wasn't everything you had confiscated?' I could give him no explanation because I did not know myself. Maybe OZNA even suspected that some British or American agency was giving money to my mother. In fact only my Swiss friends sent provisions to my mother, mainly coffee. It took me a long time to persuade my mother to write to them for it, because she was afraid OZNA would consider that an illegal link. Other friends abroad would not send me anything for fear that it would cause trouble.

Ljubljana was so near, yet barely accessible. My side of the building gave on to one of the main streets, but the surrounding wall was so high that one could see nothing except the upper floors of the building opposite – some kind of communist office. The only interesting observation I made through the window was the decline of enthusiasm for the first of May procession. By 1949 I could hear the shuffling of feet (people were too frightened not to take part) and see banners passing by, but there was no chanting and shouting. The communist cheer leaders would shout out their slogans, but mostly only one or two voices answered – to my great comfort.

I was still taken on my own for my short exercise walks and could hardly exchange even a glance with anybody. Then one morning, when I was walking round and round the lawn in the middle of the yard, I suddenly heard a female voice coming apparently from under the ground and saying: 'Good morning, Ljubo!' What was that? The guard did not seem to be paying attention. When I again passed the cellar grating from which I had heard the voice, I asked: 'Who are you?' the voice answered: 'I am Simona. Greetings from Tatjana.' She had been sent to the so-called bunkers, damp underground cells, by the OZNA physician. This man, Dr Benigar, was in charge of the prison health service, and was also director of the Emona Sanatorium for the personnel of the Slovene Ministry of the Interior (that is, Secret Police) where President Tito was often treated. Simona was being punished because she protested when Dr Benigar would not admit a very ill woman prisoner to the sick room.

When I next spoke to Simona I called: 'I should like to see you.' She climbed up to the window, but I could not see much, because there was wire netting over it. 'Give my greetings to Vito Zupan, if you see him,' she whispered when I passed by again. 'I shan't be seeing him,' I said, 'I have been alone for two years now.'

A few days later, on 17 June 1949 to be precise, the door opened and the guard from the prison office ordered me to take my belongings. When I came out with my bundle I said: 'I hope you aren't taking me to a shared room.' By then I was so accustomed to being alone that I did not want to be among people again. 'Why not?' he said. 'It will give you an opportunity of discussing politics again.'

9

Titoist re-education

The corridors were deserted when the guard marched me a floor higher to a locked and bolted door with the number 168 on it. He turned the key and opened the door, somebody came out to help me carry my belongings. Everybody shook hands with me: 'It is good to have you here!'

After a quick chat, everybody went to 'bed' again. I was given the place of honour on one of the two iron bedsteads, while the rest stretched out on the straw mattresses. On my arrival, there were only nine prisoners in the room (normal capacity five).

On the mattress near my bed was Simona's brother-in-law, Vito Zupan, so I could give him her greetings after all. We started talking and talked all through the night, I recounting my trial and expounding the ideas I had worked out in solitary confinement, and he telling me about his.

In 1948, when the Cominform crisis was at its climax, Vito, a former Partisan but no Communist, played a cruel joke on the communist notables whose nerves were tense enough as it was. He and some friends rang up Josip Vidmar, President of the Slovene Praesidium, a friend from partisan days, and told him that Tito had just resigned. That put the cat among the pigeons. The Vice-Chairman of the Slovene Government, Brecelj, a guest at Vidmar's house, phoned Kraigher, the Minister of the Interior, who was furious. Vito was arrested at his home, and when Simona protested and asked the OZNA men who would look after his two children, they took her too. OZNA confiscated all his papers and began putting together a case against him. The policemen accused him of being a 'degenerate Western writer', and his personal interrogator trampled on his manuscripts to show his contempt. They found a few poems that were rather unkind to some Slovene 'literary workers' collaborating with the Communists, and this was developed into an offence against 'Slovene national poets': Vito was sentenced to twelve years in prison.

I now had to learn a new way of life – life in a large prison room with no privacy at all. One is condemned to be with other people round the clock for weeks and months and years on end. This can be great fun, but as time wears on it becomes so tiring that prisoners used to say: 'It is not prison that is hard, it is other prisoners.' I was lucky, since I was always with decent people.

In room 168 I found a distant relative who had been sent as business representative to Trieste and then sentenced to twenty years for having 'traded in the old capitalist way'. Two Italians had been in communist prisons since the war but hoped to go home soon. There was a *Domobranci* officer, miraculously left alive, and two young Chetnik messengers.

One of our room-mates spent only the nights with us. In the mornings, he would be taken to a drawing office where prisoners with a technical education worked for enterprises such as the steel plant in Jesenice. He had been sentenced to five years' forced labour because he took part in organising a democratic opposition in Northern Slovenia. We discussed politics, but then Vito said we had better stop, because there was without doubt some informer in the room reporting everything to the OZNA Commissar who continuously tried to recruit spies among the prisoners; to report on other prisoners was apparently a sign of 're-education'.

The numbers in our room began increasing and soon reached 25. We slept by threes or fours on two straw mattresses, not knowing whether to lie across or along them. Amongst us was an engineer whose mother was Russian. This led him to say that he was in favour of the Cominform Resolution at a workers' meeting called to condemn it. Sentence: five years. There were numerous escapees – people trying to escape abroad or knowing about others trying to do it. The sentences on them were harsh – ten years or so. They were lucky not to have been shot at the border, as so many were. A former Royal Air Force NCO, who became a militia officer after the war, had a record of commuted sentences to death interspersed with escapes from prison, all because he was honest enought to rebel against the shootings. In the first month after the fighting ended, minor collaborators and many others were shot in their hundreds and he knew of shootings in abandoned pits because he came from a mining town. His father was arrested because of him.

My own father was in room No. 170 a few yards along the same corridor, and some prisoners from his room worked in the drawing office with technicians from my room. I asked them repeatedly to send him my greetings, but there was no reply. The inmates of our two rooms went for walks in the courtyard at the same time, although we marched around separately and were not allowed to speak to each other. But my father could have at least looked at me. He never did. He was obviously convinced that I was the cause of his disgrace. It seems he was ill, had high blood pressure, and prison was a terrible strain on him. As soon as a guard began to shout, he would start trembling.

In July 1949 our hopes ran high – everybody believed Tito's régime was at its end, especially as nobody expected that the Western democratic governments would miss the opportunity of overthrowing a communist one. In fact, Stalin was relentlessly pushing Tito into the arms of the West just as Tito had pushed non-communist guerrillas into those of the Nazis during the war.

In spite of pressure from all sides, Tito's Communists did not relent in their persecution of the population, but stepped it up. They introduced a law on so-called 'socially useful work' under which the political police could arrest anybody and hold him or her for two years. Vito's wife Nina disappeared in this way leaving his mother-in-law alone at home with two small children.

During that summer the police arrested hundreds of people, some at their homes, some out in the streets or sitting in a café — exactly as it had been during the occupation by the Fascists. No reasons were given for the arrests, except some most exotic ones, such as 'for having danced boogie-woogie'. Nobody knew how many people were arrested; it was said that about 10,000 were taken in Slovenia alone, though I believe this figure is too high. Hundreds of women were jailed and had to live in unhygienic conditions for several months. The fiancée of the British press attaché in Zagreb, Tatjana, was among them, having been arrested for the third time.

Among the men, there were several elderly gentlemen from my home town, several lawyers from Ljubljana, and many students. These men worked at the communist top projects: the Litostroj turbine factory, the aluminium factory in Strnišče and the Ministry of the Interior special villa and school at Tacen, near Ljubljana. They were treated badly: they remained all through the winter in the summer clothing in which they had been arrested. They were given no blankets, only cement sacks. They had to work hard, they were woken up morning after morning at four o'clock for 'gymnastics': for instance to hold each other by the ears and jump around so that often everybody's ears ended up bleeding. Another 'exercise' was to piss on each other.

Most people who knew both thought that the 'socially useful work' (DKD) was worse than Dachau, only it lasted less long. An eyewitness described how a DKD-prisoner fell ill at the Litostroj camp and the policeman in charge was told that the man had fever. 'Oh', he said, 'if he is hot, let us cool him down.' He ordered the sick man to be put in a cold bath, which killed him.

In the autumn people from our rooms began leaving for Maribor prison, among them my father. By then we had heard about the régime there. A few months after the Cominform resolution, many leading political prisoners had been sent there from Ljubljana. Before they left, they were told they would be given special treatment, so as not to forget prison if they should ever be released. Twenty by twenty, they were herded into dark rooms with the shutters nailed down. Their food rations were reduced to watery soup, which was deliberately left in front of the cell doors until it got cold. They had no parcels from home and no mail for more than six months. They, too, were in summer clothes throughout the winter and slept on the floor with only one blanket. There were rooms with Catholic priests undergoing the same treatment. After the war, about 30 priests were killed by the Communists, while 600 managed to escape. That left some 1200 in Slovenia; half of them were in prison at some stage, 300 while I was there.

In a way, this treatment was successful. Some adversaries became converted to Socialism. Very often I had to listen to their accounts of how my father exploited his workers. This did not trouble me much, because a few years of communist management had convinced me that people like my father, able to organise a profitable factory and manage it, are among the most useful in society.

Ljubljana prison was now full to overflowing. In single cells there were up to six people, but in one cell there was a grey-haired man on his own, an army general, Trampuz by name, a brother of the *Chef de Cabinet* at the Ministry of Internal Affairs. He was sentenced to twelve years forced labour for spying for the British, but the charges must have been even more implausible than normal since his trial was revoked and he was released after about four years.

At about the same time Cyrus S. Sulzberger was writing in the *New York Times* that friends of the West were being given more freedom in Yugoslavia.

At the beginning of February 1950, our room 168 was visited by a political police lieutenant-colonel, whose name we learnt later was Bravničar. He asked me: 'Sirc, do you still believe that your sentence was not just?'

'It was certainly not in accordance with the law,' I replied.

'Oh, the law, the law,' he said, 'the law always has gaps and it is up to us to close them.'

Bravnicar's strange theory agreed with some university texts I had to retype for the students among the policemen. This expert on communist law became Consul-General in Carinthia (Austria) a few months later, as we saw in the papers. The degree of infiltration of the Foreign Service by Secret Policemen was amazing. While before the war the Foreign Service had about 400 members, in the period 1945 to 1950 about 4000 men, mostly members of the Secret Police, passed through it. Some were sent abroad only for a few years, others remained 'diplomats'. It must be taken for granted that a great part of the staff of missions abroad were Secret Policemen, who indulged in political activities, propaganda for Communism, intelligence and the like.

Soon after this visit, our room was filled with people and we were told that we would all be sent to do manual work. In the event, the guards took about fifteen of us down to the courtyard. We were to dig gravel for the construction of a new floor over the laundry, and were told not to speak to other prisoners. A new storey was required to enlarge the workshops where prisoners had to produce clothes and shoes for the political police and their families and for leading employees of the prison. The demand was high because the 'new class' of customers paid little or nothing. The craftsmen were highly skilled; one of the best was the master tailor sentenced to life imprisonment for having been an officer of the *Domobranci*.

I pushed the wheelbarrow a few times and was taken aback by the variety of people in the exercise courtyard, separated from us only by iron bars. I saw a former employee of the UNRRA mission in Ljubljana, a grey-haired lady, probably imprisoned because of her work for foreigners. Professor Furlan came down to walk and made signs that all was well. Then a party of young girls arrived in several groups. Apparently the women's quarters were overflowing, with prostitutes mixed in among the political prisoners. The increased prostitution was a hard blow to communist theory, according to which prostitution was a result of capitalist social relations. It came about because many girls were brought in from villages or out of domestic service to work in offices and proved unable to cope with the paperwork. So they would be dismissed during bureaucracy-reducing campaigns and left with no job, or were offered manual work they were no longer prepared to do. For many of these unhappy creatures, uprooted as they were, prostitution was the obvious course. And the communist militia was now hunting them down.

Among the newcomers to my room was a young Italian from Trieste, Francesco Saba, a leftist who had come to Yugoslavia as a journalist, but was arrested and sentenced to several years for espionage. His father seemed to have good connections in Belgrade and was said to have seen Tito himself about Francesco, so that he was released soon after I had met him. Through him, I tried for the first time to contact my friends abroad. I wrote their addresses in Francesco's books and asked him to write to them.

Francesco had lots of books and I was longing to read them, but I was too tired in the evenings. Digging almost crushed me after three years in a prison cell. But it came to an end after about a fortnight. I was asked to translate a book on formal logic by the Soviet Professor Asmus, from Russian into Serbo-Croat. The book had been sent to Ljubljana, a Slovene-speaking town, from the federal Ministry of the Interior in Belgrade and nobody else could be found to do the translation. I stopped digging and was transferred to room No. 170.

Towards the middle of May we were suddenly told to stop work and pack our belongings and some forty of us were assembled to go to Maribor. As we were then told that we must leave everything we did not urgently need in the store in Ljubljana, this was a welcome opportunity to smuggle out my manuscripts — I put most of my books and papers in a box and innocently deposited it. It worked: mother took the box home some days later, and so the beginning of this book, a manuscript on the failure of the communist economy in Yugoslavia and the draft of my thesis on the Nuremberg trial were safe.

At ten that night the guards ordered us into a column, loaded their submachine guns, and we marched through the main gate into one of the principal streets of Ljubljana. The few people around did not pay much attention as a column of prisoners marching through the streets was common enough in Yugoslavia in 1950.

At the station we were marched along a train and ordered into carriages. I was slow, as my bundle was weighing me down, so that a young guard started shouting and threatening that he would hit me if I did not hurry up. He provoked my stubbornness, and I stopped. 'Just try to touch me!' To my amazement he quietly walked away.

After travelling all through the night, with guards standing at doors and sitting amongst us, the train made its way through a lovely stretch of green countryside and pulled up at the station in Maribor, still just a heap of rubble. We were shepherded through the town and over the bridge to the big prison building: it looked pretty hopeless even from the outside.

We were given prison uniforms and underwear and a prisoners' number. I cannot remember mine, but I do remember how unhappy I was to have to wear, for the first time, something not sent to me from outside: the suit I was given was worn and torn. I almost felt as if they had arrested me again. Two friends and I were locked in a cell said to have been, before the war, the cell of a prominent Communist, either Tito or Kidrič. It was encouraging to know that having been in prison did not preclude one from high office later. For the time being we were sitting there, looking at each other, three out of about 2000 prisoners, in a prison built for 300.

At five o'clock in the morning there was a roll-call followed by a morning walk. A mist was hanging over the courtyard, and we had to walk round in a circle without speaking. In Maribor there were always guards who tried to stir up trouble and send prisoners to the governor for punishment. Often the governor himself came to see that everybody was walking in silence and according to the regulations.

The guard in charge the first morning was not of the worst kind, so my uncle came to take me to a corner where elderly sick men were allowed to walk at greater ease. My uncle wanted me to speak to my father, but when we approached him, he turned away.

We did speak to each other the next morning, for the first time in the three years since my arrest. He had let himself be persuaded by friendly fellow-prisoners that it was not right to cut me. A sudden change came over him – he wanted to see as much of me as possible and talk to me, which was not very easy to organise. I was happy to talk to him but worried about the state of his health.

We stayed locked up in our cell for almost a month; we were taken out only once to paint slogans on streamers for Tito's birthday, and once to fill mattresses with straw. This was not exactly my forte and I was sorry for the prisoners who were to sleep on pallets filled by me. As we were pushing straw into our future beds, somebody suddenly whispered: 'Look out, Kragelj is watching!' Everybody began pushing in straw at the double.

Kragelj was the political Commissar of Maribor prison; he had the official title of assistant governor, and in fact represented the political police in the jail. A few days later, he called me to his office. 'I wanted to have a look at you, Sirc,' he greeted me. 'Tell me, is your opinion of people's authorities still as bad as it was in Ljubljana?' I started explaining my views, just for the sake of saying something. 'I see,' he stopped me after a while, 'Sirc, you really must learn sense!'

In our cell, we continued to sit around for a few more days; then a guard arrived in a great hurry. 'Are you Sirc?' he asked. 'Come on!' We almost ran to the office of a schoolmaster, a good man, who had been a teacher at the prison before the war and was now in charge of 'cultural activities'. 'Have you completed the translation of the Russian book on logic?' he asked.

'No', I said, 'I was not allowed to work.'

He shook his head: 'So start immediately, please!'

'I can't, the book and the manuscript are in the store.'

'Go and fetch it. You will work upstairs in the same room as the watchmaker. If you need anything, just tell me!'

In the spring of 1950 the Communists began showing a sudden solicitude for the rights of their prisoners. But it was difficult to believe that they had had a real change of heart, because men in charge since 1945 and responsible for many a mistreatment continued in office. Even people responsible for the mass murders of 1945 and 1946 carried on. We found out that immediately after the war Maribor prison was a kind of death camp. The inmates were made to write out long lists of people who had been groundlessly 'sentenced to death' and executed.

In Maribor I also became aware of the extent to which forced labour was used in the service of the Five-Year Plan. Prisoners were building an aluminium factory in Slovenia, prisoners were building the turbine factory of Litostroj, prisoners worked on the construction of the so-called youth railway lines between Brčko–Banovići and Samac–Sarajevo, prisoners and even women prisoners worked on the Zagreb–Belgrade motorway. There were about 30,000 prisoners, the main part of the manpower, at the construction site of New Belgrade, which the newspapers claimed would be a monument to Tito's period of our history. When foreign correspondents noticed that there was lots of barbed wire around New Belgrade, the newspapers attacked them fiercely as liars.

The Communist Party newspaper *Borba* published statistics on criminal trials on 20 June 1950. It reported that 260,000 criminal cases were heard in 1947, 220,000 in 1948, 160,000 in 1949. From the published data and from what I could see for myself, I calculated that at least one million Yugoslavs must have gone through communist prisons between 1945 and 1950, a figure equal to about one-tenth of the adult population. This would include those arrested and held for a short time without being tried. As a percentage, it is certainly not lower than in the Soviet Union during the great purge of Stalin's time. Further, approximately 300,000 people must have been massacred immediately after the war.

These figures make a telling comparison with the figures Tito gave for the 'victims of the reaction' during the first ten years of pre-war Yugoslavia, 1918-28: 24 death sentences, 600 political murders, 30,000 political arrests and 3000 political émigrés. Tito stated this in Court when he was tried for his subversive activities in 1929 and sentenced to five years' imprisonment. Had I tried to do the same at my trial, the prosecutor would have prevented me from speaking and I would probably have been shot. Nevertheless, communist propaganda called pre-war Yugoslavia 'the bloodthirsty régime of King Alexander'. To make matters worse, many Western journalists took up these lies and wrote that even if communist rule was bad, the Yugoslavs had never known anything better.

The prisoners working in the administration and I evaluated the numbers still in prison in 1950 at about 20,000 for Slovenia and between 200,000 and 300,000 for the whole of Yugoslavia. Most of these prisoners were political. The police hardly bothered with common criminals, and even when any were arrested and tried they were told they were not themselves guilty for what they had done. Those really responsible were the political prisoners: they had prevented the introduction of Socialism which would do away with criminality altogether. The governor of Maribor prison, Plos, favoured common criminals and hated political prisoners. We were ordered to take off our caps when passing him or a guard. He hated intellectuals too. He thought it was their fault he was dismissed from the *Gendarmerie* for his communist leanings and had to earn his living as a timber worker. While I was a kind of gentleman-prisoner as long as I was in the single cell, I now became exposed to the moods of the guards.

Plos called my father to his office one day and began the usual communist cat-and-mouse conversation. My father explained all over again that the charges against him had been erroneous, since he himself considered spying and informing the most vile crimes. He quoted the German saying: *'Der grosste Schuft im ganzen Land, der ist und bleibt der Denunziant.'* (The worst scoundrel in the land is and remains the informer.) Whereupon, the governor said sharply: 'I hope that you do not mean it is vile to serve as an informer to our communist authorities.'

This was not only a rebuttal, it was an invitation. In the opinion of the Communists the only clear proof of one's re-education was to become an informer, to report to them details of one's comrades' opinions. They would not even stop trying their re-education methods in the case of the sick old man my father had become by then.

As long as my father could get about, we met in the courtyard during our walks and in the hall during 'cultural' performances, so I was able to talk to him at length about what had happened. The time came when he was no longer able to come out and I had to steal away during the walks or 'cultural activity' to go to his room. One day he suddenly said: 'I believe, Ljubo, that I am dying.' I tried to comfort him, and was in fact not aware of how ill he was. By then his liver condition was so bad that his eyesight was affected and deteriorated till he could see only shadows. Eventually Captain Plesko, who was sleeping on the bed next to him and touchingly looked after him, persuaded the prisoner in charge of the prison hospital to admit him. From then on, I hardly ever saw him. I was not allowed in the hospital and succeeded in stealing in only once. I would often stand around under the windows.

My friends found out that he was to be sent to Ljubljana for treatment and I was allowed to see him off. He was so weak that I had to push him onto the rickety lorry on which he was to travel.

The desolate life in Maribor continued: our only consolation was that the civil population was not fed much better. We were given half a pound of maize bread a day with 'black water' called coffee in the morning, tasteless sauerkraut with one or two potatoes at noon and a flour soup in the evening. At noon, the meal was distributed in the courtyard and we had to come and fetch it with our own mess-tins. These mess-tins got me into trouble. I went to get my food and the guard standing near the cauldron said my mess-tin was dirty. So I went and washed it again. When I came back, he claimed that it was still dirty. At that I walked away, and he reported me to the governor.

The governor told me I must not approach his desk but must stand to attention near the door and say: 'I report to you, Mr Governor!' Then he punished me with one month without mail.

I was reported to the governor again quite soon, for not jumping out of bed as soon as the siren wailed in the morning, but this time I decided to defend myself. It made me particularly angry that I had just read that Philip Noel-Baker, the British Member of Parliament, had been entertained by Tito.

I stood in front of the governor and said that I was not aware of having done anything punishable. Anyway, I thought that it was very strange for me to be in prison for having contact with Noel-Baker while Marshal Tito was having meals with him. This was not strictly accurate: it was not Mr Philip Noel-Baker I had met, but his son. The governor was taken aback and only said: 'Yes, however, you did not socialise only with Noel-Baker but also with Dr Nagode and he has never been invited to a meal by Marshal Tito, has he? You can go!' The dinner Mr Philip Noel-Baker had with Tito thus saved me from one punishment.

It was equally disgraceful that, at a time when Yugoslav Communists were looking for better relations with the West, Professor Furlan was still in prison for having advocated just such a policy only a few years earlier. Nonetheless, the Slovene President Josip Vidmar had the effrontery to say that Furlan was in prison because he had asked for protection: he was afraid the English would murder him if he were released. So as to 'protect' him, the Slovene Communists relegated him for four years to solitary confinement, which endangered his mental balance and his physical health. A few times he was given books, but then even this 'privilege' was stopped.

My mother wrote a postcard in September 1950 saying that my father had been paroled, but was so ill that he was only being transferred from the prison part of the hospital to the general clinic. In my eternal optimism, I had the impression that his health was improving. Then, one day, Commissar Kragelj called me to his office and began talking about my father's state of health. 'Is he dying?' I asked. 'No,' said Kragelj, 'he has died. You will go to the funeral.' I went down to my friends in the courtyard and exclaimed: 'My father has died and it is all my fault!'

Just before midnight a guard came, chained my hands, and marched me in fetters through Maribor to the station. In the train, another prisoner and I sat on one side of the compartment and the guard with a sub-machine gun on his knees on the other. When the train began to fill up in the morning, people stared at us.

The sight of my father's coffin in my grandparents' house, where I spent two hours, was too painful an experience to describe.

Soon after my return to Maribor, I was told by the political Commissar that my father's guilt was negligible and that it was, therefore, entirely my responsibility that he had died: 'Had you been more reasonable it would never have happened.' My father's death was used to soften me into submission. I certainly felt guilty, but not before them, and I thought them greater scoundrels than ever.

The nightmarish life in Maribor continued. Every day when I got up I was unhappy to be alive. The only changes were a few suicides and a few attempts to escape. One who killed himself was Krautberger. I had seen him during the war among the officers of the Vth Overseas Brigade in which I had served. He was in prison for murder. Every now and again he had the so-called 'partisan' break-downs that plagued many former participants in the communist massacres. He shouted, threw himself on the ground and wept: 'They wonder why I killed the man at Trbovlje. Why did they teach me how to kill?'

In the autumn, our hearts warmed up when we read that the American journalist Sulzberger had asked Tito in an interview about the fate of Dragoljub Jovanović and other prisoners. So we had not been quite forgotten yet. We liked Attlee's visit to the Yugoslav tyrant less, but forgave him much because he was very outspoken in his comments.

Talk about an amnesty was rife again. It seemed that the West was pressing for the release of political opponents and was expecting Tito to comply if he wanted their co-operation. The Commissar had noticeably mellowed and even said to some prisoners that many sentences had been excessive and wrong. Disappointment was the more acute when on 29 November, the anniversary of the proclamation of people's democracy in Yugoslavia, hardly any political prisoners were freed, while a number of criminals were. Even among the political prisoners, informers predominated. Yet foreign newspapers praised Tito's magnanimity in dealing with political opponents. The outlook was hopeless.

My work on all sorts of translations continued in a work room where there were also the watchmaker, a former judge and Rudolf Trofenik, the pre-war secretary of the Law Faculty in Ljubljana, now imprisoned under some pretext. Soon after the amnesty, he was visited by a university colleague, Zore, formerly councillor at the Yugoslav Embassy in Washington and later ambassador to various countries, including the Lebanon and Syria. Trofenik was offered a transfer to the prison of Sremska Mitrovica, where he would take over the direction of a group of prisoners working for the Ministry of Foreign Trade. Svato Zupan and Hribar, my co-defendants, were to go with him, and they all left within a few days. In Mitrovica, there was also a department of the Ministry of Defence, staffed by prisoners of military profession, and even a foreign radio monitoring service run by linguists from among the captives. Trofenik tried to get me transferred to join his group, but the Slovene police apparently considered me so dangerous that they wanted to keep their watchful eye on me themselves.

Christmas and New Year's Eve passed in the usual desperate atmosphere of Maribor prison. In mid-January, I was unexpectedly told to take my belongings and go to the storehouse. Prisoners with their luggage were pouring into the large hall, so that it looked as if the prison building was about to be emptied. The prisoners staying behind were ordered to bring beds into the courtyards and the workshops were being dismantled in a hurry. What was happening? Were the Soviets about to invade Yugoslavia?

We had been aware of this danger, as during 1949 relations between Tito and the Cominform had worsened. Maribor is near the Hungarian border and we could not decide how the Titoists would react if attacked. They might consider us a danger to their absolute rule and massacre us, or leave us behind locked up to fall into Soviet hands. Certainly the Communists did not waver in their hatred for their political opponents at home despite their dispute with Stalin.

Fearing the worst, we debated whether we could defend ourselves, but we kept the talk to a very narrow circle because we knew betrayal would bring severe punishment. I asked some prisoners about to be released to contact Western representatives and draw their attention to our plight. But presumably nobody dared do anything of this sort.

Now many of us had been gathered in the hall since about ten o'clock in the morning, and were still there at ten at night. At eleven we were ordered into the courtyard, where we stood under floodlights. From the entrance we were watched by a number of people from the ministry in Ljubljana, among then one of the prosecutors at my trial in the uniform of an OZNA colonel and wearing a leather jacket and boots. Somebody began calling out our names.

Outside, we had to pass between two lines of guards with tommy-guns at the ready and walk to the railway line where we were crowded into waiting cattle-trucks. Some tried to guess where we were going, while I stretched out over two wooden cases and fell asleep.

When I woke, daylight was shining through the cracks. Somebody groped about in the truck and a window opened. There were guards with machine-guns in brakesmen's cabins all along the train. We were travelling along a river and eventually stopped at a goods station which some people recognised as Novo Mesto, a little town in Lower Carniola. We were taken twenty by twenty to the prison building, the local OZNA chief following the lorry in his car.

Under the gaze of the political Commissar, playing the role of a benign uncle concerned about our well-being, we went into a large prison room. Among the first, I jumped to the window, under which the river Krka flowed lazily. Beyond, there was a forest. Marvellous.

Initially the régime was mild, though for a few days we did not get any food. We were then fed enormous quantities of peas from the Western economic aid which had just started. Later on the prison administration secured some sacks of flour with attached leaflets giving the Yugoslavs the best wishes of the United States people and government.

The question still unanswered was, why had we been brought here? Novo Mesto is in the vicinity of the Rog Mountains, where after the war thousands of people were massacred and dumped in ravines by the Communists. The obvious conclusion for many was that we had been brought here in order to be 'liquidated' in the Rog should an emergency arise.

For a few months before our departure from Maribor, prisoners wanting to submit an appeal or application had been encouraged to consult the former judge who worked with me on translations. Some were sent to him by the governor and others followed of their own accord. Soon the judge began passing some of his 'cases' on to me, so that I became a 'legal adviser' in my own right, which improved my knowledge of communist criminal law. We did not believe that our legal efforts would be of great value because we knew about the intransigence of communist courts, but if the Communists wanted complaints, we were ready to use this unexpected freedom.

We needed legal texts and obtained the *Official Gazette* from the prison workshop, including an issue containing the Act on the Defence of the People and the State and covering my own trial. One prisoner had a copy of the Declaration of Human Rights adopted by the United Nations Assembly in 1948, which was incessantly invoked by the Yugoslav Communists. I quickly noticed that our judgement was not even in accordance with communist law and that it certainly infringed the Declaration of Human Rights. Article 19 reads: 'Everyone has the right to freedom of opinion and expression; the right includes freedom to seek, receive and impart information and ideas through any media and regardless of frontiers.' Article 13, par. 2 states that 'Everyone has the right to leave any country including his own, and to return to his country.' Article 20 states that 'Everyone has the right to freedom of peaceful assembly and association.'

Further, I discovered a paper by my former Professor, Munda, on criminal investigation where he described as illicit all the methods the Communist Police had applied to most of us. He claimed that psychological pressure, questioning at night, insufficient food, etc., must be considered equal to physical mistreatment. Munda dealt at length with tricks now used by communist investigators like leading questions, *captious* questions, threats and promises and concluded that all these rendered an investigation invalid.

In Novo Mesto I was well equipped to analyse my own case. During the first two months there, in crowded rooms without anything to do, I sat day after day on a wooden box between two beds writing down what happened to me during the investigation and trial and explaining its real background. I tried to hide what I was doing, afraid that the police would consider the explanation a new crime.

Why was the contact with the former Minister Šutej criminal, when he himself had never been indicted? How could opposition to the government be criminal, if the party leaders maintained that opposition was free? Were they out to trap us? And if so, was it not immoral to treat as criminals people who believed the words of the country's supreme leaders?

I wrote it all into the official copy of my indictment, because I hoped that at some stage I would be able to pass it on to my mother. When the day of her May visit approached, I packed these and a few other official papers in a box with some underwear and handed it in for checking. The guard turned over the pages of the indictment and found nothing hidden between them, while paying no attention to my handwriting in the spaces.

By the time she came next, my mother had read my explanation and at last understood what had happened: 'It must have been terrible!' Yet, in her opinion, and in the opinion of everybody she had dared ask, any attempt to prove that I was not guilty could only harm me.

She consoled me saying that a new Criminal Code was being prepared and that its promulgation would radically change our situation. Everybody was talking about this Code and even foreign newspapers were giving it a lot of attention. This longed-for Criminal Code was published in April 1951. One of the inmates was soon sent a copy by his wife. I had a look, and could only smile bitterly: the new provisions were as vague and as ambiguous as what went before. Of course, this did not prevent some Western VIPs from praising the new humane trend of the régime. Mrs Eleanor Roosevelt stated that from now on the Yugoslavs would at least know what they were allowed to do and what not. Once before, I had cursed a woman. While still in solitary confinement I read about the communist ravings of Madame Joliot-Curie which made my blood boil. I found her comments outrageous.

The *locus classicus* of vagueness in the new Code was article 118, particularly its second paragraph, reading: 'In the same way (i.e. with imprisonment of up to twenty years) shall be punished whoever spreads fascist ideas or other ideas inimical to the people and the State.' This could mean anything, in particular as the Communists interpreted in their own way terms such as 'Fascism' or 'the people': 'Fascism' meaning anything they did not like and 'the people' equated to the Communist Party. On the basis of this article, Djilas was later sentenced to seven years' imprisonment for his book *The New Class*.

In spite of the evident shakiness of communist justice, an American judge came to Yugoslavia about then and presented a communist official with a judge's wooden hammer in admiration for the work of our courts. If the people in the West could do nothing to help us, they should at least have been decent enough not to mock us!

Rumours were spreading that the imprisoned Stalin followers were being treated most abominably. When they arrived in the camp of Goli Otok they were beaten up by those who had already been converted to Titoism. To beat up their comrades not prepared to renounce Stalin was considered proof of successful re-education.

While Titoists and Stalinists abused each other, we political prisoners in Novo Mesto were permanently frightened that we would all be massacred if war broke out, and an armed clash was a real possibility then. There was the hot war in Korea, and the Soviet Union with her satellites did not spare threats to Yugoslavia. Our restiveness was increased by the feeling that our sitting in prison made no sense since our government was more and more obviously co-operating with the West. Most of us had been sentenced, if for any reason at all, because of our sympathies with the West, or for Western ideas. The only decent consequence of Tito's foreign policy somersault would have been lenient treatment of all the people sentenced in the Stalinist era, but there was little sign of leniency. Impatience made prisoners in Novo Mesto talk of mass escape.

It was little help to us when the Communists and their fellow-travellers explained that it was one thing for the communist government to be on friendly terms with the West and an entirely different one for reactionary individuals to be so. My mother was told this by President Vidmar when she went to see him and insisted that it was unjust to keep me in prison when their own foreign policy turned out to be exactly what I had stood for four years earlier. Not only did the Communists not set free people friendly towards the West, they began retracting what they had said in 1950. Then, Kragelj had said that mistakes had been made in at least seven big trials, and these would have to be revised in the light of later developments. But in Novo Mesto, he called me to his office because of what I had written on a postcard about Eleanor Roosevelt and said: 'What do you expect after all? You are all counter-revolutionaries and we shall keep you in prison as long as we choose.' He also told me that I was a fool to believe in Western democracy.

The change in communist attitude resulted largely from inaction by Western governments. All those who knew Yugoslavia in 1950 were convinced that the Titoists were terrified of Stalin and that the West could have obtained not just the release of political prisoners, but other political concessions as well. The West, though, did not seem to care about their fellow-democrats in Yugoslav prisons, or for democracy. When a friend tried to intervene for me with the United States Ambassador in Belgrade, George Allan, his Excellency said: 'We cannot interfere with Yugoslav internal affairs. If we did, Tito would go back to the East.' At that time Tito could not go back to the East, and later, when he could, he went there in spite of Western non-intervention. Yet the West could have done much for us, if it had cared to. A case in point is the fact that the Slovene Communists released my co-defendants Furlan and Snoj unprompted in the spring of 1951, as they thought this would please their new benefactors. Most people thought it so self-evident that I would follow that I was seen in the streets of Ljubljana – so visitors told my fellow-prisoners.

The Communists, who knew about the dilemma we were in after the honeymoon between Tito and the Western governments started, often asked ironically: 'Why are you so much in favour of the West? Don't you see that the West has abandoned all of you?'

At the end of June 1951, we were all unexpectedly transported from Novo Mesto back to Ljubljana. There I was locked up with four other prisoners, Styrians, in a small room, a walled-off part of a corridor. These Styrians told me a lot about the 1945 massacres of the Croats returned from Carinthia, something like 40,000 or 50,000 killed around Celje.

A fortnight later I was transferred to a bright room, a former guardroom with two big windows, neither nailed down nor whitewashed. I was to share this room for about half a year with a former journalist, Branko Vrčon, whom I knew by name, and Dušan Spindler whom I knew only from the report of his trial in the newspapers.

Just before we left Novo Mesto the federal chief of police, Ranković, made public a report 'On the Further Strengthening of the Administration of Justice and the Rule of Law'. It was first broadcast, and later printed in *Komunist* (the Party magazine) for 1951. According to Ranković, the task of the Communists was 'to strengthen the rule of law and resolutely to suppress any arbitrariness and any unlawful decisions regardless of who took them and in what form.' He described exactly what had been going on since the so-called liberation. Ranković then admitted that 'local administrative or Party bodies put pressure on courts and thus violated their independence and turned the courts and the judges into their own technical apparatus.' He concluded that all this was contrary to the basic tenets of our party and State leadership.

The foreign press acclaimed this statement as a great step forwards; in fact it was monstrous hypocrisy. Ranković must have known all along exactly what his subordinates were doing and issued the appropriate instructions himself. In line with well-known communist tactics, he condemned the misuses with a straight face when they became too widely known and put the blame on subordinates. Again in line with communist tactics, he did nothing effectively to stop the abuses or to repair the consequences of those committed before. I knew masses of prisoners sentenced on the basis of false accusations; however, I heard of only two cases of trial revision.

Ranković's remonstrations, of course, did not apply to big political trials, such as mine, since the Communists proclaimed the likes of us to be counter-revolutionaries, and counter-revolutionaries had to be re-educated. The official biography of Tito states that re-education of political prisoners is a monstrosity 'because it would mean that they had to give up their convictions'. But then, the Communists consider only their imprisoned comrades political prisoners, while prisoners under Communism are deemed to be scoundrels as they oppose the Communist Party, the only salvation of the world.

I did not trust Ranković – my experience was too bad – but his speech gave a new impetus to my wish to do something about myself. I began pestering my mother to see a lawyer and contact my foreign friends to ask them for affidavits about the real nature of my friendship with them. She refused to do any such thing because she was afraid that it would only cause more trouble.

Up to 1951, it had never occurred to me to enter a useless legal argument with the authorities. I had never even thought of the possibility of freedom. Now all this talk about the 'rule of law' made me decide to fight my case, even if it had nuisance value only.

My mother had thought of it before but obviously did not know the conditions in jail. Otherwise she would hardly have suggested that I should submit to 're-education'! I could even surmise that my family were angry at my supposedly making fanatical anti-communist speeches, because every time my mother enquired about my release, she was told: 'Out of the question. He is an enemy. He refuses to be re-educated.'

I could not explain to my mother what re-education meant in communist language. Three things were required: First, a prisoner had to admit to his guilt even if the accusations were not true at all. Second, he had to pay lip-service to the wisdom of the Communist Party and its leaders. And third, he had to report on his co-prisoners. Up to 1953, hardly anybody had been pardoned without being considered an informer by his fellows. Exceptions were only made if there were strong State reasons, or interventions. In all other cases the commissars did their best to break the prisoners' self-respect.

Of course, the Communists would never say what constituted their brand of re-education. On the contrary, they would deny its existence and not mention the truth even to the prisoners who were expected to get re-educated. Their art of governing consisted of frightening the governed into doing what the Communists want without having even to mention it. A prisoner trying to prove to the Commissar that he was re-educated by pointing out that he worked hard, would be told: 'Work is not enough!' Everybody in prison knew, in fact, that the ultimate condition for getting out was to become an informer.

Eventually I did persuade my mother to get in touch with my foreign friends and try to obtain affidavits from them. She wrote to New York, to the former American Red Cross representative in Yugoslavia, and went to see the British Vice-Consul in Zagreb. This friend, Ted Kay, was friendly and sympathetic but was afraid to try doing anything for me. 'We are afraid', he said, 'that a British intervention could only do harm. The best he can do is to "reform". He may pay any lip-service necessary to Communism. Everybody will understand this under the circumstances.' I was livid. Obviously the British did not know, either, what 're-education' meant, and I felt forsaken by everybody.

I was not aware that the first British post-war Consul in Ljubljana, Frank Waddams, was working behind the scenes. Although he had given up the Foreign Service, he did what he could when he heard about the trials of Professor Furlan and myself. In a letter to *The Times* he explained the true nature of our relations. When the Foreign Office maintained that British intervention could only make things worse for us, he exclaimed: 'What could be worse than a death sentence?' He kept on interceding for us and found a Conservative Member of Parliament, Tufton Beamish, later Lord Chelwood, willing to write repeatedly to the Foreign Secretary asking what had been done about Professor Furlan and me. This led to the British Ambassador in Belgrade enquiring about us. Frank Waddams also enlisted Konni Zilliacus and other leftist British MPs to help. Zilliacus talked to Ranković himself and was shamelessly told that Furlan and I had evidently been doing a job in British Intelligence, although the British Consulate may not have known about it, as he put it.

I am certain that these interventions were a great help. Had I known about them when I was in prison, I would have been much happier.

10

Half-hearted rule of law

The next three years were taken up with attempts to obtain my release. My mother worked indefatigably once I had persuaded her to try: she found lawyers to pursue my case, wrote letters, submitted applications and contacted my foreign friends.

All this time the country's economy was being propped up by the West, whose aid alleviated the worst effects of government policy. But the diplomatic rapprochement led only to Westerners' being persuaded of the virtues of the régime, not in their taking any steps to help liberate their Yugoslav friends from prison.

The first lawyer to see me was a Croat relative, in August 1951. The guard took us to one of the offices; when he left us we both stared at the holes in the boarded walls. The office looked like a broadcasting studio. After some twenty minutes, a stranger came in and sat down without uttering a word. We both felt increasingly ill at ease and when the lawyer went I felt most frustrated. The lawyer must have too because he let me know, 'It is not time yet.'

The reply to each of my mother's next three applications in 1951 was invariably a printed form. The conditions in the Act on the Implementation of Punishment did not apply, it stated, since I had not yet served half my prison term. My mother pointed out to the Ministry of the Interior that some of my co-defendants had been paroled in spite of this and that, anyway, the Act envisaged exceptional parole. There was no shortage of 'legal possibilities', if anybody was to be imprisoned, but the Communists were seemingly hard put to find a legal basis for anybody's release. In my case, they also claimed that I was 'stubborn'.

One application was rejected in spite of previous consultation with the nominal Head of State, Dr Ribar, a friend of the Croat branch of our family. He was to sign the decision as Chairman of the Praesidium of the People's Assembly of the Federal People's Republic.

The journalist in our cell was determined to get out, and play-acted a conversion to Marxism in a way that often made me lose my temper. Dušan Spindler, the third man, was very honest, but also very naïve. Although a monstrous injustice had been done to him, he was still a convinced Communist. All injustices were due to 'subjective errors', he insisted. For the first time I had an insight into that terrible thing, the communist 'religion', and how it could distort a sincere man's thinking.

The economy went from bad to worse; there were constant food shortages. The leaders themselves were clearly aware that it was all the fault of the system, but their incessant changes were ineffective because they did not touch the Marxian fundamentals. I laughed and said that the government did not know what it was doing. Dušan objected and claimed these never-ending alterations were due to fast economic growth. Capitalist countries were exceedingly sluggish, while in communist countries legislators could not keep up with progress.

Both my fellow-prisoners were taken aback when, despite allegedly favourable developments, the currency had to be devalued from 50 dinars per dollar to 300 dinars per dollar. I was convinced it was worth even less from reading all the economic news.

There followed the great transformation, the master stroke of Titoism, meant to show how progressive it was compared with Stalinism — the State began 'withering away' by a simple device: the government was renamed the Executive Council in parallel with the governments of all constituent republics; for instance, the government of Slovenia became the Executive Council of the People's Republic of Slovenia. Dušan was enthusiastic. 'You see', he triumphed, 'how right Marx was about the disappearance of government! There is no government any more and the State has begun withering away.'

I thought it far more interesting that the new Chairman of the Slovene Executive Council was none other than the previous Minister of the Interior, Boris Kraigher, a general of the Secret Police. Niko Šilih, hitherto Chief of the Slovene Branch of the Secret Police, who had interrogated me during the investigation, became the new Secretary (not Minister, because the State was withering away) of the Interior. The State seemed more firmly in the hands of the Secret Police than ever. Later, when Šilih became Chairman of the Parliamentary Commission for Internal Affairs, another acquaintance of mine, Mitja Ribičič, became the Secretary of the Interior. He was promoted from Chief of the Slovene Secret Police; before that he had been the People's Prosecutor for Slovenia.

There was more and more talk about workers' councils and communes which were supposed to make Yugoslavia a genuine Marxist State in the teeth of Stalin. All federal parliaments were given a second chamber, the Chamber of Producers, with mandates proportionate to output. It is clear that a worker in a modern factory with enormous capital produces (or, by the way, should produce) more than a peasant with a plough. At worst, this is a negation of Marx's doctrine on surplus value; Kardelj admitted freely that it was a device to strengthen the domination of the working class.

Despite this, the Western public seemed to think highly of the Yugoslav régime and its army, and illusions about a forthcoming free election abounded.

'What?' said Dušan with disgust. 'Free elections! How can you expect a group of men who know exactly what the future will bring and what is necessary for the happiness of the people, to bow to the hazards of an election!' Their knowledge clearly also entitled our Communists to use cunning and violence to keep themselves in power; but they took a different line when Stalin, confident that it was he who knew the future, used the most monstrous lies against Titoists. The trade-union leader, Djuro Salaj, wrote: 'Of course, it is proper to use lies in the struggle against class enemies, but we are no class enemies.'

During the preparations for the November amnesty, Drew Pearson, an American journalist, caused much excitement by sending Marshal Tito a question on Cardinal Stepinac, who was still serving a fifteen-year sentence after falling out with Tito. Under pressure from Western public opinion, the Communists, who at that time depended entirely on aid from the West, released Stepinac from prison and interned him in his home village of Krašić. The West could well have pushed through any demand for change — had it tried to.

In our room, Dušan was shocked that 'war criminals like Cardinal Stepinac' were being released, while I remained in prison. Initially, he had considered me a spy, but after long talks he concluded that I was not a criminal at all, an idea not easy for him to digest. Earlier on I had almost hit him with a chair when he said that I was to blame for my father's death since I had opposed the communist government, the only one capable of bringing happiness to mankind, and the police naturally had to silence me. But when he decided that I was not guilty, he loyally supported all my efforts to get the truth about my case known. 'Don't believe that I approve of your political opinions,' he said, 'but I find that it is not fair to keep people in prison under false accusations. Of course, I remain a Communist.'

On his insistence, I wrote a note drawing the attentions of 'whom it may concern' to the many remaining prisoners sentenced only because of their democratic leanings. Dušan smuggled it out to my mother. She did not dare do anything about it till February 1952, when she wrote a letter to the UN Secretary-General, Trygve Lie. If the letter ever arrived, nothing was done about it.

Dušan's helpfulness conjured up a new atmosphere between us. I helped him write down the story of his own case and inserted the required legal passages. What he told me in his naïvete surpassed anything I could have imagined.

Dušan came from a Slovene nationalist family — he was a teacher, two of his brothers were career officers. As soon as the Germans occupied Northern Slovenia the three brothers went into the resistance, the two officers were killed by the Gestapo, while Dušan spent a while in Mauthausen. Once home, he started recruiting for the so-called Styrian partisan division near his home. He soon heard that most of the men sent by him had allegedly been killed by a commissar. Being an old Communist with some influence, he succeeded in alerting the party heads, and a few leaders were punished for excess of zeal. It transpired that the commissar had acted on a warning from headquarters to the effect that nationalists were trying to infiltrate the ranks of his division. He decided that Dušan's recruits were the infiltrators and, it was reported, had eight men – some say more – killed. It was rumoured that he murdered a few – entirely innocent – himself by clubbing them to death.

Dušan fell ill, and the story was forgotten, but he recovered in time to be appointed the first mayor of liberated Maribor, the second largest Slovene town. In his honesty, he made another mistake – he accused army officers billeted in Maribor flats of illegally removing furniture and had the accusation broadcast. He was removed from his mayorship and demoted to a lowly job where the commissar caught up with him. Dušan was indicted of having been instrumental in 80% of all Gestapo successes in Styria (whatever this meant) and sentenced to life imprisonment. His wife and his sister-in-law (whose husband had been shot by the Nazis) were also sentenced to four and two years, respectively, for collaboration with the Gestapo. Everything became clear when we found out that the commissar was, in reality, a high official in the Secretariat of the Interior.

In the autumn of 1951, I was asked by a Secret Policeman to teach him English. I could hardly refuse, and there were also some benefits: he brought me the odd copy of *The Economist* and some English books, including Hillary's *The Last Enemy*. More policemen followed, but early in 1952 they suddenly all stopped coming. Of course I wondered why and talked about it to my friend Slavko Zovič. He jumped and asked me to describe my student. 'That is he,' he exclaimed and became all excited. It turned out that I had taught English to Colonel Winkler who, six years earlier, had kidnapped Slavko in the middle of Trieste under the noses of the British and the Americans. This same Winkler had now himself taken refuge in Trieste, having become tired of Communism in Slovenia.

Dušan's case was not the only piece of police insanity that came my way. Ranković's criticism of illegality prompted a review of the cases of imprisoned foreigners. I was ordered to translate the records from the German. There was a poor Austrian woman arrested when she came to visit her brother. In her confusion, she admitted to having been sent by the Gestapo just before the war to kill Anthony Eden when he visited Belgrade. She consorted with a friend of Himmler, but was finally imprisoned by the Gestapo. In prison she was recruited by the Israeli secret service, and met the Polish Countess Radziwil who worked for the Vatican. This nonsense made me laugh, while Dušan was horrified by the evil doings of capitalist spies.

A few days later, I was given new minutes in which the unfortunate woman, who had by then spent five years in prison, explained that her original story was pure invention based on stories in twopenny illustrated magazines. The 'gentlemen' (as she put it) who had interrogated her shouted and threatened her so much that she confirmed anything they wanted.

In February 1952, the political Commissar, Kragelj, told me I would have to answer some written questions and suggested the answers should be detailed because they were most interested in my views. There were about two hundred questions, on everything from my grandfather's activity in our home town before the war to refugee politics in Switzerland in 1944. Surprisingly, I had never been given a questionnaire before, though it was common practice.

It so happened that I had just felt offended by a new book which referred to my trial and claimed I had said that our underground group was in favour of collaboration with the enemy. I used my answers to point out that this was false and that the Court could have established that if it had cared to. I wrote: 'Of course I was wrong to expect the most elementary decency from the Court. The Court did not bother to look at the documents but limited itself to construed interrogation minutes.'

On another question I wrote: 'It is possible that I stated something similar during the interrogation by the Secret Police.... If somebody who has not been allowed to sleep for weeks is tortured hour upon hour with leading and *captious* questions, he will, in the end, confess to anything to be left in peace.'

I made acid remarks about the 'leading role' of the Communists in the resistance, saying that the Swiss considered us 'savages and fools' because we fought each other in a national emergency. I claimed that our group was attacked from all sides because we tried to mediate between the fighting factions. 'If my behaviour during the war may be called criminal,' I concluded, 'anything may be so labelled.'

I handed thirty typed pages to the Commissar, who accepted them with a kind smile. For a fortnight there was no reaction, which made me think they had swallowed it, but then I was dragged to the prison governor who shouted: 'What a swinish thing have you written!' I muttered about having been invited to write down my views. 'Nobody is interested in your views', he shouted and punished me with a month without mail, parcel or visit.

I emerged ever so happy. What is a month without privileges compared with the Governor and the Commissar having no better argument against what I had written than punishment. My room-mates were amazed, because apparently nobody had ever been punished for his replies to the questionnaire.

Questionnaires and autobiographies were part of communist psychoanalysis, but I had an inkling that there was more to it. In a room opposite our prison wing, two mysterious teams of prisoners were at work. Could their work be linked with the interminable questionnaires? It occurred to me that they must be engaged in some kind of historical research for the police. Step by step I discovered that, in the winter of 1949–50, the Secret Police had isolated some prisoners in two cells, given them a large part of the police archives and ordered them to write papers on various aspects of the recent past. Soon they were told that their papers were fine but that they should make them more 'operational', which they understood to mean that they were supposed to help the police arrest and put on trial more 'war criminals'. The task was repulsive to most and some actually fell ill. Eventually the 'top secrecy' veiling the two teams was downgraded: the prisoners were allowed to walk with us and finally came to live among other prisoners, only going to work in separate rooms.

A change of room-mate brought me an editor of the Trieste Titoist Slovene newspaper and Dr Slavko Stojković. Stojković had been a diplomat before the war and afterwards had taught law at the Economics Faculty in Belgrade; he was a veritable encyclopaedia. He had come on holiday to Slovenia with his family, was arrested on suspicion of intending to escape abroad and sentenced to eight years, of which he served three. His wife had a nervous breakdown. Their two sons also spent several months in jail.

There was no end to interesting discussions, and funnily enough, we had books which could hardly be described as pro-communist. I was even given *A History of Western Philosophy* by Bertrand Russell, and Stojković *The Managerial Revolution* and *The Machiavellians* by Burnham. Although not agreeing with Burnham's theories about managerialism, I rejoiced that somebody in the West already understood what Communism was all about.

In another surprise move, a priest turned up in our cell. This was Dr Stanko Lenič, former secretary to the Bishop of Ljubljana, Dr Rozman, who had left the country in 1945. So far Lenič, like most other imprisoned priests, had been doing heavy physical work. They worked with other people, but had separate accommodation. Among priests were included Protestant pastors and many Jehovah's Witnesses, who had spread in Slovene industrial towns and were severely persecuted.

Dr Lenič had been in solitary confinement for a few months because of his alleged bad influence on other priests. The police pressed him to join the Association of Saint Cyril and Metod, a kind of priests' trade-union, and to condemn his war-time superior, the Bishop of Ljubljana, as a war criminal. Dr Lenič refused, saying that the Yugoslav bishops had prohibited membership of the communist-organised priests' association and that he could not in good faith condemn Bishop Rozman because he knew better than anybody that everything he had done was with the best intentions. The police attempted to soften Lenič by depriving him of his breviary and by sending him among us laymen. He had been sentenced to twelve years for failing to report a clandestine visitor from Austria.

I spent the following two and a half years, until my release, with Dr Lenič. I would probably never have become so closely acquainted with a priest otherwise and Dr Lenič would not have been among laymen, particularly liberals, for such a long time. He admitted that he was rather apprehensive about living among us, but later enjoyed it. This 'co-existence' turned out very useful to us all, although that was the last thing the Communists intended.

My mother always hoped that something would happen, and that I would be freed as some of my co-defendants had been. It was hard not to believe this if one read the papers, brimming over with criticism of Soviet inhumanity and disregarding the fact that the same 'inhuman methods' were still being applied in Yugoslavia. She went to see the British Consuls in Zagreb in the summer of 1952, when they agreed that what was happening to me was excessive. The Consulate officials, including the Consul-General, were kind, yet they said they could do nothing themselves, but would draw the attention of their superiors to my fate. Mother also visited Dr Šubašić. He too said he could do nothing, as did Dr Politeo, a lawyer who had defended Tito when he was sentenced to five years' imprisonment for subversion before the war.

Dr Politeo's answer was the more significant in that he was able to defend Tito properly under 'the blood-stained dictatorship of King Alexander'. Tito had then refused to recognise the Court because he said he recognised only the jurisdiction of the Communist Party: in short, he made a political speech. This contrast did not prevent the Western press from lamenting the fate of Tito and his comrades under the monarchy without ever comparing his fate with what Tito had done after the war. Vernon Bartlett, for instance, wrote that the dictatorship in pre-war Yugoslavia 'was worse than we had ever imagined'. Mrs Eleanor Roosevelt even said, in reviewing Dedijer's *Biography of Tito*, that Communism was the only hope for Yugoslavia.

In September 1952, Anthony Eden was to come to Belgrade. At this juncture, our Communists could no longer claim that their relations were with the British workers' government and therefore of no concern to bourgeois prisoners. My mother wrote a letter signed on behalf of Wives and Mothers in Yugoslavia. In spite of the generous aid of the West she said, there were still people in prison because of their Western leanings. The details were known to the British Consulates, best of all to the consuls who were in the country from 1945 until 1947.

I doubt whether Anthony Eden ever saw my mother's letter but she told me that political prisoners were specifically mentioned during the talks. A little later my mother smuggled letters abroad: our Swiss friends received one and went to see the British Minister in Berne, only to be told that the British could not interfere with the internal affairs of another State.

The next lawyer to come was Stanko Mohorič, a young man of my own age, who from then on loyally supported me and risked much from the unpredictable communist attitude towards lawyers. Lawyers had often been punished for defending their clients instead of helping the Court to convict them. Astonishingly, we were allowed to talk freely in the presence of a guard.

Mohorič thought it best to submit a proposal for 'an extraordinary reduction of sentence', as provided for in the Code of Criminal Procedure, and quoting attenuating circumstances which had come to light after the trial. I drafted the first proposal myself, saying my father had been sentenced and died although not guilty and that my mother had been illegally deprived of most of her personal belongings; and that Marshal Tito himself had admitted that Yugoslav foreign policy was wrong at the time when I was arrested. According to *Dnevnik* of 10 September 1951, he said: 'In our former policy we made the mistake of relying entirely on the Soviet Union....'

The lawyer watered down my draft; he eliminated my mention of the change in foreign policy, instead he referred to my former illness and to the effect it allegedly had on my mind, to the fact that 'during the war I continuously tried to help in bringing about an agreement between anti-occupation forces' and to the death of my father after three years in prison. This application was submitted on 1 November 1952.

During 1952, far-reaching economic reforms were being introduced because the Communists themselves had realised that it was impossible to plan in the teeth of 'objective economic laws'. The play of the free market returned to the economy under the name of 'automatism' or a 'Socialist market' policy. It fell to me to explain the working of 'automatism' to prisoners at the regular cultural meeting in September. A complicated 'affair' followed. Somebody told the Commissar that I was propagating economic liberalism. The Commissar himself did not understand much about this and consulted other prisoners. Nobody found out what the Commissar finally reported to his superiors.

The Court's refusal of my request came at the New Year 1953, and read: 'The proposal for an exceptional reduction of the sentence is not substantiated. The prisoner's acts were among the worst crimes against the people and the State and were so defined also in the new Criminal Code. In view of the importance of these crimes, the Court of Appeal considers that the circumstances enumerated by the prisoner ... would certainly not have been a reason for a milder sentence in the sense of Art. 296 of the Criminal Code. The report from the Ministry of the Interior says that the health of the prisoner is good, that there is no active tuberculosis at present and that he needs medical attention only from time to time. Moreover, the report shows that the prisoner is ill-behaved, that he had to be disciplined three times because of not heeding warnings, that he is, politically, a bitter enemy of our social system and that he persistently criticises our political and social order in the most ruthless terms with the intention of preventing other prisoners from reforming. These circumstances, which prove that the punishment has had no re-educational effect on the prisoner so far, clearly speak against any reduction in sentence.'

So that was that! This was in line with a statement of the leading communist woman, Vida Tomšič, in the autumn of 1952, to the effect that there could be no democracy for the reactionary remnants. And all this time the talk about democracy in Yugoslavia continued unabated in the West. I was livid — the more so as I had read in Tito's biography that Tito refused to apply for parole in old Yugoslavia, claiming that one of its conditions was 're-education', in his view an insult to any political prisoner.

In a letter smuggled to my mother I explained that I was not mad, as she might think reading the decision of the Court, but that I had never been cautioned and that the three disciplinary measures were for two trivial offences and for giving 'swinish' answers to the questionnaire after having been expressly asked for my views. 'I find it outrageous that such nonsense be brought up in a decision of the Supreme Court,' I wrote.

I wondered what influence I could have had on other prisoners apart from the ones in my room. During the walks I much preferred to do gymnastics. My talk about 'automatism' was presumably an example of my attempts to convert people to anti-Communism. I was in good company then; the economic dictator, Kidrič, had recently said: 'The new economic system should be based on objective economic laws and avoid, if possible, the administrative throttling of these laws.'

At the beginning of 1953, the census included a question about religion, and it turned out that between 85% and 90% of people considered themselves members of religious communities. My form was filled in by a prison employee, who asked me: 'Do you believe in God?' I said: 'Yes, I do!' He repeated: 'Do you indeed believe everything about eternal life and all that?' I said: 'Yes, I do.' Since several of us were questioned simultaneously, some of my comrades, no longer quite certain about 'eternal life', heard my answers and followed my lead.

This census was a failure for the Communists, because it showed clearly that a very large part of the population must still be opposed to them after eight years. It was clearly oppression pure and simple to prohibit the celebration of religious holidays, especially making Christmas a working day. Small wonder that prisoners were scandalised at the Anglican Archbishop Fisher attending a reception in Britain, in honour of Marshal Tito. The papal nuncio, too, was present at the celebration of the anniversary of communist Yugoslavia in Paris in 1951.

A new kind of prisoner began turning up by 1953, the so-called economic criminals, people who stole things from enterprises because they could not live on their meagre wages. The Communists never tired of talking about the factories belonging to the people, and were being taken all too literally.

Stalin died in March 1953, but his death did not brighten our prospects. When Tito visited London I felt personally humiliated by his reception there. Churchill said that ideologies could not prevent people being friends, because only deeds counted; as if acts did not spring from ideas, in particular with the Communists.

At about the same time, Labour MPs were bludgeoning Franco, demanding the release of political prisoners. Yugoslav newspapers commented: 'One thing is certain: the entire democratic world should help the suffering Spanish people to free themselves from Fascist fetters, which have been weighing them down for the last fifteen years.' But when it came to American support for emigrants from satellite countries they protested, because the Yugoslav Communists obviously did not wish these countries to cease being communist, but at best wanted them to become independent of Moscow.

Britons who had figured in my trial now came to Yugoslavia and earned different descriptions: John Gibbs, then a 'major spy', came as a BBC reporter to tape-record 'big construction sites, factories and co-operatives', and Seton-Watson, the 'dangerous agent' of my interrogation, turned out to be a 'pioneer of Yugoslav-British rapprochement'.

Kidrič, the economic dictator, died in April. As his funeral was broadcast, tears came rolling down the face of the good Spindler, of a touching communist faith. Kidrič was Prime Minister of Slovenia during the 'liquidation' of tens of thousands of people. His wife was chief of the Secret Police, which included murder squads, during the war. In his funeral oration, Tito claimed that Kidrič had 'burnt himself out working'. I reflected that had he worked less the economy might have been in a better shape.

In the autumn of 1952, my mother tried writing directly to Marshal Tito asking him to intervene for me. An answer came from the Ministry of the Interior of Slovenia, advising that we should apply for a revision of the trial if we considered there had been illegalities. Theory was another matter: a much-advertised article about socialist ethics appeared claiming that Lenin's moral precepts (e.g. anything is good if it leads to Communism) were 'one-sided'. The writer advocated tolerance and stressed that the differences between Yugoslavia and the Soviet Union lay not in their beliefs but in the way they were implemented. The hypocrisy of it was enough to drive one mad. Another example came to light again at the same time: the declaration of Tito's National Committee of August 1944, denying that its aim was 'the establishment of Communism as falsely claimed by our enemies'. So the Titoists had brazenly contradicted themselves, persecuting people for opposing something they themselves said they did not want. They publicly declared themselves in favour of Communism only in 1948, after I had been in prison for a year.

The provocation to go for revision was grave, but the Communists probably thought that we would not dare try. The Commissar effectively warned me off in March 1953: 'Why do you want a revision?' 'I am still in prison in spite of all that has changed in the country,' I said. 'Oh, oh, don't be so naïve. You know very well that things are decided here rather than in courts.'

I refused to be frightened into submission, and my mother went to Belgrade with an application for the revision of my father's trial and mine. My lawyer had enumerated irregularities committed by the Court, pointing out its wrong conclusions and citing witnesses and other evidence. My mother was received courteously by the Federal People's Prosecutor, but his Slovene aide dismissed her with: 'What do you expect? All these people are spies. They also collaborated with the enemy during the war.' I was upset and thought it was time to show I was not forsaken by everybody. My mother wrote to the British, American and French Consulates in Zagreb and asked for affidavits from my friends, explaining that my contacts with them were entirely normal. I also decided to expand some points in the application and sent more data to my lawyer. By then I had come into the open and sent the two letters through the Commissar.

The Federal Public Prosecutor was about to leave for a session of the UN Commission for Human Rights just then and I was again shocked at communist hypocrisy, when he stated that Yugoslavia was firmly in favour of these rights and of international control of their implementation. Yet my lawyer was not allowed to see my file at the Supreme Court although Yugoslav law expressly entitled him to.

We did not have to wait long for the decision. It read that 'no reason or legal argument could be found for opening fresh proceedings in the case of prisoner Ljubo Sirc'. In these three lines they dismissed two applications, one of eight pages and one of six pages of arguments.

Meanwhile the affidavits of my British friends arrived, but there was no answer to my mother's request for statements from the Americans and the French. The affidavits asserted that 'our relations were of a purely social character', and had formally passed through the British Foreign Office and the Yugoslav Embassy in London. Despite this, my mother did not have the courage to submit them to the authorities, as she had heard rumours that highly placed persons were outraged by my impertinence.

One letter she did enclose in her next application was from Anneliese, a German woman I had known in Perugia during the war. She was prompted to write as she had come across Professor Furlan's daughter in the United States in the forties. Anneliese was appalled to hear that I was in prison, since she remembered me as an ardent patriot, eager for my country's liberation. Her letter did not help either.

In mid-1953, I was summoned to the Commissar who — to my surprise — was beaming with benevolence. He informed me — to my no smaller surprise — that my father had not been released because he was dying, but because he had a positive view 'of our reality' — the usual jargon for the communist régime. He suggested that I should follow my father's example and picked on my claim that I was a liberal: 'If you are such a good liberal, you should help us in our struggle against clericalism.' When he noticed that I found this understanding of liberalism odd, he went on: 'You must help us in some way. We want to re-educate you and re-education means acts not simply words. You know this perfectly well, but you cynically pretend not to understand.'

I was not in prison for any particular reason, he explained, but because I was 'an enemy of the people'. My 'ideology' made me hate Communism although I could have had a successful career under the present régime had I been more amenable.

In the end Kragelj asked me to write yet another *vita* and explain what motives had set me against the Communists. Again, I threw caution to the winds and wrote openly about the development of my ideas, almost as in this book. I blamed the Yugoslav Communists for their biased collaboration with Stalin and described my fears that Yugoslavia would become involved in a war against the West on the Soviet side, one the Communists could not but lose. Whether my views were right or wrong, I remarked, was another question, but they were most certainly not criminal. I concluded that I hoped frankness would pay. The Commissar accepted my 24 pages but said nothing, which I considered a good sign.

Not for long. Spindler and I were seen separately and confronted with the accusation that we had smuggled letters out of prison. A ridiculously light punishment was followed by the prison governor sending us to the bunker for a fortnight for this 'swinish thing'.

So down we went to the cellar where we were locked up in two separate cells. The bunker was unpleasant, but my real worry was that this affair had spoiled my chances of being released in the November 1953 amnesty. I asked to see the Commissar and started talking eagerly: 'You must not be surprised that I smuggled letters; how else could I have told my mother what had happened during the trial?' He shook his head: 'You must not hope that we shall set you free as long as your mother sends letters of protest abroad.' The police had found my mother's appeal to friends in a train bound for Austria. A relative travelling abroad took my mother's message, unscrewed a plate in the WC on the train, hid the paper behind it and replaced it. When the train had reached Austria, the relative wanted to take the letter out, but it had disappeared.

A few days later, my mother was called to the police headquarters in Ljubljana. She was shown into an empty room and, when she turned round, two soldiers were standing there with tommy-guns pointed at her. My mother reacted violently by screaming and shouting: 'You have murdered my husband. You have taken all we had. You are still keeping my son in prison. You have done to us every evil you could. And you still won't leave us alone.' Everybody fell silent and after a while she was allowed to go.

A new Code on Criminal Procedure was adopted in September 1953. Hopes ran high because the new provisions were rumoured most humane and advanced and also opened the possibility for the Supreme Court to decide on the revision of trials, but, alas, only of those concluded after 1 January 1954. Another hope gone.

Yet the chances that I might be released still seemed fairly good. On my autobiographical notes, the Commissar commented: 'We knew little about the West, so that some mistakes were inevitable. Also we were fighting for our lives. What is important is that we have stopped using terror. Had we not, we would have lost everything.'

The exchanges ended with repeated advice that I should, since I was a liberal, help the Communists to fight clericalism. The Secret Policeman 'reponsible for the priests' wanted me to persuade Dr Lenič to be more co-operative. In his turn, Dr Lenič was put under pressure to talk Bishop Volk into being more conciliatory, when he, Dr Lenič, was released.

Both Dr Lenič and I thought the interest the Commissars were taking in us was a good sign. These dreams came to an abrupt end when, late one evening in mid-October 1953, we heard a procession shouting: 'Long live Trieste! Down with England! Down with America!'

The next day the papers reported that the British and the Americans intended to hand Trieste to the Italians. To prevent any repercussions on me, I wrote a letter of protest to the British Consulate in Zagreb. The Commissar refused to forward it, saying it would only make matters worse.

The Communists had every intention of turning the Trieste problem into a weapon against so-called 'internal enemies'. As it raised the nationalist feelings of many Slovenes, it would help the Communists put the blame for the loss of Trieste on their opponents. Professor Furlan, living in a little town up the Sava valley, was attacked by a mob raised by the police. Shouting 'Furlan and his English friends have sold Trieste to the Italians' they put him in a wheelbarrow and nearly wheeled him into the river, but his wife very courageously stopped them.

'Have you heard what happened to Furlan?' mused the Commissar. 'You had better be on good terms with us lest something similar happens to you.'

In prison, the priests were manoeuvred into a very awkward situation. Many Catholic prisoners were promised lenient treatment (the annual amnesty was two months away) if they claimed that it was the Pope who wanted Trieste to become Italian. Anybody asking whether this was true was shouted down. Then a resolution condemning the Pope was drawn up and the priests were asked to sign it. They refused, with one or two exceptions, and were pilloried as traitors.

Spindler in his naïveté disclosed the secret hopes of the Communists. 'What we want you to do', he explained to Dr Lenič, 'is to sever relations with Rome and establish a national Church.' Deprived of their international link, the Catholics would be toys in Communist hands.

The method for breaking prisoners was to encourage their hopes for an amnesty, let them have a breakdown when these hopes failed, and then make other promises – and also demands for 'co-operation' – when their morale reached the lowest point.

The Commissar asked me to write about 'unresolved questions' between myself and the people's authority, which I took to mean such things as my mother's belongings' being taken from her. The Commissar told me that what they were interested in was the unresolved question of my future 'co-operation' with them. Dr Lenič and I were asked to translate Pattee's *The Case of Cardinal Stepinac* by the end of November, the usual time for an amnesty.

On the actual day, we were all nervously sitting around, but nothing happened until five o'clock in the afternoon. Then only one of our room-mates was called out with his belongings. The consolation was that he was Mr Matelic, one of the nicest men I have ever met. That night nobody slept, since it is difficult to accept after years in prison that there is no hope of an early end to the torture.

What incensed me most was the communiqué in the press: 'Full amnesty was not granted to those who, during our national revolution, participated in the killing of our citizens.' I asked the Commissar whom I had killed or helped to kill. 'Don't be so pernickety,' he riposted. 'Do you want us to say: "Full amnesty was not granted to those who, during our national revolution, participated in the killing of our citizens and to Ljubo Sirc?"'

'You see,' he continued, 'we must keep you in prison because you are intelligent and you are an enemy. Therefore we cannot be satisfied with statements only. We want acts.' 'What kind of acts?' I interrupted. 'What kind of acts! Don't play the innocent! We are a secret service and you know very well what secret services are interested in!'

A few days after the amnesty I was happy to hear Spindler called out of our room with his belongings. We caught sight of other prisoners, including my uncle, Captain Pirc, standing in the corridor waiting to be released on parole. The guard let me step out and shake hands with him.

A new prisoner joined us in December, a member of the Communist Police. The Commissar had told me prison was a terrible nervous strain on him, could I and my fellow prisoners help? A tall chap with roaming eyes and obviously very ill at ease walked into our room. Some capricious higher authority insisted that he be put with us, although he had fought this order tooth and nail for fear he would meet people he had sent to jail. And he considered it beneath his communist dignity to be with political prisoners. He was an UDBA Major whose girl had married a higher-ranking UDBA man. He had denounced the husband as a Gestapo collaborator, but the husband had him sentenced to six years in prison for abusing his official position.

Most political prisoners were moved after this to the new prison at the castle of Ig, not far from Ljubljana. Ten other prisoners, mainly priests, were waiting in our room. It was clean, and the view from its windows simply wonderful with the Krim mountain near Ljubljana covered with pine forests, and high mountains in the distance.

The main topic of the moment was the articles by the Vice-President of Yugoslavia, the 'crown-prince' Milovan Djilas, in the party paper *Borba*. Djilas came out for real democracy and against discrimination of the type which says: 'The law rules supreme in Yugoslavia, but there can be no law for our enemies.' In my view, the articles were somewhat confused and at times it was far from clear what Djilas meant, probably the effect of his Marxian training, and possibly also of his reluctance to offend his comrades.

The Secret Police major stood between two beds and mused: 'We shall have to learn everything from scratch when we come out if it continues like this!' The Communists were all called to see the Commissar, and when they returned, they stated one after another: 'Djilas' theses are all wrong.'

Soon we were listening to the trial of Djilas by the Central Committee of the Communist Party. It was sad to hear Djilas' former friends and comrades attacking him, one after another, for having taken the slogans about equality and legality seriously. Djilas at first appeared to resist, then caved in. Many were shocked by his behaviour, but they probably did not realise what it meant to stand alone, confronted by a body of former friends criticising you in the name of ideas you had ardently believed in yourself not so long ago. As a former Communist pointed out to me, Djilas was probably also aware that he had gone too far and that his head was at stake if he did not 'repent'. His expulsion from the Central Committee killed off any possibility for real democracy in Yugoslavia, if one had ever existed. It was a refusal to recognise that the Party leaders were mortals like anybody else, and a restatement of the dogma that they, and only they, knew 'what is necessary for the happiness or mankind' or in this case at least, of the Yugoslavs.

But 'liberal' Communism was to continue. This brand of Communism shares with Stalinism the conceited idea that communist leaders are so much 'wiser' than ordinary mortals that they have to be their 'teachers'. The enforcement of their 'teachings' was milder because the population was restive, and this persuaded the Communists they had to change tack if an explosion was to be avoided. They also realised that their grip on the country could be relaxed without any danger to the party. As for allowing other parties, the leaders maintained that another party in Yugoslavia would be anomalous, because there was no party, as such, in the country since they had renamed the Communist Party of Yugoslavia the League of Yugoslav Communists.

At the beginning of 1954, the Commissar suggested I should submit a new application for extraordinary reduction of sentence, and seemed to approve of my draft. I sent a copy to my mother to comfort her since her life was becoming more and more difficult. I often wondered how she managed to make ends meet and send me parcels, about which I felt very guilty.

The Commissars were aware of my state of mind and tried to push me into collaboration. I was asked to give reviews of foreign political events, intended to force me to toe the communist line. I somehow succeeded in keeping out of trouble; at least the prisoners never accused me of making communist propaganda. The lectures were to encourage the discussion of political matters and induce prisoners to vent their real views. Once I heard the 'prison educator' giving orders to the 'chief librarian' to take notes on what prisoners said during the debate.

Very appropriately, on 13 May 1954, we celebrated the tenth anniversary of Tito's Communist Police, which was then called the UDB-Administration of State Security. Its earlier names were Army of State Security and Department of People's Defence (OZNA). To mark the happy occasion, we prisoners had an extra goulash and were 'free' for the day, that is, we sat in a circle in the inner court and husked switches for the basket-making workshop, which was what we had to do 'voluntarily' on all 'free' days.

The anniversary was also marked by awarding the Order of People's Hero to several men who had killed 'enemies', mainly political opponents of the Communists, during the war by attacking them in the streets. This was a very bad sign, because it indicated that the Communists, far from being ashamed of their terrorist methods, were holding back only for the time being.

I translated my last book in prison, *Assessment of Men*, a study on recruiting for the US Intelligence Service. Earlier books about coding were followed by a whole series of American college handbooks on psychological adjustment. I had translated the Interpol warrants of arrest for years.

At some stage we got émigré newspapers, and in 1954 a full translation of *The Conspiracy of Silence* by Weissberg-Czybulski found its way into the prison library. To nobody's surprise, the administration at first tried to prevent us from reading this account of events in the Soviet Union during Stalin's purges. When I did read it, I had the impression that I was reading about what happened to me, and I expect others did too.

The Court rejected my application at the end of February 1954, saying that the objective and subjective state was no different from that established in the judgement. I fumed, under the impression that the Commissar was pulling my leg. Without delay, I prepared an appeal to the Supreme Court in Belgrade, but the Commissar said that I should not insist on their forwarding it because my application had been sent to the Executive Council in Belgrade for a full amnesty. An amnesty was apparently a much better answer than any court ruling. There were obviously mistakes in my judgement, as Kragelj had intimated before. He said the decision would take two to three months, so I withdrew my appeal.

I could imagine my mother's feelings on hearing my application had been rejected. As far back as 1951 she had said: 'This is a fate worse than death!' In the meantime she had become more tired, contracted asthma and run short of money. My grandmother would pay me one visit a year, usually in August. In

1954 she was too ill to come, and died a month later aged 84. My mother wanted me to come to the funeral, but the request was rejected, and I did not want to go anyway.

Dr Ljuba Prenner, a woman lawyer from Ljubljana who was working on my case together with Stanko Mohorič, also came. She was a courageous woman who had herself spent a long time in prison. But neither she nor anyone else could do anything. In the summer I was visited by my father's cousin, Vinko Franchetti, the brother of Lado whom the Communists killed after having called him up in Split. Both were sailors and Vinko somehow finished up in Monaco, so I insisted on seeing him because I thought foreign visitors helped.

For years my mother had been looking out for a chance to approach Marshal Tito and speak to him personally. This was in line with the popular belief that dictators are much better than their régimes and that they do not know what is going on. Therefore just a few words of explanation should be enough for the dictator to correct the wrong. In the autumn of 1954 my mother almost succeeded in speaking to Tito, in a café in Kranj. She approached his table, but when she began speaking, Tito looked at her with his cold eyes of steel, and somebody next to him got up and led her away. It was Jože Vilfan, Tito's Secretary-General. He took my mother by the hand, led her out and said: 'You must not disturb the President. He is on holiday.'

It was now three years since Minister Ranković had made his famous speech about mistakes in the administration of justice. My patience ran out, and I wrote again to Commissar Kragelj at the end of September. 'I could understand the way I was treated in 1947, but I am unable to understand it now,' I wrote. 'Imagine those extremists who, in 1944, advised me not to go back, laughing not only at me, but also at the people's authorities; they are free, while I have spent almost eight years in prison.'

I enclosed letters for the Slovene Secretary of the Interior, Mitja Ribičič, and Jože Vilfan. I stressed that I had often been warned not to refer to legal provisions and not to demand that the rule of law be observed, because this would only harm me. I could not accept these warnings because if I did I would have to believe that the top Yugoslav leaders who often spoke about legality were ordinary liars. I never had an answer.

The decision of the Federal Executive Council arrived, signed by the police boss Ranković, at the beginning of October; my sentence had been reduced from 20 years' to 15 years' imprisonment. This was a mockery and a very bad sign, since I could hardly expect that after this reduction I would be included in the amnesty due not quite two months later. My mother was desperate. Up till then the answer to my requests used to be that the superior authorities could do nothing because of bad reports from the prison administration. When the former Chairman of the Federal People's Assembly, Dr Ribar, talked about me to the communist leader Moša Pijade, he was told: 'What can I do! The prison administration reports about Sirc are so bad.' In 1954, the prison administration seemed to support my application – and the result was the same.

Before I was handed the decision I had seen Kragelj, who said he had come to Ig especially to talk to me, and was most friendly. He explained at some length that my contacts abroad could be very useful to the State. Kragelj implied that I should renew these connections and 'advise Yugoslav authorities on foreigners' opinions'. He wanted me to draft a project on this task, with a list of my foreign friends and acquaintances.

My first impulse was to refuse, as I saw they wanted to get me on a slippery slope and eventually make me a regular agent. On reflection, I decided the task could be useful, as it would enable me to see foreign representatives without difficulty. I drafted a letter, claiming that it was odd to ask somebody imprisoned because of friendship with foreigners to renew his good relations, but if I could be certain that there was no danger of going to prison again I was 'ready to take up my social relations with foreigners and to draw the attention of the Yugoslav authorities to their impressions and reactions regarding Yugoslav policy in the same way as, for instance, British Labour Party members inform the British government about foreigners' opinions.' Then I listed my acquaintances abroad.

'On the other hand', I added, 'I am in no way ready to do anything which would in any way suggest intelligence, agentship, provocation etc.' I went on: 'For this reason, I would also wish to deal in the sense of this letter with some political rather than an intelligence body, so that there could be no mistake about the nature of my advice.'

I did not wish either to be bound by anything but the law, and my reports should be entirely voluntary. Further on, I said: 'It is impossible for me to be disloyal towards my personal friends, and to get out of them things they would otherwise not be ready to tell by means of tricks. If one desires good relations and friendly contact with foreigners, one must be sincere oneself.' I concluded that it would be better to discuss this matter after my release, since Kragelj anyway said that it was in no way related to it.

Kragelj arrived a few days later and said: 'That won't do, Sirc. I am quite willing to accept your letter as it is, however I cannot take it to the Secretary of the Interior, Ribičič. He would be angry.' Kragelj advised me to write a humbler letter and suggested some additional points. Uncertain as to whether these suggestions were conditions for my release, I preferred to fall into line and leave second thoughts for later. I repeated the passage about British Labour members but I dropped the point about not wanting to have anything to do with intelligence organs. At Kragelj's express demand I added: 'I am ready to bring to the attention of the authorities the opinions of émigrés learnt from any correspondence to them. I emphasise that I do not desire to cause personal mischief to anybody.'

Kragelj also asked me to insert: 'If, by chance, I should learn anything about some spy or other criminal, I shall feel obliged to denounce him.' I insisted that my warnings should be entirely voluntary, but had to drop the condition that I should feel bound only by the law. Kragelj now seemed satisfied.

A few days before the anniversary of the Republic, on 29 November, he came again and told me that I would be set free. 'First have a good rest,' he said. 'After about a month, come to see me. Just ring me up before you come. My telephone number is 21–405. I work at the villa in Župančičeva 11.'

I hardly slept a wink on my last night, nor did anyone else.

On 28 November 1954, we were taken out of our room early and were thus spared hours of anxious waiting. As I walked out, I felt like an actor on the stage with everybody looking on. I could shake hands only with the nearest. When the freedom candidates were herded in the hall, almost all our old friends were there, but only one priest.

Finally the 'educator', Kebe, made a little speech, told us how grateful we should be to people's authorities for their clemency and asked us to sign a resolution of thanks. I did not feel the slightest gratitude to people who had held me in prison for seven and a half years, and simply passed the resolution on. So did a few of my friends.

At dusk the trucks rolled through the main gate and sped over the moor of Ljubljana towards the town. We were unloaded behind the railway station and dispersed without much ado. I dragged my two bundles to the house of Dr Žirovnik but, unaccustomed to shoes, I developed blisters over those few hundred yards. Although my relatives were not expecting me, a crowd assembled within half an hour to celebrate my returning. Somebody telephoned to tell my mother and she came at once by taxi.

In Kranj, relatives and neighbours were also assembled at my grandparents' house, since our own had been confiscated. I could not sleep for the first few nights, but talked and talked with my mother till I was struck by the fear that there might be microphones in the wall common with the next house.

Towards the end of December 1954, I went to see Commissar Kragelj at the villa in Župančičeva 11. A board gave it as a department of the Secretariat of the Interior, Administration of Border Traffic and Foreigners: quite obviously the headquarters of the intelligence service for abroad. Nothing much transpired. When I said I was ready to visit foreigners in Zagreb and Belgrade, he advised postponing it somewhat so as not to arouse suspicion.

Apart from trying to obtain compensation for my mother's illegally confiscated property, I had to do something to earn my living. I found some translation work, but difficulties soon cropped up. I was offered the job of translating tracts on agriculture from the Danish, and hastily started acquiring a working knowledge of the language, but I heard no more. It occurred to me that the member of the delegation who had brought them from Denmark belonged to the Slovene Union of Agricultural Co-operatives. Its president was Viktor Avbelj, the public prosecutor at my trial.

On another occasion, I was to accompany a group of American sales experts, serving as interpreter and translator of their lectures. Nothing came of it. The employee responsible for the arrangement telephoned in my presence to the Secretary of the Slovene Chamber of Commerce. I could hear what the man on the other end was saying. 'What, Sirc?' he said. 'No, no work for Sirc. He is guilty that his father died in prison.' This secretary was one of the leading officials in the Ministry of Industry when my father worked there. Therefore he should have known better. Other former colleagues of my father's were not of the same opinion, as I could feel from the way they shook hands with me in the streets.

I visited several Western consulates and embassies at the end of January 1955. Everywhere I showed officials translations of the letters I had to sign before being released. The counsellor of one embassy accompanied me to the door and said: 'Thank you for being so decent!' It was not as smooth everywhere though. Consul X would not give me an introduction to Consul Y who did not want to receive me. 'How could I give you an introduction after you have told me that you have signed an obligation to co-operate with the Communist Police?' he said. I too had misgivings and was very cautious. Often foreign officials caused great difficulties for local people; either they were careless or they preferred being on friendly terms with communist authorities to protecting the vital interests of their fellow-democrats living under Communism.

In May 1955, I had just come out of an embassy and was walking along a street in Belgrade, when I noticed three men in Soviet NKVD uniform with a civilian. A bare month later, the Soviet 'collective leadership' in the persons of Kruschev, Bulganin and Mikoyan visited Yugoslavia. I saw them as they drove through Ljubljana on their way to Bled. The citizens were ordered to give them a very cool reception, but our hearts froze. What did this visit mean?

When I saw Kragelj next, he lectured me on the clumsiness of Kruschev. 'He got drunk at Bled,' he said, 'and talked about the atomic bomb. He told the people around that it was a splendid weapon and that it would do no harm to drop one on somebody one day.' A few weeks later, Kragelj said casually to a friend of mind: 'Everything is not as black in the Soviet Union as it is often said. Their technical achievements are wonderful.' What Kragelj said only reflected the words of his chief, Kraigher. The rapprochement with the Soviet Union was well under way.

When I saw that translations would not keep me, I began looking for a permanent post, but this also proved difficult. The newly-founded Economic Institute of Slovenia was looking for a research worker, but I was told that all the posts were taken. In a law library, I was given to understand that it would harm them and me if they proposed me for employment there. I thought that these two cases were perhaps exceptions. However, I became suspicious when the same thing happened again. A friend of my father's approached the director of a textile export firm, a Communist. The director said he would like to employ me; however, a few days later he said that 'his superiors' had told him he could not give a job to Sirc. I was not employable by a firm importing pharmaceutical goods either. Eventually I applied for the post of law *rapporteur* with the Chamber of Commerce in Kranj. (The latest development was that there was a Chamber of Commerce in every town.) The secretary was willing but his superiors would not have it.

I received a curious letter from Kragelj in September 1955: he had been informed that I had applied for a job with the power network administration in Novo Mesto – I had never done anything of the kind. He went on that he had approved. 'However', he wrote, 'I believe that Novo Mesto is a little bit out of the way.' He asked me to see him and suggested that I should take a job in Koper on the border near Trieste. 'There an occasion will soon crop up for you to go at least as far as Trieste', he concluded.

What was he after? Did they want to send me abroad to do some dirty work for them after having duly compromised me? The next time I saw Kragelj, he said little about Koper, but began questioning me about my former fellow-prisoners, among them Professor Furlan. It was high time for me to clear out.

11

Postscript: Uphill struggle in freedom

On 1 November 1955, I escaped from Yugoslavia to Italy over the snow-covered hills, and made my way to Rome via Udine and Venice. With me was a former fellow-prisoner, Stanko Kamenšček, an Air-Force officer. A native of the Slovene-settled territory under Italy before the war, he had had trouble with the fascist authorities and there was some danger that he might be imprisoned if he stayed in Italy. So a Slovene priest and I accompanied him to the French border above Menton where he crossed into France without difficulty.

Before Stanko left, we had both been to the British and United States Embassies where we were promised support provided we could regulate our status with the Italians. Now I was on my own, but the Italian authorities in Rome still began behaving in a nationalistic way, which I found inexplicable because I had persuaded myself in prison that the whole of Western Europe stood solid *vis-à-vis* Communism. It needed six months of combined efforts by my father's war-time lawyer Avv. Salvatore Mastracchi-Manes, the Slovene priest in Rome, Monsignor Robič, the Swiss representative of the UN Commissioner for Refugees and the British to get me an Italian travel document for refugees. The Roman bureaucrats claimed I was a British spy and that the British should look after me. The least kind part of this prevarication was that the Italian authorities uncritically took over the communist Court's description of my doings. From what Avv. Mastracchi-Manes told me, they took particular exception to my having gone to the British Embassy before reporting to the Italian authorities, and calmed down only when he said that it was on his insistence that I had been to the British first.

While waiting for the Italian document, I was shooed off to Perugia, which was rather sad in the winter months. I lived on money supplied by my good friends and sometimes also by the lawyer. This borrowing was possible because I hoped that I would get at least the money my father had paid for Turkish cotton in 1941. It was deposited in a Swiss bank because the Turks could not deliver the cotton. With the help of a Swiss lawyer, I found the money and was paid 60% of the amount (100,000 Swiss francs) while the Turkish suppliers kept 40%. The Soviet foreign trade authorities had also deposited the dollars paid for the cotton they could not deliver (because of the war) in an American bank, but the Americans did not return it to the owners: they handed it over to the Yugoslav Communists.

By the time I was paid the money in Switzerland I could go there on an Italian travel document, but I still could not go to Britain because I had no British visa. It took me quite a few months to obtain one. I chose Britain as my final destination not only because I had forged some links with this country and I thought very well of it, but also because I had a second cousin, Elsie Sirc, in London. She was the daughter of a great-uncle, my father's uncle Louis who, in the time of the great European migrations West, had left via Trieste for the Canary Islands (of all places), met an Englishwoman there, married her and settled in London. Elsie guaranteed my upkeep and provided all sorts of documents, but such was the fear of excessive immigration then that it still took an inordinate time for me to reach London. I got there in September 1956.

In between, I wandered around Europe on temporary visas, except in Western Germany, which had abolished visas for refugees. In Paris, I met a largish group of Yugoslav exiles of my own age. They invited me to dinner so that I could give them a run-down of the situation in Yugoslavia. They were visibly perplexed when I explained that Socialism does not work and that the economy is conducted, in spite of self-management or, better, because of self-management, along lines which must end in disaster. Later I was told that quite a few of my newly found friends thought that I must have been so blinded by my hatred for the Titoists that I was no longer able to talk sense.

A prominent Yugoslav living in London, Vane Ivanović, arranged for me to meet John Hughes at the Ritz Hotel in Paris. He was the Chairman of the Free Europe Committee, a semi-official American organisation for the area. We had a very interesting discussion, but by then the US State Department no longer considered Yugoslavia a communist State in the sense that it was part of the international communist conspiracy, so exiles from there were of no great interest.

In the end I reached London, stayed with Elsie in her house at a pleasant park near Lewisham and began looking for a job. Surprisingly fast I was appointed Serbo-Croat and Russian monitor at the BBC Monitoring Service in Reading. After a spell of one and a half years there, I was happy to leave. My knowledge of English turned out to be less good than I myself had imagined, but I also found some of the criteria for worthwhile news funny, no doubt because I thought I knew more about Communism and Titoism than the news bosses in Reading.

It was a relief when my young Swiss friend, Vincent, invited me to Switzerland to complete my doctorate in economics and promised to finance my studies. To my amazement, I was invited to an office in London and told they would have to deprive me of the British travel document I had acquired in the meantime, if I did not intend to stay in Britain and work. In the end, they let me go and keep it.

The University of Fribourg was where I had spent a semester during the war, and I returned there. I chose to work on a dissertation on the policy of economic development in communist Yugoslavia, and I had some difficulty in finding a supervisor. The Fribourg professors, for obvious reasons, did not know much about the subject. This, however, did not prevent one of them, a Catholic Marxist, from objecting to my criticism of Marx in my first essay. Fortunately, he was never asked to mark anything of mine again, and I ploughed on, mostly arranging material I had collected by patiently reading communist newspapers over my years in prison. There were objections that this was not a scientific approach, that I should quote serious studies rather than newspapers, so that I had some difficulty in explaining that communist contradictions showed up most clearly in articles written from a short-term point of view. No attempt was made at hiding there, whereas in scholarly papers concealment was much easier. There was a lot of trouble for me in various seminars, where quite a few students reacted unpleasantly to critical views on Socialism. Probably I established myself by passing my oral doctorate examination *summa cum laude,* so I was able to carry on my writing with more assurance.

By then my mother had joined me. She had come in 1957 and 1958 for a short time only. For journeying to Britain she had almost as much trouble obtaining a British visa as with her Yugoslav passport. What she had to say on her arrival in Switzerland was alarming. Somehow, the secret police in Slovenia had found out that Western authorities were frequently rather unpleasant to me and had moved to make use of this. My mother was told that I could easily be issued with a Yugoslav passport if I was prepared to return to the agreement stipulated before my release from prison. It did not require much imagination to see that they could compromise me, even without my consenting to anything, in the eyes of the Swiss and the British. I hastily reported the messages to the Swiss police and to the British Embassy in Berne.

Then I settled down to writing my thesis, with my mother acting as an almost over-zealous typist and cook. We lived in a small one-room flat overflowing with paper in the Grand' Rue. I was in such a hurry to finish that I gave notice for the flat much too early. So we spent quite a while in a Murten lake cottage belonging to my Swiss friends. The document was finally handed over to the University authorities, and we departed for London.

Before I had finished my studies, I was offered a post by the Paderewski Foundation in New York, a subsidiary of the Free Europe Committee. I would be paid to go to East Bengal, East Pakistan as it then was, to teach economics at Notre Dame college, affiliated to Dacca University and run by American Holy Cross Fathers. I was looking forward to this experience.

I felt very happy among my Bengali students and among the Holy Cross priests. I lived with them until moving to a house along the Elephant Road in the suburbs. The man who was the principal of our College, Father Ganguly, soon became the first Bengali bishop. This gave me the additional advantage of inheriting his bicycle. Professor M.N. Huda, later Minister of Finance, invited me to teach international economics at the University proper. I was delighted when I had a chance to do Notre Dame College a good turn. It so happened that I knew the then West German Minister of Overseas Aid, Walter Scheel, later President of the Federal Republic, from the Liberal International. I wrote to him about the work of the Holy Cross Fathers and how greatly it had impressed me. As a result of this testimony, and, no doubt, some investigation by the Germans themselves, the College was given 1 million marks which it put to good use and to the eventual benefit of Bengali Moslem students.

The Pakistani government was staunchly anti-communist during my time there. I myself was eyed with suspicion by the police until I showed them reports on my death sentence in *The Times*. Then the President of Pakistan, Ayub Khan, stopped in Belgrade on his way to West Germany, and the Yugoslav Communists charmed him into believing that they had discovered the final answers to all the ills of underdevelopment. Till then, all printed matter in Serbo-Croat or Slovene had been disappearing – I had received few of the Yugoslav newspapers to which my mother had subscribed for me. Now delegations were coming from and going to Yugoslavia. Talk was rife about how Bengali agriculture had to be 'mechanised' and organised in co-operatives just as in Yugoslavia. This was, of course, sheer nonsense, which I tried to explain in an article in the *Pakistan Economic Journal* describing the abysmal failure of Yugoslav agriculture under Communism.

For specific Bengali reasons the failure there of these methods would have been even worse. Fortunately, the Bengali experts, especially M.N. Huda, soon recognised this and stopped listening to Titoist advice.

When I returned to London I wrote a longish article about the harmful influence of Titoism on Pakistani agriculture, but nobody would publish it in English; it was printed in German by the Swiss East-Institute in Berne, directed by Dr Peter Sager who became a good friend. While still in Dacca, I was particularly assailed for my views on development by two American experts from Harvard, advisers to the Pakistani government. They told me I should study Paul Baran, an American Marxist, if I wanted to understand the problem of economic progress.

My stay in Asia had two highlights: my visit to Rangoon for Christmas and another to Nepal for Easter. In Burma I was impressed by the friendliness of the Burmese and saddened by a group of visiting Chinese, all dressed up in Soviet-type uniforms. I went to Kathmandu at the invitation of Sir Leonard and Lady Scopes, friends from Ljubljana days. Sir Leonard was now British Ambassador in Kathmandu. They told me I had just missed a Yugoslav Himalayan expedition led by Stane Kersnik, my former assistant prison governor.

After a year in Dacca, I was invited to stay for another year. I would have liked to stay, but was afraid that I would have trouble finding a permanent job in Europe if I delayed my return much longer. I felt somewhat out of my depth and there was nobody to guide me. I worked at replacement jobs at the BBC Foreign Services in Bush House, but that could not last beyond the end of the summer. It seemed that I was about to miss all boats and I seriously considered becoming a tourist guide.

In prison, I had once translated an article from *Encounter* for the Secret Police and my eye had been caught by another piece written by Salvador de Madariaga. It was an enormous encouragement for me; although I no longer remembered what it said, I was determined to find the author when I was free in the West and I did. He sent me to John McCullum-Scott, the Secretary-General of the Liberal International, which started my long association with this organisation. The first conference I attended was the 1957 one in Oxford.

It was my considered opinion that it was nonsensical for Yugoslavia to tackle its problems by inventing specific solutions. I thought it should align itself with Western European political currents, represented at the time by the Socialist, Liberal and Christian-Democratic Internationals. They had a lot in common, of course and, in my view, should have co-operated in many respects, but my own choice was the liberals.

A natural consequence was to form a Yugoslav group, which made me turn to two new friends I had made during my studies. Adil Zulfikarpašić lived in Fribourg. He had come from Austria after leaving Yugoslavia in 1946 because he could no longer stand the behaviour of his communist comrades. Although a scion of a Bosnian aristocratic family, he became a Communist in high school, spent a horrific year in a Ustashi jail and, after he had been exchanged for captured Pavelić officials, became the Commissar of a partisan division. Vlado Predavec had been on the opposite side, one of the few Croats in the headquarters of Draža Mihailović. His father, a leader of the Croat Peasant Party, had died before the war. There existed also an East European Peasant International, but I thought there was no future in this as the number of peasants in all countries was shrinking fast.

Vlado, Adil and I organised a Federation of Liberals from Yugoslavia, and we joined the Committee of Liberal Exiles within the Liberal International presided over by Salvador de Madariaga. Prominent members included the Czech, Hubert Ripka, the Romanian Gafencu and the Polish Count Edward Raczynski. We hoped that many more Yugoslav exiles would join us, but too many could never make up their minds where they belonged. Of the Serbs, only Nenad Petrović came.

The core of the Liberal International in the 1960s consisted of politicians with clear views on political matters, including Communism. Some of the liberal parties had less acceptable views, but this is bound to happen in any large organisation. The most typical of the parties soft on Communism was the Danish Radical Venstre. It was led by Hermod Lannung who, as a young attaché at the

Danish Legation in Russia, had known Lenin and thought that because of this the Communists had a soft spot for him. The likeable old man sometimes drove me mad. Some of the British liberals were so much enamoured of Tito that one of them told me I did not represent anybody, since Yugoslavia was truly represented only by him. Certain high-ranking Liberal Party members were inclined to share this view. Adil and I had a heated discussion with one of them, whom I heard again giving vent to his enthusiasm for communist planning, even at the end of the 1960s.

In 1961 I was in London with no job. Fortunately, many of the leading members of the Liberal International were also members of the Mont Pèlerin Society, an international association of liberal (with a small 'l') philosophers, economists and political scientists. This led me towards the Institute of Economic Affairs in London, at this time still in Eaton Square. I was taken on as a temporary researcher by Ralph Harris (now Lord Harris of High Cross) and I made the acquaintance of Antony (later Sir Antony) Fisher and Arthur Seldon. I helped Seldon and Harris in the writing of a chapter of their book on advertising and produced my first piece to be published in Britain in the collection of essays on *Communist Economy Under Change*. The book reviews, including the little they said about my own contribution, were on the whole favourable, but Alec Nove, later to become a good friend, had some harsh words for me in *International Affairs*. He thought what I had written showed far more clearly that I detested Titoist Socialism than that I had any valid arguments against it.

This was a foretaste of the trouble I would have with my writings. My thesis in Fribourg had been accepted with the grade *cum laude* after long delays. The supervisor was so uncertain as to what I was saying about the failings of the Yugoslav economy that he kept postponing the final decision. In the end he yielded to Professor Biucchi who thought that the thesis was satisfactory, although he was himself left-wing and forever talking about the young Marx.

But the thesis had to be published. It made the rounds of several publishers and was invariably returned as exaggerated and biased and not doing justice to the successes of the Yugoslav economy. Finally I met Professor Wilhelm Roepke at the Graduate School of International Studies in Geneva, a hero of mine since I had read his *Die Lehre von der Wirtschaft* (Teachings on Economies) in the Berne hospital in 1943. I was not disappointed. As soon as I explained what my claims in the dissertation were, the Professor approved of them and gave me a letter for Professor Fritz Meyer, the editor of the *Ordo Jahrbuch* in Bonn, where a shortened version was printed in 1962.

The time came for me to move on from the Institute of Economic Affairs which was naturally more interested in altering the course of British economic policy than in publishing studies on Eastern Europe. Two lectureships were advertised at Queen's College, Dundee, part of the old university of St

Andrews. The interview delighted me because I was much impressed by the educated Scots spoken by the Vice-Chancellor, Sir Malcolm Knox; a temporary lectureship was offered me and I accepted. Professor Archie Campbell told me in a jocular way that the decision to appoint me was difficult, 'because we don't like foreigners here, and I do not mean your being a Yugoslav; we do not like the English either.' I had to work hard, since I was not accustomed to the British way of university teaching. As my special subject, I took International Economics; I had touched on it in Dacca, but I had to deepen my knowledge.

I still remember with pleasure some of my first British students and the times at Dundee. But I could not resist the temptation when Andrew Skinner, a Dundee friend who had left for the University of Glasgow a year before, came to tell me in 1965 that the Glasgow Department of Political Economy had an opening for an International Economics specialist. I applied and was given the job. Apparently some Glasgow dons considered my appointment as the arrival of a 'paleolithic liberal' (*Steinzeit-Liberaler*). But I was on the same wavelength (or almost) as the head of Department, Professor Tom Wilson, and also his predecessor, Professor Macfie, so I felt at home. I had just missed Ronald Meek, a Glasgow senior lecturer, then appointed to Leeds, who was a fervent Communist and whose book *Studies in the Labour Theory of Value* made my hair stand on end. To my amazement Professor Meek offered me a senior lectureship at Leeds which I might have accepted had I not been keen on Glasgow.

At Glasgow, I was, of course, linked to the Soviet Institute which had been in existence for some time. One of the first things I did for the Institute was to write an article on Soviet agriculture. It was in reply to some curious notions I heard at a meeting from the German Professor Raupach, who thought that if big estates were the proper form of land holding in Prussia, the same should be true of Russia. My analysis was based, as I put it, on rational economics – mainstream economics as taught at Western universities. The editors sent the piece back with the remark that I must not call one version of economics 'rational'. When I corrected this 'mistake', the article was printed. This was a first warning that criticising communist aberrations was not easily accepted.

In fact I was told just this in so many words by an impeccable source – Professor Fritz Machlup of the University of Princeton, but originally from Vienna. 'Do not be too critical of Communism,' he said when I talked to him at the Mont Pèlerin Society meeting at Semmering, 'it will make it difficult for you to get university jobs.' I was somewhat bewildered but had no intention of tempering my questioning of communist economic tenets. I considered that to be my life task, especially as they were so obviously ruinous.

The first Mont Pèlerin Society meeting I attended was in Knokke. There I began my friendship with a young German economist, Armin Gutowski, who later became one of its leading lights. There was no shortage of other luminaries at these get-togethers — Hayek, Haberler, Stigler, Friedman, Buchanan, Hutt, Nishiyama. The interest in communist economic affairs was not exactly overwhelming; in fact, we often had to fight for a slot in the time-table for a discussion of Eastern Europe. I still cannot quite grasp why this should have been so. But there was one prominent member, Professor Warren Nutter, who had clear-cut ideas about the communist approach to economics, and the two Poles in the society, Eugen Zaleski and Andrzej Brzeski, and I were grateful to him.

In 1969, the meeting of the Mont Pèlerin Society was in Venezuela, and I was invited to read a paper on economic development. I grasped this opportunity and was amazed that my contribution was praised — I think by Peter Bauer (later Lord Bauer) among others — because there was otherwise so much wishful thinking about developing countries. After my return from Bengal, I tried to place a script on my observations abut the economic problems of East Pakistan, but was invariably turned down because people did not want to read this kind of realistic stuff, as a German publisher told me. Nebulous thinking prevailed.

A paid trip to Caracas was an opportunity to visit North America and see friends there. I travelled to Toronto, Cleveland, New York, Washington, Denver, San Francisco, Los Angeles, Phoenix, New Orleans, Miami, over to Venezuela, back to New York and home to Glasgow. The size of the country impressed me, and I was glad that the Americans (at least those I came across) were friendly and sober people since the future of the world, to my mind, depended on their steadfastness.

True, by 1969, the menacing communist Soviet iceberg had started melting. Not only did the Hungarians revolt in 1956; at the beginning of the 1960s the communist growth rates became endangered and quite a few East European economists, in particular the Czechs, began looking for new ways forward.

In 1966 I was invited to Florence to attend an East-West meeting organised by the CESES (Centre for Socio-Economic Studies) in Milan. Its director was Renato Mieli, a former secretary to the Italian Communist leader Togliatti, who had become disenchanted by communist teachings. He succeeded in bringing together a considerable number of Western specialists on the Soviet Union and Eastern Europe and East-European economists. Two Soviet economists, Professor L.M. Gatovsky and A.I. Pashkov, were also present, and perhaps the most memorable event was a somewhat strident exchange of views between a Russian and the Czech economist, Oldřich Kyn, something unheard of.

A year later, in September 1967, when we all met at Rapallo, the atmosphere was different. The Russians promised to come but did not, the Poles would not or could not because they had no exit visas, the Hungarians strangely added some Stalinist water to their otherwise up-market wine. The only carefree Easterners were the Czechs and the Yugoslavs. From Yugoslavia there were

Rudolf Bićanić and Branimir Šoškić who talked about the need to introduce socialist shares. Kyn dwelt on responsibility in enterprises, which would most easily be established if there was a relationship akin to capitalist ownership, but it would have to be different because ownership was not permissible under Socialism.

In the summer of 1968, we learnt why the Poles and the Hungarians were so cagey at Rapallo. The wrath of the Soviet leadership fell on Czechoslovakia and some of our acquaintances from the CESES meetings turned into refugees. But their attitudes were still strange. On the spur of the moment, I wrote a book on the *Economic Devolution in Eastern Europe* in which I added – after the Soviet invasion of Czechoslovakia – that one can do everything with tanks except reform an economy. Yet a friendly Czech took me to task because I did not quote Marx from his full writings but only from a selection of passages. For him the communist sage was still the *fons et origo* of all wisdom, to be approached with reverence, while for me Marx was indeed the source and fount, but of all mischief.

Ota Šik also found his way to Glasgow – his criticism of the Soviet system was unsurpassable; in the end he had to apply it as the Czechoslovak Minister of Industry. But his reform plans were so similar to what the Yugoslav Communists claimed they were doing, that they could hardly work any better. The biggest surprise for me was when I went to a meeting with Czech philosophers at Dunblane, only to be told by someone – I cannot remember whether he was Czech – that I had richly deserved my death sentence in Yugoslavia since I did not believe in Socialism.

President Tito of Yugoslavia had similar worries. He had consented to the Soviet intervention in Hungary because, as he said, Communists (most of them Communist Policemen) were being killed in the streets of Budapest. The Czechoslovak 'Communism with a human face' frightened him even more. He decided to tighten the screws. The first man he chose to be Federal Prime Minister was the popular Slovene, Stane Kavčič. But this moderate man refused point-blank, in a way unprecedented for a communist country. Who better as a second choice then, than my old acquaintance Mitja Ribičič, a colonel in the Secret Police!

Ribičič immediately started talking about class-consciousness and such like, which did not prevent him from coming on an official visit to London. As soon as I got wind of his arrival I wrote down an account of my 'encounters with the Yugoslav Prime Minister' which my old Slovene associate and friend, Dušan Pleničar, printed as a leaflet on six pages and we distributed it to the British press. There was an immediate result – journalists began ringing me up and enquiring whether I indeed knew the Prime Minister, and indeed I did.

But then the British powers-that-be stepped in. The questioning of the Prime Minister's past stopped and some papers went into counter-attack, especially

Lajos Lederer in *The Observer*. While I wrote that Ribičič's past was well known in Slovenia, he called him 'Mitja the misunderstood' whose integrity only reprobate exiles like me could call into question. *The Observer* did print my letter explaining that I was an exile primarily because Mitja's police were trying to press me into becoming a communist agent. When Ribičič heard that Ion Ratiu had invited me to the international press lunch in his honour, he threatened that he would not attend if I was there. So I was invited to disinvite myself.

The Special Branch were most polite when they asked me to come for an interview at St Andrew's Square in Glasgow. They wondered where I would be on the day Ribičič was to arrive in Britain. I said I was going to ski and I really did, so that quite a few of my telephone conversations with London journalists were conducted from the Blacklunans lodge at the foot of Glenshee. The police then asked me whether I would report it to them if I knew that somebody was going to kill Ribičič. 'But, of course,' I said, 'I do not want him to die, I want him to live long burdened with his black conscience.'

Mitja Ribičič was made to feel most welcome by the British authorities. While it is encouraging that the British make all these efforts to maintain friendly relations with Yugoslavia, I would question whether it was strictly necessary to honour a former Secret Policeman who pursued class enemies and of whom many people have horrific recollections.

Somewhat earlier, in 1967, I had a similar brush with another of my interrogators. I travelled to Tunisia to work on this text with Ronnie Mathews who unfortunately died before we got anywhere. While I was staying with him, he invited me to go to a reception at the Indonesian Embassy. There he introduced me to the British Ambassador who began praising his Yugoslav colleague, Niko Šilih. 'Oh, yes,' I said, 'I know him quite well. He would come and sit down on my bed, when I was allowed to sleep, during the interrogation. And when I jumped up, he would say: "And how do you feel Sirc, now that we are going to hang you?"' The Ambassador muttered that this shed an entirely different light on Šilih, who was meanwhile seen approaching. He and I were so taken aback by our sudden encounter that we shook hands, upon which the British Envoy led him away as if to tell him something important.

While Ribičič was in London, back in Yugoslavia the terrain was being prepared to oust groups of younger and more sensible communist leaders. A number had succeeded in establishing themselves at the level of the constituent Yugoslav republics. They harkened to the voices that were prevalent in Prague before the Soviet intervention; this alarmed Tito and also Kardelj, who *ex post* explained that the 'Prague spring' could not have ended differently because some of the Czechoslovak Communists were beholden to bourgeois democracy.

In 1971, the Croat leaders were pushed aside at the very moment of Queen Elizabeth's visit to Yugoslavia. I would have thought that Tito would not want to display his ruthlessness against what was, after all, a democratic development in spite of nationalistic overtones. But general approval in the West of his action soon became clear from the newspapers.

In the early 1970s, the Western ministries and public were at a complete loss about Yugoslavia. Two preoccupations seemed to prevail: on the one hand, Yugoslavia was to be used as an example to other East European countries on how to make themselves independent from Moscow. On the other, Western officials were afraid of Yugoslavia falling apart along nationalist lines and creating a dangerous vacuum leading to armed strife. These fears went so far that the Western governments were prepared to support anything Tito did, regardless of how ruinous it was for his country. They could never summon the courage to evaluate the situation in Yugoslavia critically, and either devise some better policy themselves or give support to Yugoslav groups that came up with constructive proposals.

Economically Yugoslavia was sliding into ever-greater chaos, while all official sources in the West sang the praises of the wonderful economic progress it was achieving and advocated that Tito should be given more money. This appraisal was common to most institutions, from NATO to the OECD. I could not help wondering what this stance was supposed to achieve. One thing it did achieve was a general craze for self-management. Without much doubt, the Western economies were in a spot of trouble at that time and many people, not necessarily Socialists, thought that workers' management would be a solution. I sat through many meetings and symposia trying to warn and to explain that the success of self-management in Yugoslavia was not what it was thought to be, and reaping hostile reactions for my efforts.

Tito and Kardelj themselves realised that concessions must be made to nationalism in Yugoslavia if it was to be overcome, and this found expression in the appropriate articles of the 1974 constitution (whatever one might think of this product of Kardelj's). Yet Western policy-makers could never quite grasp this need, and forever preached more centralism and more central authority – a trend which can only play into the hands of the crudest Communists. Of course it is not easy to dissuade them from this approach as long as Yugoslavs of different sorts behave like intransigents, not wanting to talk or listen to one another.

From the beginning of my exile, it had been clear to me that the Yugoslav opposition at home and abroad, or dissidents of any kind, would not be able to do much if their various national groups did not co-operate. I shared this view with my two friends from Switzerland, Adil and Vlado. We thought it necessary to explore the differences between Yugoslav nations as a factor to take into account when their mutual relationship was to be organised. There obviously had to be a working relationship because the Serbs, the Croats and the Bosnian Moslems intermingle to a bewildering extent; and the Slovenes and Macedonians are exposed to great dangers from their neighbours if they remain on their own.

The task was to work out a programme designed to change Yugoslavia into a community of nations without neglecting either their differences or their common interests. In 1963 a meeting for this purpose was called by Vane Ivanović at Stansted near London.

The important feature of this get-together was that it was held under the auspices of the pre-war Croat leader Vlatko Maček. He was too old to be present in person but he corrected in his own hand the draft agreement submitted by his secretary Branko Pešelj, by then an American attorney and professor at Fordham University. Also present was Miha Krek, the leader of the Slovene People's Party in exile. This party was undoubtedly the largest Slovene party before the war, but was dislodged by the Communists through cunning and violence. Of the Serbs, there were in particular Boka Vlajić and Desimir Tošić.

The so-called Stansted agreement recognised the right of all Yugoslav nations to self-determination and secession but also underlined that, in the opinion of participants, it was in their interest to stay together. It also tried to provide some new solutions to facilitate the symbiosis of Yugoslavs such as polycentrism, an arrangement for federal authorities not to be all centralised in the same city but distributed amongst capitals, e.g. the government would be in Belgrade, the parliament in Zagreb, the supreme Court in Ljubljana etc.

Many years later, in 1979, Adil Zulfikarpašić and I met a number of friends with a view to widening the circle of those working for an agreement between Yugoslavs. In Zürich we discussed the possibilities with two Serbs from Paris, Dragaš Kešeljević and Marko Krstić, two Croats living in Germany, Zdenko Antić and Marijan Batinić, and the Bosnian Moslem Teufik Velagić, turned wise by long imprisonment. Dragaš Kešeljević was the Yugoslav commercial attaché in Warsaw when my father was there with a trade delegation just before his arrest, but soon defected. Marijan Batinić was involved in Mihajlo Mihajlov's attempts to organise an independent journal in Yugoslavia and thus our link to him. The first Democratic Encounter was called to London by co-incidence for the day when Tito died in May 1980.

The next Democratic Encounter was supposed to take place in Paris in the autumn of 1980. The French authorities forbade it, although they were quite happy to allow émigré street demonstrations at the same time. The Titoist Secret Police was also active: in Paris they sent out additional fake invitations. Had the meeting taken place, it would have been a great success, with some 40 people present. The French attitude to democratic exiles is very strange, because it is deemed that a *raison d'état* is involved and that foreign totalitarian governments must not be offended, as would happen if serious exile groups were allowed to deliberate on French soil. More than this, I was expressly asked by the editor of *Politique Etrangère* to write an article on Yugoslavia. But it was never published and I have never been told why.

Events in Yugoslavia were of great concern to us and we all followed closely the imprisonment of Milovan Djilas and Mihajlo Mihajlov. When Djilas came out of prison for the second time (in 1967), I wrote to him, and he answered after a while, saying he understood that I was not a real 'emigrant'! Soon afterwards, two members of the Mihajlov Zadar group came to Glasgow and finally Martin Dewhirst, a Glasgow colleague, brought me the news that Djilas was coming to London in October 1968 and that I should come to meet him at the Cumberland Hotel in London. We sat together for four hours discussing the future of our country.

From then on, I had intermittent contacts with Djilas, mostly through the Belgrade lawyer Joro Barović, a former partisan officer dismissed for having sided with Djilas. We were talking about how to speed up democratic developments in Yugoslavia. We last met in Venice in 1975. Soon afterwards Barović died when a lorry collided with his car. Most people think that he was deliberately killed.

Djilas's son Aleksa came to London in the 1970s and was eventually invited to attend the Democratic Encounter of 1982. There was even some excitement about it, as the National Liberal Club, where the meeting was to be held, received a telephone call threatening a bomb explosion. The callers were quite possibly the Titoist Secret Police — in hiding in London. Aleksa kept quiet all the way through the proceedings, stressing that he was only an observer, but when asked what he thought about it all, he said that it was really not up to us, people exiled from Yugoslavia for many years, to discuss its future. Only people at home were entitled to engage in these debates. I could not understand how a young man without political experience could say such things in front of people who had suffered in Tito's jails for their religious and political beliefs.

When some prominent Russian exiles organised the Resistance International, Yugoslavia was at first represented by Mihajlo Mihajlov, but when he retired, young Djilas was chosen. I wanted to protest that a student was no replacement for a prominent exile, but then thought better of it. However, somebody told Aleksa about my initial reaction, and also that I had said Djilas should not behave as if he had never been a Stalinist. Consequently, Aleksa telephoned me and said that, with the knowledge of his father, he was breaking off all links with me because I was an anti-Communist.

I no longer knew what to make of the two Djilases. Things became somewhat clearer when I carefully read *Encounter* for September–October 1983. On page 27 there was part of an interview with Milovan Djilas by Michael Charlton who asked him, amongst other things, whether there was some sense of repentance growing within him. Djilas answered:

> No, I have never felt any repentance. I think that Westerners over-estimate the violence in Communism as something very decisive, in the sense of inhuman.

> Violence is part of any politics, and Communism is of course strongly connected with such ideas. But I think the essentials are those utopian conceptions as I told you. For example, if Stalin had really succeeded in creating a perfect society, nobody would have reproached him for his crimes...

And he went on:

> That was the war, the Revolution. I did my duty as did the other Yugoslav leaders. They created a revolutionary Army. This isn't easy; it can't be done without some conflict, some cruel methods even...

So that was that. This man, whom the whole world praised, still defended violence. The communist leaders were only doing their duty — their duty to whom? Stalin, communist revolution or what? Was it their duty to start a 'class war' while the country was occupied; to kill tens of thousands, hundreds of thousands, for no better reason than that they wanted absolute power so as to bring Stalinism to Yugoslavia — a system which condemns itself by its inhumanity?

Instead of admitting that there were deep inconsistencies in the behaviour of Yugoslav Communists, Djilas claims to this day that the only thing worse than orthodox Communism is orthodox anti-Communism (*South Slav Journal*, summer 1987, page 35).

When I attended the regular autumn Slovene meeting at Opčine near Trieste in 1984, I was asked by Professor France Bučar of Ljubljana whether I would be willing to contribute to an enquiry organised by the Ljubljana journal *Nova Revija* on how to resolve the Yugoslav crisis. Of course I was thrilled to be invited to write for a publication in my home country although still an exile.

By then *Nova Revija* had made a name for itself and for its editors Rupel and Grafenauer as a forum for discussion of all problems by Slovenes and often also by writers from other parts of Yugoslavia. It also played a part in bringing into the open the ghastly circumstances surrounding the extermination of 12,000 *Domobranci* in 1945. The question was raised by the philosopher Spomenka Hribar, originating from a communist family, but unable to forget the collective guilt. Mitja Ribičič, who was presumably involved in most police actions in Slovenia, of course talked of his having done his duty as 'a soldier of the revolution' etc. Without much doubt, this discussion cleared the atmosphere in Slovenia more than anything else had.

My contribution for the *Nova Revija* was soon ready. It said that the present economic system was unworkable and enumerated the reasons why, as in my other writings; it explained why political democracy is required if private enterprise is to flourish, and then came out for Slovenia to remain in the Yugoslav community with as much independence as possible but co-operating freely with the other regions. Apparently this did not go down too well, because in 1985 when the complete paper arrived, nationalism was rife. This was unfortunate, in so far as it would be much easier to get rid of Communism finally if Yugoslav nations understood that it is Communism that hampers their development, rather than accusing each other. Why nationalist shrillness should have arisen where it was muted for decades, I do not know, but I do not like it, either in Slovenia, or in Serbia, Croatia or wherever. I think I am a patriot but this does not mean that I have to talk nonsense and fail to see the better side of others.

My paper was not only received, it was also passed on to printers and it was typeset. Then the authorities stepped in, in the person of Jože Smole, the chairman of the People's Front of Slovenia. He said that my contribution could not be printed because I was an enemy of the people. *Nova Revija* conformed, but twice printed material on the exchanges that took place. These included my letter to Smole telling him that he should stop calling those who wish to help to resolve the crisis, 'enemies of the people', when the misery is caused uniquely by the Communists themselves and their fancy notions.

My first contact with Kosta Čavoški, a researcher in Belgrade, came in 1983. I had been helping Nora Beloff who was writing a book on Yugoslavia. She had been there and returned with a typescript discussing the way in which Tito's party did away with all opposition immediately after the war. I was amazed that the new generation of scholars in Yugoslavia was sufficiently interested in these happenings for Vojislav Koštunica and Kosta Čavoški to write about it. I sent them whatever material I had handy but some of it did not arrive. To my even greater amazement, the re-written typescript by Koštunica and Čavoški was published in Belgrade soon afterwards, which seemed a clear proof that there was a very liberal faction in the leadership of the Serbian Communist Party. In this climate, some members of the Serbian Academy of Sciences, with the support of younger intellectuals such as Kosta and Vojislav, organised a Committee for the Defence of Freedom of Thought and Expression. Through it they began defending people from all over Yugoslavia persecuted because of their views.

In 1987, this Belgrade Committee came up with a petition (all their interventions are couched in this form): after the rehabilitation of some communist victims of the endless Titoist miscarriages of justice, it was the turn of non-Communists. Our trial was expressly mentioned. There followed another petition devoted exclusively to the question of re-trying Nagode and co-defendants, including myself.

It was taken up by the Slovene university students' papers, *Tribuna* in Ljubljana and *Katedra* in Maribor. In addition, the Executive Committee of the Slovene Writers' Society wrote on our behalf:

> The committee supports the pleas for re-trial of *Stara Pravda* [old justice – a slogan of Slovene and Croat peasants during the *Jacquerie* in their part of the world], the trial of which was staged in Ljubljana in 1947 with trumped-up charges. It was modelled on the fraternal Stalinist purges and helped the new rulers to settle accounts in a hurry with a group of Slovene patriots and intellectuals who did not belong to the Party. They were turned into criminals and traitors ... since some victims of this trial are still alive, our society should apologise to them for the suffering wrongly inflicted on them.

More than that, *Tribuna* was the first in Yugoslavia to publish anything written by me. It was the translation of my letter printed in the London *South Slav Journal*, taking to task all those who were now saying it was useless fighting Hitler. There followed excerpts from my memoirs printed in Slovene in 1968 by Dušan Pleničar under the heading *Nonsense and Sense*, the nonsense of the title being the communist claim that they knew all the answers. *Tribuna* printed seven instalments and finished one with a sharp demand signed by Ivo Žajdela, a student, that I should be rehabilitated, which reads in part:

> Why is it necessary today to bring up all the problems relating to the trial of Nagode and all other similar trials...? Nagode's trial was a classic Stalinist trial – right here in Slovenia...
>
> The demand for complete rehabilitation – moral and material – is therefore self-evident, both the rehabilitation of Črtomir Nagode and of all the others sentenced with him. There is, of course, the logical request that immediately after rehabilitation, Ljubo Sirc be allowed to enter his native Slovenia, and the syntagma 'Slovene political émigré' be re-appraised at the same time...
>
> The 'struggle' against that party-political arbitrariness is the decisive 'struggle' for young people. If we yield here, then we can no more than dream of a better future.
>
> In several of its issues *Tribuna* has been publishing extracts from Ljubo Sirc's book *Nonsense and Sense*, which came out in Great Britain in 1968 [*sic*!]. I, myself, in fact, see absolutely nothing objectionable in that book, but I am, nevertheless, distressed to find out that, 40 years after the liberation, the Slovene Party and its historiography cannot provide a qualified or impartial insight into the Nagode trial. An influential Slovene historian (I shall not name him) has stated that he does not want to say anything for the public about the Nagode trial. It is significant how much of the past there still is in the present.
>
> The extracts from Sirc's book about the Nagode trial published in *Tribuna* mention frequently the name of the high-ranking Slovene politician, Mitja Ribičič, who is also well known as a poet and as Partisan Ciril. Let Mitja Ribičič explain what his role was in Nagode's trial!

It all looked as if there was a real probability of a re-trial. Dissent in Slovenia was widening and was at least partly supported by the Slovene government and party bodies. The Slovene public prosecutor had the courage to talk back to the Federal Public Prosecutor, refusing to take his orders and threatening to call in the Slovene parliament. While all this is applauded by the intellectual dissenters in other republics, there is no evidence of the popular support for it being as great as it is in Slovenia, which creates tensions. It is difficult to understand why this should be so. Is it because elsewhere the repression apparatus is still in place, or because, as some Slovenes claim, there is less concern for freedom?

Yet, the situation in Yugoslavia has become preposterous. The Communist Party is hanging on to power by the skin of its teeth, although it is by now obvious that communist tenets must lead to the worst kind of misery, and that since Tito's death their Party has no authority left. Nobody in authority is capable of anything except perhaps feeble attempts at oppression, as when the communist Army tried to intimidate the Slovenes by accusing three Slovene journalists of revealing military secrets. It is time for the Party to give up.

The ineptitude of the Communist Party in running the Yugoslav economy was the subject of a book I wrote in the 1970s. Again I had trouble in placing it, but fortunately in the end an editor at Macmillan's picked up the typescript and published it within a short time in 1979. Being immodest, I can say that this was one of the rare books that predicted the complete collapse of the Yugoslav economy before it happened. Many people told me they were aware my predictions had come true.

If the Yugoslav communist authorities had had their way, the book would never have been published. In the autumn of 1974, two policemen in mufti appeared at my mother's house in Kranj – she used to spend one year with me and one year in Kranj – and asked to see her passport: one of them took it and put it in his pocket saying that she would never see me again if I did not stop slandering Yugoslavia.

Of course, I had no intention of interrupting my study of the Yugoslav economy, and therefore resorted to another, far more efficient, method of publicity in dealing with totalitarian régimes. I started writing to everybody I knew all around the world, asking them to write either to Tito himself or to the nearest Yugoslav Embassy and protest against their treatment of an old woman; my mother was over 80 by then. It is especially worth mentioning that Lajos Lederer, and a Swiss journalist who had once described Ribičič as a liberal, both intervened privately. A great help was my Indian colleague and friend, Radha Sinha, who mobilised some people in India. The secretaries in the Adam Smith Building, Glasgow, collected hundreds of signatures. Yet, how decent people can misunderstand matters of which they have no experience is shown by the refusal of a neighbour to sign a petition, saying: 'We cannot get involved in quarrels among foreigners.' Others, in more elevated positions, thought that the loss of my mother's passport was not sufficiently earth-shaking for them to do anything.

The *Guardian* ran the story of my mother in its gossip column. At any rate, the interventions worked. Out of the blue, a Swiss friend, Yvonne Losinger, received a letter from Tito's office announcing that her protest had been received and sent on to Slovenia for action. Within a few days the two policemen came to see my mother again and wanted her to ask me some questions on their behalf. She of course said she could not ask me any questions since she was in Kranj and I was in Glasgow. 'That's easy to remedy,' and the policeman took the passport out of his pocket and put it on the table. When my mother arrived, I wrote to the Prime Minister of Slovenia expressing the wish that the authorities should write to me personally if they had any questions.

My mother spent another quiet year with me, went back to Kranj, came again to Glasgow for my wedding to Sue, and saw her granddaughter Nadia at a time when I could easily have had grandchildren myself. She was ill, though, and she knew it. But she still wondered whether she could go back to Kranj once more to take leave of her sister and her niece, whom she loved dearly and who were her support in difficult times.

Eventually, the doctor said that her state had stabilised and that she could go to Kranj for a month, but not longer if she wanted to return. Sue and I had agreed she would die with us. Everything was organised – I would accompany her to Heathrow where she would take the Yugoslav plane for Ljubljana while I would fly on to Germany for a lecture tour. According to the time-table, she would have left Glasgow just before 11 o'clock in the morning and would land at Kranj (the airport for Ljubljana) at 4 o'clock, a travel time of four hours, taking the time difference into account.

Everything went wrong. The plane was three hours late and flew to Zagreb. My mother still went, so that I last saw her being wheeled along an endless airport corridor.

Then I telephoned Halka, my mother's sister, to go to Zagreb, 150km away, to fetch her. They found her exhausted and disoriented. After this journey, there was apparently no question of her coming back to Glasgow. She died in May 1978, having seen Sue and Nadia again, but not me – I was waiting for them in Carinthia. Since my mother's body was transported to Graz in Austria for cremation, I went there to stand beside her coffin for a while. I was full of remorse – I should not have let her go back, but what was the use. I could never do anything right when it came to my parents.

In the 1970s it was far from clear that left-wing policies did not work. It was not just that in Britain Edward Heath was again replaced by Harold Wilson; people still believed that, in spite of their permanent reforms, the communist-run countries were doing very well and were the model for the future. Since the students' revolt in 1968, it was perhaps no longer believed that one had to copy the Soviet Union exactly, but some kind of less-than-clear alternative was still the order of the day. Because I did not agree with this, many people believed me to be not quite right in the head — all of which also had consequences for my career.

Most knowledgeable people advised me to leave the university as soon as I could, if I wanted to take up something else. In the event, I took early (but not very early) retirement in 1983 and organised a Centre for Research into Communist Economies with the help of Lord Harris and many others, especially my professional colleagues willing to serve on the Academic Advisory Council. The Centre looked serious enough to attract the minimum of funds required for its functioning from a few American and British foundations. The pupose was and is to do for communist countries what Ralph Harris's Institute of Economic Affairs did for Britain — to publish critical scholarly assessments of communist economic theory and of the performance of individual communist countries. The task cried out to be done because Western observers were holding their fire to an almost ridiculous extent when faced with communist matters, and in some instances did not even seem to know what fire they possessed in the form of normal economic theory. The hesitant approach to communist 'economics' did great harm to the population of communist countries. The response to the establishment of CRCE in communist countries appears to confirm this diagnosis, because many social scientists there offered to help.

In 1987, after two years of almost suspended animation, Mikhail Gorbachev came out forcefully in favour of what he calls *glasnost* and *perestroika*. He and his associates are obviously aware of past blunders, at least those committed by Stalin. But are they also clear about where they are going, or rather, where they have to go if they really wish to lift the population of their countries out of their present poverty and dejection? It is to be hoped that they are and that they have the courage of their convictions, but concerned people should make sure that they are reminded of it again and again.

There are some hopeful signs. Recently I have been invited to attend scholarly meetings organised by the Institute of World Economics at the Hungarian Academy of Sciences. So, in March 1988, I went to Eastern Europe for the first time since my escape from Yugoslavia in 1955. The occasion was a conference in Györ on alternative socialist models and I was able to discuss freely the necessary conditions for a functioning economy. My contribution was recorded in the proceedings. Similarly, in January 1989, I visited Warsaw and talked about Polish problems both with dissidents and with members of the Economics Institute of the Polish Academy of Sciences and of the Economic Advisory Council to the government. At a recent conference in Sopron, Hungary, I seem to have startled everybody by claiming that any transition to a market system must not be dragged out but should be instantaneous, in the way Erhard reformed the German economy in 1948. In spite of this, a group of alert young Russian economists present in Sopron said that they thought I should be invited to visit the Soviet Union in order to explain my views to audiences there.

There remains Yugoslavia. In fact, I have recently received an invitation to attend a conference on Yugoslavia at the turn of the century. The conference is to be held in Belgrade at the end of May 1989 by the Yugoslav Association of Sociologists. It remains to be seen whether or not I will be allowed to enter my home country.

INDEX

Alexander I, King 9, 10, 12, 144
Allan, George 151
All-Slovene Union 30
Ambrož (Švent) 97, 99–105, 107, 127–8
Anders, General Wladyslaw 51, 53
Anić, Dr Srečko (Dr Felix Engel) 42–4
Antić, Zdenko 186
Aube, L' 49
Avbelj, Viktor 102, 107–8, 111, 173
Avšič, Colonel Jaka 25, 28

Badoglio, Marshal Pietro 38
Bakarić, Vladimir 93
Baran, Paul 178
Barović, Joro 187
Bartlett, Vernon 160
Batinić, Marijan 186
Bauer, Peter (later Lord) 182
Beamish, Tufton (later Lord Chelwood) 153
Bebler, Dr Aleš 24
Belgrade 10, 15, 19, 81–5, 89, 90, 91, 169, 178
Beloff, Nora 189
Benedik, Judge Valentin 34
Berne 41–2, 44, 177–8
Bevin, Ernest 1, 97
Bićanić, Rudolf 183
Biucchi, Professor Basilio 180
Bleiweiss, Janez 6
Bogomolov, Colonel 75
Bonn 180
Borba 143, 168
Bratianu, Constantin (Dinu) 121
Bravničar, Colonel 140
Brecelj, Dr Marijan 137

Brilej, Dr Jože 93
Brzeski, Andrzej 182
Bučar, France 188
Buchanan, James 182
Bulganin 173

Cachin, Dr Marcel 46–7
Campbell, Archie 181
Catholic People's Party 31, 37
Čavoški, Kosta 189
Česenj, Lieutenant Marko 43
Charlton, Michael 187
Chetniks 26, 32, 39, 42, 45, 51, 53, 69, 71, 138
Churchill, Sir Winston 44, 46, 81, 88, 91, 117, 134, 162
Communist Party 12, 23, 24, 26–7, 35, 46, 49, 54, 62, 67, 73–4, 82, 94, 99, 129, 132, 134, 150, 152, 168
Črnomelj 65–8
Croat Peasant Party 9, 12, 82, 91, 93, 179
Croats 8, 12, 15, 32–3, 87, 151, 179, 185, 190
Czechs 8, 182

Dacca 177–8
Daily Worker 76, 77
D'Amato, Major 100, 111
Damjan, Dr Viktor 124
Danish Radical Venstre 179–180
Davies, Ambassador Joe 41
Deakin, F.W.D. 34
Delo 31
de Madriaga, Salvador 179

Demokratija 81, 82
Dewhirst, Martin 187
Djilas, Aleska 187
Djilas, Milovan 34, 35, 79, 150, 168, 187–8
Dnevnik 161
Domobranci 43, 45, 62, 69, 70–1, 76, 79, 80, 91, 188
Dundee 180–1

Eagon, Captain 52
Economist, The 67
Eden, Sir Anthony 43, 157, 160
Ehrlich, Professor Lambert 30
Emmer, Fanouš 26–7
Engel, Dr Felix (Dr Srečko Anić) 42–4

Figaro, Le 49
Fisher, Archbishop 162
Fisher, Sir Anthony 180
Florence 182
Franchetti, Lado 170
Franchetti, Vinko 170
French League for Human Rights 88
Fribourg 44, 176–7, 179
Friedman, Milton 182
Furlan, Professor Boris 2, 43, 86, 98, 100, 106, 111–16, 118, 122, 125, 141, 145, 151, 153, 166

Gafencu 179
Gambara, General Gastone 35
Ganguly, Father T.A, (later Archbishop) 177
Gaser, Paul 128
Gatovsky, L.M. 182
Geneva 46
Gestapo 77, 79, 92, 127, 128–9, 156–7
Gibbs, Captain John 86, 113, 123–4, 163
Gibbs, Tatjana (née Korun) 86, 96, 115, 123–4, 136, 139
Glasgow 181, 182, 183, 192
Glušič, Colonel Andrej 91–2
Gorbachev, Mikhail 193
Gouzenko, Igor 48

Grafenauer, Niko 188
Grkić, Colonel 102, 108–9, 111
Grol, Milan 81–2, 84, 85, 110
Guardian, The 191
Gutowski, Armin 181

Haberler, Gottfried 182
Harris, Ralph (now Lord) 180, 193
Harrison, Hubert 59
Hayek, Friedrich 182
Heath, Edward 192
Herriot, Edouard 88
Heuman, Gabriel 86
Hitler, Adolf 13, 20, 31, 37, 69, 80
Hočevar, Mrs Pavla 106, 107, 133
Hoptner, Jake 86, 100, 112
Hribar, Elizabeta 106
Hribar, Spomenka 188
Hribar, Zoran 106, 147
Huda, M.N. 178
Hughes, John 176
Humanité, L' 49
Hutt, William H. 182

Ilić, General Ljubo 50
Ivanović, Vane 176, 186

Jančiković, Dr Toma 90–1, 103, 110, 122
Jesenice 79, 96, 138
Jones, Major 36
Jovanović, Dragoljub 84–6, 94, 102–3, 108–9, 110, 111–2, 121–2, 146
Jovanović, Slobodan 37, 110
Juretić, Monsignor Augustin 44

Kamenšček, Stanko 175
Karadžić, Vuk Stafanović 130
Kardelj, Edvard 34–5, 84, 87, 103, 114, 131, 155, 184, 185
Katedra 189
Kathmandu 178
Katja, Boh (née Székély) 95, 98, 99, 105, 108, 112, 116, 117, 119, 123–4, 127
Kavčič, Stane 183
Kavčnik, Professor Leon 2, 106, 109, 113, 116

Index

Kay, Ted 90, 153
Kebe, prison educator 172
Kern, Captain Ivan (later Rear-Admiral) 37, 39–40, 50–1, 55
Kersnik, Stane 123, 124, 130, 178
Kešeljevič, Dragaš 186
Khan, President Ayub 178
Kidrič, Boris 3, 21, 22, 28, 29, 77, 79, 80, 87, 94, 103, 127, 132, 134, 162–3
Knokke 181
Knox, Sir Malcolm 181
Kocbek, Edvard 34
Koce, Jure 37
Korošec, Prime Minister the Rev. Dr Anton 9, 12
Košir, Mirko 127, 128
Koštunica, Vojislav 189
Kragelj, Commissar Jože 142, 144, 150, 158, 163–8, 170–2, 173–4
Kraigher, Boris 93, 137, 155, 173
Kranj 4, 7, 13, 15, 16, 57, 70–1, 93, 100, 170, 172, 191
Krek, Dr Miha 53, 186
Krstić, Marko 186
Kruschev 173
Kulovec, the Rev. Dr Fran 12
Kumelj, Metod 106
Kyn, Oldřich 182–3

Lajovic, Vid 106
Lannung, Hermod 179–80
Lederer, Lajos 184, 191
Leibnitz 71–2
Lenič, Bishop Stanko 159, 166–7
Lenin 134, 163
Leskošek, Franc 103
Lewis MP, Arthur 81
Liberal International 179–80
Liberation Army 51, 56, 61
Liberation Front 20–2, 23–5, 26–7, 33, 34, 70, 90, 100, 107, 132
Lie, Trygve 156
Life magazine 113
Liepschitz 1, 104

Ljubljana 1, 3, 11, 12, 14, 16–19, 21, 24, 26, 29–30, 33, 35, 38, 40–1, 43–5, 57, 69, 71, 74–80, 82, 86, 89–90, 93ff, 140
Ljudska Pravica 73
Lokar, Miloš 19, 24
London 186
Losinger, Yvonne 191

Maček, Ivan 12, 15, 44, 84
Maček, Vlatko 186
Machlup, Professor Fritz 181
Majaron, Dr Ferdinand 65, 74
Mandić, Father Dominik 32–3
Maniu, Juliu 121
Manning MP, Mrs Leah 83
Maribor 130, 141ff
Marseilles 7, 51, 52
Marx, Karl 80, 126, 130–1, 134, 183
Mastracchi-Manes, Salvatore 175
Matelič, Miro 167
Mathews, Ronnie 184
Mauriac, François 49
McCullum-Scott, John 179
Meek, Ronald 181
Meyer, Fritz 180
Mieli, Renato 182
Miha, Colonel Mihič 67
Mihailović, Colonel Dragoljub (later General) 24–5, 28–30, 33, 35–6, 41, 43, 44, 46, 88, 179
Mihajlov, Mihajlo 186–7
Mikolayczyk, Stanislaw 3
Mikoyan 173
Milan, Lieutenant 116, 119
Milice Patriotique 47
Milok, Dr Zdravko 46, 48–9
Mohorič, Stanko 160, 170
Moslems 185
Mont Pèlerin Society 180, 181, 182
Moore, Lieutenant 53, 54
Moscatello, Monsignor Nicolò 33
Moscow 13
Munda, Professor 149
Mussolini, Benito 18, 38

Naglič, Captain Vlado 45
Nagode, Dr Črtomir 2, 3, 19–23, 25–8, 34–5, 43–5, 71, 78, 81, 88, 90–2, 94, 101, 106, 110, 112, 113, 115, 122, 189, 190
Nagy, Ferenc 3, 121
Naples 54
Nedić, General Milan 25
National Cotton Council of America 89, 99
National Committee (Tito's) 42, 44, 51
New York Times 140
Nishiyama 182
Nizier, Colonel 47–8
Noel-Baker, Captain Francis 90, 145
Novak, Major Karel 25, 30, 33–4, 35–6, 39
Nova Revija 188
Nove, Professor Alec 180
Novo Mesto 148ff, 174
Nuremburg trials 124–5
Nutter, Warren 182

Ogris, Albin 94
Oswald, Stane 127–8
OZNA 80, 116–17, 123–4, 126–8, 133–5, 137–8, 169

Pakistan Economic Journal 178
Paris 49, 50, 176, 186
Paris Peace Conference 87
Partisans 31, 36, 39, 41–3, 54, 56–7, 61, 67, 69, 70–1, 76, 79, 80, 90, 108, 114, 135
Partonić, Andreja 49, 50
Pashkov, A.I. 182
Paul, Karadjordjević, Prince 9, 14
Pearce, Major 59, 66–7
Pearson, Drew 156
People's Assemblies 91, 154
People's Front 82, 84, 91, 189
Perugia 30–2, 100, 104, 111, 175
Pešelj, Branko 186
Pesjak, Jože 26
Peter II, King 14, 15, 60–2, 83

Petrović, Nenad 179
Pijade, Moše 131, 170
Pirc, Captain Boris 29, 32, 43, 167
Pirc, Ciril (grandfather) 4–8, 17
Pirc, General Franjo 88
Pirc, Captain (later Colonel) Metod 45, 56–7, 88, 98, 106
Pirc, Zdenka 5 (*see also* under Sirc)
Platts-Mills MP, J.F.F. 82
Pleničar, Dušan 183, 190
Pleško, Captain 145
Plos, Governor 144–5
Politeo, Dr Ivo 160
Politique Etrangère 186
Pravda 19, 20–3, 25–9, 30, 33–4, 43, 108
Predavec, Vlado 179, 185
Prenner, Dr Ljuba 170
Prešeren, France 6–7
Presterl, Martin 128
Purić, Božidar 46

Raczynski, Count Edward 179
Radić, Stjepan 9
Radica, Bogdan 113
Ranković, Aleksandar 151–3, 157, 170
Rapallo 182–3
Ratiu, Ion 184
Raupach, Hans 181
Reader's Digest 113
Ribar, Dr Ivan 154, 170
Ribičič, Colonel Mitja (Ciril) 95–7, 101, 106, 118, 155, 156–7, 170–1, 183–4, 190
Ripka, Hubert 179
Robič, Monsignor Pavle 175
Roepke, Wilhelm 125, 180
Ronko, Major 104, 116–19
Roosevelt, Mrs Eleanor 149, 150
Rožman, Bishop Gregorij 159
Rupel, Dimitrij 188
Rupnik, General Leon 41, 45, 124
Rus, Judge Jože 23, 27

Saba, Francesco 141

Sager, Peter 178
Salaj, Djuro 156
Savić, Kirilo 85–6
Scheel, Walter 178
Schellenberg, Walter 45
Scopes, Leonard (later Sir) and Mrs 86–7, 89, 178
Scott, Captain 58–9
Seldon, Arthur 180
Semmering 181
Serbian Democratic Party 82
Serbs 8, 12, 18, 25–6, 36, 42, 44, 85, 102, 179, 185, 186
Sergeychik 66
Seton-Watson, Hugh 102, 163
Sevšek, Governor 127–8
Šik, Ota 183
Šilih, Niko 99, 101, 104, 117, 118–19, 155, 184
Simčič-Marko, Marjan 102
Simović, General Dušan 14, 15
Sinha, Radha 192
Sirc, Elsie 176
Sirc, Franjo 1, 2, 9–10, 13–14, 15, 32, 78, 89, 99, 103, 104, 106, 113, 119, 123, 138–40, 142, 144, 146, 164, 175
Sirc, Ljubo 95, 101–2, 104, 106, 109–11, 117–19, 121, 127, 129, 134, 136, 140, 142–4, 164, 167, 171, 173–4, 190
Sirc, Louis 176
Sirc, Sue 192–3
Sirc, Vinko 5
Sirc, Zdenka 5, 70, 94, 112, 116, 118–19, 123, 126, 134, 145, 149–52, 154, 160, 163–5, 169–70, 172, 177, 192
Skinner, Andrew 181
Slovene Liberation Front 37
Slovene People's Party 15, 186
Slovenes 4–6, 8, 9, 18, 21–2, 24, 28–30, 46, 62, 64, 76, 84, 87, 100, 107, 133, 145, 166, 185, 190–1
Slovenski Poročevalec 110–11, 112–13

Smole, Janko 74
Smole, Jože 189
Snoj, France 78, 90, 112, 113, 151
Sokol 20
Soškić, Branimir 183
South Slav Journal 188, 190
Spindler, Dušan 151, 154–7, 165–6, 167
Split 55–6, 57–8, 60–1
Stalin 128–30, 134, 138, 143, 156, 162, 188
Stare, Bogdan 106
Stepinac, Archbishop (later Cardinal) Alojzije 44, 156
Stepišnik, Vladimir 127
Stigler, George 182
Stojković, Slavko 159
Sremska Mitrovica 147
Šubašić, Ivan 46, 50–1, 53, 60, 81, 91, 93, 117, 132, 160 (*see also* Tito-Šubašić Agreement)
Šutej, Dr Juraj 32, 33, 81, 91, 93, 103, 110, 149
Svetina, Tone 31

Tatjana – *see under* Gibbs
The Observer 184
The Times 122, 153, 178
Thorez, Maurice 49
Tito, Marshal Josip Broz 2, 34, 36, 44, 46, 51, 53, 60–1, 66, 75, 77, 81–2, 90–1, 130, 132, 134–5, 137, 144, 146, 150–1, 156, 160–2, 163, 170, 180, 183–5, 186, (*see also* Tito-Šubašić Agreement)
Tito-Šubašić Agreement 47, 50–1, 55, 58, 63, 65–6, 81, 91, 93, 100
Togliatti, Palmiro 182
Tolbukhin, Marshal Fyodor Ivanovich 71
Tomšič, Vida 161
Topusko 62–3
Tošić, Desimir 186
Trampuž, Boris 93
Tribuna 189, 190
Trieste 19, 35, 43, 71, 75, 84, 87, 166, 174

Trifunović, Miša 92
Trofenik, Dr Rudolf 147
Turk-Gorazd, Franjo 133

UDBA 167, 168, 169
UN Relief and Reconstruction Agency 1, 58, 66, 84, 88, 89, 98, 125
Ustashi 9, 25–6, 31, 35, 42, 63–4, 179

Vauhnik, Colonel Vladimir, 28, 45
Velagić, Teufik 186, 187
Vidmar, Josip 87, 93–4, 137, 145, 150
Vilfan Jože 27, 170
Vlajić, Boka 186
Vode, Angela 106, 110
Volk, Bishop A. 166
Vrčon, Dr Branko 151

Waddams, Major Frank 75, 80, 86, 153
Wattenwyll, Colonel 45
White Guards 31, 33, 40

Wilson, Harold 192
Wilson, Professor Tom 181
Winkler, Colonel 157

Yugoslav Liberation Committee 49, 50
Yugoslav-Soviet Friendship Society 2

Zajdela, Ivo 190
Zaleski, Eugen 182
Zalik, Martin 102
Zalokar, Marko 75
Zhukov, Major 75
Ziliacus MP, Ronny 153
Zirovnik, Dr Janko 107, 172
Zovič, Slavko 57
Zulfikarnašić, Adil 179–80, 185–6
Zupan, Simona 133, 136–7
Zupan, Dr Svatopluk 106, 147
Zupan, Vito 133, 137–8
Žužemberk 76